ARGUMENTATION

Reasoning in Communication

ARGUMENTATION

Reasoning in Communication

J. VERNON JENSEN
University of Minnesota

D. Van Nostrand Company
NEW YORK CINCINNATI TORONTO LONDON MELBOURNE

D. Van Nostrand Company Regional Offices:
New York   Cincinnati

D. Van Nostrand Company International Offices:
London   Toronto   Melbourne

Copyright © 1981 by Litton Educational Publishing, Inc.

Library of Congress Catalog Card Number: 80-50230
ISBN: 0-442-25396-6

Published by D. Van Nostrand Company
135 West 50th Street, New York, N.Y. 10020

10   9   8   7   6   5   4   3   2   1

To Irene Khin Khin

Preface

This book is intended for courses in Argumentation or Argumentation and Debate, whether at the lower or upper division level. It should also fulfill the needs of courses in Applied Logic and Argumentation in departments of Philosophy, English, and Journalism. The book is appropriate as well for the debater and for students in adult education courses.

The book's primary goals are at the heart of the liberal arts tradition: thinking logically and communicating clearly and effectively. Both theory and practice are stressed. Theory is brought into the practical arena for appreciation and application. Scholarly literature has been put into simple and familiar language, and examples are used to clarify concepts. Examples are drawn from the interests of the students rather than from those of the author, from formal debate propositions, or from quoted excerpts from magazines or other sources.

Students are encouraged to formulate positions as they study the material. They may agree, disagree, or discuss in classroom sessions what has been written. An extensive annotated bibliography is included at the end of the book to encourage those who wish to read further.

The text begins with the nature of argumentation and the importance of ethics. Chapter 3 surveys the Toulmin system of analysis of argumentation, introducing the elements of claim, data, warrant, backing, qualifier, and reservation. Chapters 4 and 5 explore the numerous subclaims possible when analyzing problems and proposing solutions. Chapters 6 and 7 discuss classifying, gathering, evaluating, and recording evidence. Inductive and deductive reasoning are analyzed in Chapters 8 and 9. Pseudoreasoning is probed in Chapter 10, and receiver analysis and source credibility are covered in Chapters 11 and 12. A chapter discussing the organizing of argumentation includes briefing and a survey of case and debate formats. The last three chapters discuss refutation, language in argumentation, and the oral presentation of argumentation. At the end of each chapter are exercises designed for writing or speaking assignments or for class discussion. Instructors may want to shift the order of the chapters to suit their purposes or the needs of their students.

Sensitive to the unfairness inherent in the traditional utilization of only masculine pronouns, I have used plural subjects where possible and have balanced the number of male and female examples throughout the book.

An Instructor's Manual, available from the publisher, contains methods of teaching, roles of the teacher, means to aid student and teacher interaction, a suggested course outline, suggestions for evaluating speeches, and examination questions.

I wish to acknowledge numerous colleagues at the University of Minnesota in the Speech-Communication Department, especially Robert L. Scott, Ernest G. Bormann, and William S. Howell, and in the Communication Program, Daniel V. Bryan and Jean Ward. They have helped create a stimulating and supportive atmosphere in which to work. Hundreds of students have indirectly contributed more to this book than they or I fully realize. I wish to thank Judith Joseph, of D. Van Nostrand Company, for her encouragement and advice, Maggie Schwarz for helpful editorial guidance, and Sandra Riekki and Susan Kellogg for excellent typing. I appreciate the helpful suggestions of the following reviewers: Dencil R. Taylor, Midwestern State University; George Hinshaw, Northwest Missouri State University; Ronald J. Matlon, University of Massachusetts, and Patricia L. Garrighan, State University of New York at Oswego. Finally, I wish to thank my wife, Irene, son, Donald, daughter, Maythee, and son-in-law, John, for their enveloping love, which makes this and any enterprise worthwhile.

Contents

16 ORAL PRESENTATION OF ARGUMENTATION   299

ARGUMENTATION

Reasoning in Communication

1 Introduction to Argumentation

Importance of Argumentation and Debate
Definition of Communication, Argumentation, and Debate
Values of Argumentation and Debate
Basic Concepts in Argumentation and Debate
Summary
Exercises

IMPORTANCE OF ARGUMENTATION AND DEBATE

It is customary to assert how important argumentation and debate are in democratic societies, and although this may seem commonplace, it is a fundamental place to begin. When Americans travel abroad or simply pay heed to the news of the day, they are made painfully aware that there are numerous countries on this planet which have authoritarian governments, of varying political orientations, which lack a parliamentary debating process in national decision-making, and lack a trust of open and free expression of dissent. These regimes send opposition leaders into exile or to prison or worse, whereas parliamentary democracies honor the opposition by giving it a responsible role, and some governments even pay the Leader of the Opposition an additional special salary.

In the spirit of the ancient Athenians, modern democracies continue to echo the outlook and commitment expressed by Pericles: "...instead of looking on discussion as a stumbling-block in the way of action, we think it an indispensable preliminary to any wise action at all."[1] Modern

1 Thucydides, *The Peloponnesian War*, trans. R. Crawley, intro. J. Gavorse (New York: Modern Library, 1934), p. 105.

1

democracies not only share Aristotle's faith that "things that are true and things that are just have a natural tendency to prevail over their opposites,"[2] but also share his realization that truth and justice need trained rhetoricians to help win the day.

This spirit of free expression has been transmitted to the United States via the deeply rooted English heritage. Listen to Peter Wentworth, the fiery Elizabethan orator, seeking to make parliamentary debating more free from interference from the Crown in the late sixteenth century:

> If the envious do offer anything hurtful or perilous, what inconvenience doth grow thereby? ... By the darkness of the night the brightness of the sun showeth more excellent and clear; and how can truth appear and conquer until falsehood and all subtleties that should shadow and darken it are found out?[3]

The seventeenth century literary giant, John Milton, did much to develop the *free marketplace* concept, that is, that people ought to be free to express their various ideas, just as people are free in a marketplace to display their various products. The eloquent late eighteenth century forensic orator, Lord Erskine, gave forceful impetus to the faith that in a contest between truth and falsity, "truth will spring from the collision."[4] John Stuart Mill, the famous nineteenth century philosopher, emphasized that "since the general or prevailing opinion on any object is rarely or never the whole truth, it is only by the collision of adverse opinions that the remainder of the truth has any chance of being supplied."[5] In the twentieth century, Sir Winston Churchill used to like to point out that parliamentary democracy was the worst possible form of government—until you had looked at the other options! Contemporary oratory in London's Hyde Park reminds us that free speech is alive and well.[6]

In the United States the First Amendment to the Constitution stands as a basic pillar to our democratic edifice: "Congress shall make no law respecting an establishment of religion, or prohibiting the free exercise thereof; or abridging the freedom of speech, or of the press; or the right of the people peaceably to assemble, and to petition the Government for a redress of grievances." We have tried, with varying degrees of success,

2 Aristotle, *Rhetoric*, trans. W. Rhys Roberts (New York: Modern Library, 1954), 1355a.

3 Speech in the House of Commons, February 8, 1576, *British Orations* (New York: E.P. Dutton, 1960), p. 7.

4 Speech in the Court of King's Bench, December 18, 1792, *British Orations*-, p. 137.

5 "On Liberty," in Haig A. Bosmajian (ed.), *The Principles and Practice of Freedom of Speech* (Boston: Houghton Mifflin, 1971), p. 60.

6 See J. Vernon Jensen, "London's Outdoor Oratory," *Today's Speech*, 15 (1967): 3–6.

to perpetuate the premise that people are capable of self-government, that sovereignty ultimately resides with them, and that individuals have the right to explore and express ideas freely. We have tried to put into practice the notion that ideas publicly tested will lead to wiser decisions, to peaceful change, to programs which will secure acceptance and commitment from the widest possible portion of society. Committed to the premise that the majority should rule, we nevertheless, recognizing that majorities may be wrong and may change their minds, are equally committed to the free expression of minority views. The right of dissent is our greatest assurance that, in Wentworth's metaphor above, the sun will conquer the darkness. To use another figure of speech, democracy has been compared to a raft, whereby water is always splashing over it but it always stays afloat; whereas authoritarian governments may look like a sturdy vessel for awhile but eventually sink. History is filled with sunken dictatorships, once arrogantly riding the waves in false glitter and pomp. To ensure that the raft stays afloat, we need to combat effectively the three fundamental enemies of the democratic process, that is, the enemy centered in the will (apathy), the enemy centered in the mind (ignorance), and the enemy centered in the spirit (intolerance).

Decision Making

Rational decision-making is important in a host of everyday, informal communicative situations as well as in formal legislative debating chambers or in the overarching milieu of society. As Crable put it: "Argumentation is not only important because of its potential in a free society but also because it permeates so much of human activity."[7] Each day we have to make decisions: What clothes should I wear? Should I skip class? What should I eat for lunch? Should I go to the library to study? Should I write a letter to the editor of the campus newspaper? Should I go to a movie tonight? Other, more major decisions are also ours to make: What college or university should I go to? What political candidates should I support in the coming election? What religious affiliation should I commit myself to? Should I live in a dormitory, in an apartment, or join a sorority/fraternity? Should I marry before graduating? Should I purchase a new stereo set? Should I work or travel during summer vacation? In all decisions, large or small, we know we have to decide, for not to decide is to decide. We thus engage in intrapersonal argumenta-

7 Richard E. Crable, *Argumentation as Communication: Reasoning with Receivers* (Columbus, Ohio: Charles E. Merrill, 1976), p. 4.

tion, that is, we debate with ourselves, and we engage in interpersonal argumentation with others, and the outcome of such efforts can be highly significant in our lives and in the lives of those around us.

Surely in the vast majority of cases, though admittedly not in all, life's decisions are arrived at more wisely if we use our rational powers to the utmost; carefully formulated decisions are generally more reliable and preferable, and are more likely to stand the test of time. We recognize that we humans will probably be pushed and pulled by our selfish interests and ignorance, by pressures from peers, by submission to authority figures, and by a host of other nonrational factors in our decision-making unless we can assert our independence and make decisions based on our own rational processes.

Thus, as Ziegelmueller and Dause have put it: "If we believe that logical factors should prevail in individual and social decisions, then we must have a commitment to training in argumentation."[8] Centuries ago Plutarch focused clearly when he asserted that learning, rather than good ancestry, riches, glory, beauty, health, or strength, is the most important possession that human beings can acquire, and that reason and speech, the two most distinctive components of human learning, particularly needed to be nurtured.[9] That is precisely what argumentation and debate courses attempt to do.

Being so central to our national heritage and to our everyday communicative needs, it is not surprising that argumentation, debate, and forensic activities long have been an integral part of our curricular and extracurricular educational scene.[10] Today a strong interest in argumentation courses and debate and forensic activities is apparent, and in addition to the long-established exchange debates with Oxford and Cambridge, American debaters are participating in tours in such countries as New Zealand, the Soviet Union, and Japan.[11] Japan is

8 George W. Ziegelmueller and Charles A. Dause, *Argumentation: Inquiry and Advocacy* (Englewood Cliffs, N.J.: Prentice-Hall, 1975), p. 9.

9 *Plutarch's Morals*, rev. trans. William W. Goodwin (Boston: Little, Brown, 1878), pp. 12–13.

10 See David Potter, "The Debate Tradition," and Annabel D. Hagood, "Forensic Honor Societies," in James H. McBath (ed.), *Argumentation and Debate: Principles and Practices* (rev. ed.; New York: Holt, Rinehart and Winston, 1963), pp. 14–47; Richard E. Rieke and Malcolm O. Sillars, *Argumentation and the Decision Making Process* (New York: Wiley, 1975), pp. 277–82; and George V. Bohman, "Rhetorical Practice in Colonial America," Marie Hochmuth and Richard Murphy, "Rhetorical and Elocutionary Training in Nineteenth-Century Colleges," L. Leroy Cowperthwaite and A. Craig Baird, "Intercollegiate Debating," in Karl R. Wallace (ed.), *History of Speech Education in America* (New York: Appleton-Century-Crofts, 1954), pp. 60–79, 153–77, 259–76.

11 Unpublished papers presented by John D. Saxon, Lucy M. Keele, David Congalton,

enthusiastically becoming involved in debating activities through their extracurricular English Language Clubs. Debate in Great Britain has traditionally been handled by students themselves in their Debating Unions, outside of the regular curriculum, but in the newer polytechnic universities, debate and curricular communication offerings are reflecting American influence. We, in turn, have been influenced to some degree by the British style of debating.

DEFINITION OF COMMUNICATION, ARGUMENTATION, AND DEBATE

Communication

Argumentation should be viewed within the overall framework of the human communication process. The basic paradigm of communication can be expressed in the single question: Who said what through what medium to whom for what purpose, despite what distractions, with what result?

The who is the person encoding (sending) the message, whether speaker or writer. The what is the message, which could be carried via such mediums as the voice (that is, manipulated sound waves), nonverbal cues (such as gestures, body movements, or facial expressions), or writing. These in turn might be mediated by radio, television, the telephone, or a public address system. The words or nonverbal cues operate as symbols, that is, they stand for something else. The word "table," for example, stands for that object. The word is not the object. Words and nonverbal cues do not have meaning in and of themselves, for meaning resides in the minds of the people engaged in the communication transaction. In the above question, the to whom is the decoder (recipient) of the message, whether listener or reader. Sender and receiver interact continually, with the latter sending at least nonverbal cues which the initial encoder incorporates into her subsequent statements, and on and on in a dynamic, continuous process. The general purpose would be to inform, persuade, or entertain, and the specific purpose would of course be narrowed to the particular objective of the movement. Distractions such as noise, poor handwriting, crowded

and Ronald J. Matlon at the annual convention of the Speech Communication Association, November 12, 1979, in San Antonio, Texas; Matlon, "Japan and the CIDD [Committee on International Discussion and Debate]: The 1978 Tour," *Spectra*, 15 (February 1979): 12.

conditions, or competing communicators could significantly distort or modify the message. Each communicator, of course, has his own inner distraction mechanism, a filtering screen made up of his values, experiences, knowledge, and biases, through which the message may be distorted or significantly modified. The results are both the short- and long-range effects of the communicative transaction.

For many years now the human communication process has been appropriately depicted as a circular, bilateral transaction between at least two people, rather than the older, less-satisfactory image of the unidirectional process whereby a communicator delivered some message to someone else who simply absorbed it, much like a messenger handing a note to someone without receiving a response to it.

Argumentation

Rieke and Sillars define argumentation well when they say it is "that ongoing transaction of advancing claims, supporting them with reasons, and the advancing of competing claims with appropriate support, the mutual criticism of them, and the granting of adherence to one."[12] Argumentation is a human communication process which emphasizes the rational (logos) while at the same time recognizing the importance of the appeal to the credibility of the arguer (ethos), and the appeal to the emotions of the audience (pathos). This textbook reflects that proportioning, for eight chapters (3–10) deal with claims, reasoning, and evidence; whereas only one chapter (11) discusses ethos, and one chapter (12) analyzes pathos. Argumentation, of course, occurs in informal, interpersonal, everyday interactions as well as in public discourse and in formal debating situations.

To distinguish argumentation from persuasion, it can be stated that the above proportioning is reversed, in that persuasion stresses ethos and pathos, while to a lesser degree acknowledging the role of reason. Persuasion is mainly concerned with the effect of the communicative effort on the audience. Propaganda can be considered large-scale persuasion, where only one side of a case is presented in a sustained campaign, and it is aimed at a mass audience.

We ought to correct the negative image that many readers probably have of the term argumentation. In our colloquial expressions we speak of an argumentative person as one who is troublesome, unfriendly, quarrelsome. This picture of course should be dispelled, for an arguer, in our technical use of the term, is one who is engaged in the above

12 Rieke and Sillars, pp. 6–7.

process of presenting and examining claims and reasons. Furthermore, it would be helpful to define a quarrel as a communicative exchange in which countering claims are exchanged with virtually no supporting reasons and with virtually no examination of each other's claims.

Debate

Debate is a specific application of argumentation. It is structured advocacy in a formalized situation on a specific proposition. The issues are crystallized into two mutually exclusive opposing positions on some claim of fact, value, or policy. These types of claims are clarified in chapter 3. The advocates on both sides have equal time and equal opportunity to present their points and to respond to those by their opponents. Judgment on the strength of the respective cases is rendered by a judge, a third party, either singular (a judge in a courtroom or in an academic debate) or plural (a jury or multiple judges in an academic debate). Central to the process of debate, whether it be in the courtroom, legislative chambers, on the public platform, or in an academic debate tournament, is the concept that the advocates are not trying to change each other's views, they are trying to influence some third party on whose decision they place great value and whose decision is binding.

VALUES OF ARGUMENTATION AND DEBATE

We have briefly sketched the importance of rational decision-making to democratic society in general. Here we want to summarize the specific benefits of educational debate to the participants. A serious and active debater stands to gain valuable experience and training in investigative procedures, analytical skills, synthesizing, impromptu analyzing and synthesizing, speaking, and courage in risk-taking. These values will be highly significant in the individual's growth as a scholar, critic, and communicator, will provide excellent skills for most jobs and professions, and will help the individual to play a significant participatory role in community, state, and national affairs.

Training in Investigative Procedures

The vast amount of research that is necessary for a debater to ferret out information from newspapers, pamphlets, periodicals, documents, and books develops the student's ability to utilize more efficiently the abundant resources of the library. Chapter 6 discusses the process of information-gathering. Searching for data of course takes debaters outside of the library, too, and they learn to interview people in the community with skill and confidence, and simply become more sensitive to the radio, television, and current newspapers and magazines as sources for relevant information. Engaging in such investigation, debaters develop an eagerness to get to the bottom of things, but also come to realize that even the most thorough investigation will still probably be incomplete. These attitudes and skills obviously have a direct application to the student's other classes and endeavors as well.

Skill in Analyzing

Debate provides experience and training in analyzing the various materials discovered. Finding information is only the first step, for one must learn to evaluate the facts and opinions accumulated. One learns to separate the important from the trivia, the relevant from the irrelevant, the recent from the outdated, the reliable from the unreliable, the strong from the weak, the sound from the unsound. The process of testing evidence is discussed in chapter 7, and much of the textbook is devoted to developing soundness of reasoning. It is one thing to discover information, but it is quite another thing to discriminate intelligently and evaluate what one finds. Debate definitely helps the participants to do so.

In developing one's ability to analyze, debate nurtures the scholarly approach of looking at both sides of all the issues. Indeed, it teaches us that most issues have more than two sides. It is the spirit which Harrison Salisbury, the highly respected journalist and author, recently gave credit to his alma mater, the University of Minnesota, for having inculcated in him:

> It was...a heels-dug-in attitude toward the world, not accepting beliefs or doctrines or movements simply on their credentials but subjecting them to a skeptical kind of scrutiny....It was...the long hard look, the deliberately provoked argument to see what each side had to say, the determined search not for just two sides of a question but a third or even a fourth side; an independence from political cliches and a determination not to be bound by the past or by any stereotype of the future.[13]

One learns to arrive at conclusions carefully and methodically, demanding of oneself and others solid evidence and sound reasoning. Rigid

13 Harrison E. Salisbury, in Chester G. Anderson (ed.), *Growing Up in Minnesota* (Minneapolis: University of Minnesota Press, 1976), pp. 71–72.

preconceptions and motives are rigorously scrutinized. One learns to disagree without being disagreeable, to challenge ideas and not the person. The analytical spirit, at the heart of what it means to be a scholar, is at the heart of the debating experience.

Skill in Synthesizing

To be able to take things apart (analysis) is fine, but we also need to know how to put them together (synthesis). The latter is thus the intellectual companion of the former, and debate gives the participant excellent experience in both. Debaters are forced to build a coherent case out of the isolated bits of data. A pile of bricks does not make a building; a human being has to put them together in some meaningful form. Debaters gain experience in arranging their information, in structuring their ideas in a purposeful manner. Constructing a well-organized case is discussed in chapter 13. Through reasoning, debaters come to see relationships and patterns which at first were not apparent. The skill of composing, of putting things together, is a fundamental value derived from debating.

Skill in Impromptu Analyzing and Synthesizing

It is common to assert that debating gives one practice in thinking on one's feet. Indeed it does. In the dynamic cut and thrust of debate, participants gain valuable experience in responding immediately to questions and claims, in extracting quickly the relevant data from one's storehouse, and in effectively communicating it under pressure. It is one thing to be able to gather and organize data in the long weeks of calm prior to a debate, but it is quite another experience to listen perceptively, to present evidence in the flash of the moment, to defend one's claims, and to spot weaknesses in the opposition's case in the heated exchange of an actual debate. Debate is one of the very few instances where a college and university student can get such training in intellectual dueling, for unfortunately few classes provide it. If students are lucky enough to have intellectually stimulating companions, then they may get a similar valuable experience in college bull sessions, as C.S. Lewis, author and theologian, experienced as a student at Oxford. He excitedly wrote to his close friend back home in Ireland: " … you can have no idea how the constant friction with other and different minds improves one."[14]

14 C.S. Lewis to Arthur Greeves, April 11, 1920, in Walter Hooper (ed.), *They Stand Together: The Letters of C.S. Lewis to Arthur Greeves* (New York: Macmillan, 1979), p. 270.

Skill in Speaking

Educational debate obviously provides excellent opportunities for participants to develop and polish their skill in speaking. Chapter 16 will discuss this in detail. The endless rehearsing, practice sessions, intrasquad clashes, intercollegiate tournaments, and presentations before a general public audience help debaters develop a fluency and effectiveness which otherwise would lie undeveloped and unpolished. Development of such skill and confidence and poise obviously carries over into other scholarly endeavors, into other public-speaking situations, and into everyday activities.

Courage in Risk-Taking

The courage to expose oneself to intellectual and emotional risks is significantly strengthened by debate experience, for the very essence of debate is that participants voluntarily place themselves in a situation in which their ideas and statements are open to immediate challenge by a trained opponent. This willingness to risk, in the short run, possible defeat in a contest, or, in the long run, serious modification of one's views, values, and commitments develops a moral courage which is difficult to acquire in any other context. To state one's views in the presence of one's opponents and await their inevitable counterattacks takes courage. Debaters put themselves in the role of what Ehninger and Brockriede call "a restrained partisan," that is, debaters "stand poised between the desire to maintain a present view and willingness to accept the judgment a critical examination of that view may yield. ... [They enter into] ... a consciously induced state of intellectual and moral tension."[15]

Potential Dangers in Debate

Citing the impressive values of debate experience should not blind us to a number of possible dangers. By focusing on only two alternatives, debating can lock a person into a rigid two-value orientation, lacking sensitivity to multiple options in social and personal problems. Beginning with a conclusion, that is, with a ready proposition which is to be advocated, debating may not inculcate sufficiently the attitude of searching for the best possible solution. Debate tends to stress disagreement by

15 Douglas Ehninger and Wayne Brockriede, *Decision by Debate* (2nd ed.; New York: Harper & Row, 1978), p. 29.

forcing participants to make clear just how they differ from the opposition, instead of stressing the areas of agreement. Debate may encourage participants to be unnecessarily pugnacious. All too often, in tournament situations the focus on winning vastly overrides being concerned about serving the truth. Short-range victory takes precedence over long-run success. Participants may glory excessively in verbal eloquence. Early in the nineteenth century, Richard Whately, British rhetorical theorist, warned:

> When young men's faculties are in an immature state, and their knowledge scanty, crude, and imperfectly arranged, if they are prematurely hurried into a habit of fluent elocution, they are likely to retain through life a careless facility of pouring forth ill-digested thoughts in well-turned phrases, and an aversion to cautious reflection.[16]

These dangers in nineteenth century British debating societies are to be acknowledged as potentially lurking in twentieth century American debating circles as well, but they can be easily overcome with a wise and conscientious program of debating training.

BASIC CONCEPTS IN ARGUMENTATION AND DEBATE

To make our study of argumentation and debate more understandable, it is necessary at the outset to clarify some basic concepts in the field. Thus, it is important to define what is meant by such things as issues, presumption, burden of proof, proof itself, a *prima facie* case, and probability.

Issues

Issues are central, inherent questions imbedded in the subject being discussed, not something tangentially created by the arguers. The arguer's case is an outgrowth of how she answers these vital questions. An issue is larger than an argument, for an issue may be made up of many arguments. Issues are phrased in the form of a question; they are to be explored and answered by the advocates. Be they in the courtroom, in an academic debate, or in any informal situation, the advocates who can best come to grips with the issues usually will be the most successful.

16 Richard Whately, *Elements of Rhetoric*, Douglas Ehninger (ed.), (Carbondale, Ill.: Southern Illinois University Press, 1963), p. 27. This work was originally published in 1828.

Stock issues are those basic, standard questions which apply to virtually any proposal put forth as a solution to some problem. These stock issues are: Does a problem exist? Is the problem significant? Is the problem inherent in the status quo? What is the proposed solution? Is the plan workable? Will the plan bring significant benefits? Chapters 4 and 5 present a detailed listing and analysis of questions that an advocate might probe when grappling with these stock issues.

Issues are also classified into other categories. We speak of *potential* issues, that is, the whole universe of possible, relevant issues in any given subject, with the understanding that time and space do not permit the advocates to deal with all of them. The *contested* issues are those actual issues on which a particular debate is conducted, and the *ultimate* issue is the one central issue, often arrived at during the cut and thrust of the debate, on which the winner of the debate will often be decided. *Admitted* issues are those that are waived, that is, the opposition does not choose to contest them.[17]

Presumption

Presumption is the recognition that what currently exists, the status quo, that is, the prevailing beliefs, practices, institutions, or systems, will continue to exist unless good and sufficient reasons are put forth why they should not. For example, the current practice of using gasoline in automobiles will continue until some different source of propulsion, such as Gasohol, can be demonstrated to be more feasible and beneficial. Presumption does not say that the status quo deserves to exist but simply that it likely will; that is, presumption is descriptive, not prescriptive.

The status quo has time on its side, that is, it has existed over a certain period of time. It has concreteness and tangibleness on its side, that is, it is in actual existence. It is assumed to have widespread acceptance or it would not continue to exist. Change involves considerable cost in terms of effort, money, and thought. For example, we may ask ourselves whether we should buy a new pair of shoes, but reluctant to spend the money, time, and effort in purchasing a new pair, we opt to keep the shoes we have. Change involves risk; it is better to live with a known defect than to propose a solution whose effect, no matter how apparently laudable, cannot be guaranteed. In short, the status quo has an inherent strength which will enable it to continue until an opposing idea or program is able to dislodge it.

17 For a longer discussion of issues, see Austin J. Freeley, *Argumentation and Debate: Rational Decision Making* (4th ed.; Belmont, Calif.: Wadsworth, 1976), pp. 50–59.

It should also be noted, however, that in many situations the proposer of new policies gains presumption rather easily, and the persons who would forestall the new proposal are reluctant to do so, for a variety of reasons. A person may appear to be standing in the way of progress or may be perceived as being personally motivated to block someone else's plan. It also is often assumed that the proposer has thought the subject through, knows what she is talking about, and thus, especially if she is trusted and if people do not desire to investigate the subject further, her proposal is merely rubber-stamped by others present. Also, people may not want to antagonize the proposer, not only because of the immediate unpleasantness that may occur but also because the proposer's vote or goodwill in the future might be needed. The seemingly mundane can also be very important here, that is, the audience may be tired, anxious to go home or eat or relax, and hence are quick to give an affirmative vote on whatever is being proposed. But having noted this, it should further be suggested that, really, the minute a proposal is made it sort of becomes the status quo. For example, the minute John is nominated for some office, other people are reluctant to nominate others for the above reasons, and his nomination becomes an immediate status quo which others are reluctant to alter.

There are varying degrees of strength, of course, to any given status quo, for some are more susceptible to change than others. For example, the practice of driving on the right side of the road is more deeply entrenched in our society than is the practice of driving at a maximum speed of 55 miles per hour. It would be considerably easier to change the latter than to change to driving on the left side of the road. The degree of strength of the presumption will thus vary with each item.

Richard Whately is still a helpful authority to turn to in clarifying presumption, for he thoroughly analyzed and succinctly described the concept:

> There is a Presumption in favour of every existing institution. Many of these (we will suppose, the majority) may be susceptible of alteration for the better;...No one is called on (though he may find it advisable) to defend an existing institution, till some argument is adduced against it.[18]

His military analogy further clarifies the point:

> 'Presumption' in favour of any supposition, means...a pre-occupation of the ground, as implies that it must stand good till some sufficient reason is adduced against it....A body of troops may be perfectly adequate to the

18 Whately, p. 114.

defence of a fortress against any attack that may be made on it; and yet, if ignorant of the advantage they possess, they sally forth into the open field to encounter the enemy, they may suffer a repulse. At any rate, even if strong enough to act on the offensive, they ought still to keep possession of their fortress. In like manner, if you have the 'Presumption' on your side, and can but refute all the arguments brought against you, you have, for the present at least, gained a victory.[19]

Burden of Proof

This is the opposite side of the coin from presumption. It is the burden, the task, of the person who wants to change the status quo to demonstrate convincingly that the present situation should be altered. Where presumption is descriptive, burden of proof is prescriptive. As Whately expressed it,

> ...the 'Burden of proof' lies with him who proposes an alteration; simply, on the ground that since a change is not a good in itself, he who demands a change should show cause for it....[His] argument ought in fairness to prove, not merely an actual inconvenience, but the possibility of a change for the better.[20]

In an educational debate, if the judge perceives the teams to be equal, the decision goes to the negative team, the one defending the status quo, for the affirmative team has the burden of proof to demonstrate a clear advantage to their case. A boxer who challenges the champion has to win the contest; a draw (a tie) results in the status quo continuing, that is, the champion remains champion until defeated.

Those who accuse have to prove their case. In the courtroom the burden of proof rests on the prosecution, for the defendent is presumed to be innocent until proven guilty. A student who claims a professor is unfair has the burden to prove those charges. A teacher who accuses a student of cheating has to prove that charge, for the student is presumed to be innocent until satisfactory proof is forthcoming. The burden, the risk, then, is appropriately on the accuser, for this protects people from irresponsible and unsupported charges.

Proof

We have clarified what the burden is, but we still need to discuss more specifically just what proof itself is. "Prove it to me" is a challenge we all

19 Whately, pp. 112–13. For a different perspective on presumption, see Ehninger and Brockriede, pp. 139–41.
20 Whately, p. 114.

have had to measure up to in a variety of situatons. What is proof to one person may not be to another. Thus, proof is not some inherent quality in the message but, rather, depends on the audience dimension. Proof is the winning of assent from the audience, measured by statements of agreement, nonverbal cues such as head nodding, or actions, such as purchasing the advertised product.

A helpful metaphor is to say that the arguer seeks to gain the adherence of the audience, which depicts an image of two entities sticking together; thus the participants come together in their views, just as two objects are made to stick together by some adhesive glue. Another useful metaphor is to say that proof is that which is necessary to move an individual over the threshold from nonacceptance to acceptance, just as when we step over the threshold of a door, we move from the outside to the inside, or vice versa. The evidence and reasoning which causes members of the audience to cross over the threshold, or to adhere to the claims of the arguer, serves in that instance as proof.

It is as if there were a chemical reaction whereby some members of the audience but not others react to the message so as to accept the soundness, the truthfulness, of the claim. For example, experimental findings have won the adherence of a number of people to the contention that smoking is indeed harmful to one's health; that same evidence has not been proof to other people. The prosecuting attorney says that the evidence proves that the suspect did indeed rob the bank; the defense attorney says that the evidence does not prove it. The judge or jury has to decide in their own minds whether proof is present or not. Student A says that Professor X is incompetent, as he or she is disorganized, gives poor tests, and is a dull speaker; but Student B does not feel that these bits of evidence prove the accusation. A brother tells his sister, "OK, you've proved it to me, now let's see you prove it to Dad!"

We must realize, then, that proof is individualized, whether the communicative transactions are in dyads, small groups, large audiences, or even mass audiences. We are seeking to get individuals to adhere to our claims, and of course if the audience factor is large, we then hope that a large number adhere. But however large the number, they are still individuals who determine whether or not something is proof.

Sometimes, of course, nothing will satisfy individuals as being proof, especially on extremely important subjects. A firmly committed anti-abortionist refuses to believe the arguments and evidence of the opposition, and parents may refuse to believe that their child is not capable of straight "A" schoolwork. The audience, thus, may occasionally make demands for proof so strong that no arguer is likely to meet them.

Prima Facie Case

When people advocating a change of the status quo present a case which is powerful enough to win the desired adherence from the audience, or to force a defense of the status quo, then they have presented a prima facie case. *Prima facie* means "on the face of it," or "on first appearance," and it is a logically adequate case, then, whose proof is strong enough to establish itself in the eyes of other people. It is the minimum needed to establish a desired case. It is potentially strong enough to push the present occupants off the high ground, to revert to Whately's analogy.

Probability

In making decisions in informal or formal contexts we operate on a continuum of certainty, which can be illustrated by the following diagram:

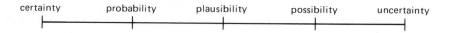

If we and our audience are truly certain about something, then there is no need to engage in argumentation. Likewise, if we and our audience are totally uncertain, then we are unlikely to. But in virtually all of our human communication we are dealing with degrees of certainty, which are expressed as probably, plausibly, and possibly. What we are engaged in as arguers is to move the audience along that continuum to coincide with where we stand, or at least closer to it than they are intially. Since certainty is not present, since our knowledge is incomplete, our perceptions limited, and time and space restricted, we have to take a stand on less-than-perfect grounds. This should make us more tentative about our assertions, more tolerant of the views of others, and more committed to the open marketplace of ideas in order that truth might be better served.

SUMMARY

Argumentation and debate are at the heart of democracy, and each needs the other. With our democratic roots in Greece and Great Britain, we in the United States endeavor to nurture the notion of a self-governing open society. Argumentation and debate are also central to our everyday decision-making on personal and community problems. Our colleges and universities in their curricular and extracurricular offerings do much to further training in argumentation and debate.

As one area of communication, argumentation is that process which emphasizes the rational, presenting and evaluating reasons and evidence in support for claims, for the purpose of winning adherence. Debate, a specific application of argumentation, is structured advocacy in a formalized situation on a specific proposition. Training in debate, and in argumentation in general, brings numerous benefits, such as increased skill in gathering information, in analyzing and evaluating the material accumulated, in synthesizing the data into a coherent, well-constructed case, in impromptu analyzing and synthesizing (thinking on one's feet), and in speaking, as well as in developing courage in the type of risk-taking inherent in placing oneself in a communicative situation in which one's ideas and statements are open to immediate challenge by a trained opponent.

A number of basic concepts in argumentation and debate need to be clarified at the onset. These include an understanding of what is meant by issues, presumption, burden of proof, proof itself, a *prima facie* case, and the concept of probability.

EXERCISES

1. Interview some members of the debate team at your school. Do they agree or disagree with the values and potential dangers of debate as discussed in this chapter? Would they add some further points? Share your findings in an oral report to your class.

2. Keep a diary of argumentation as you observe it in everyday experiences during the next five days. Summarize in a 500-word essay some of your major conclusions. Attach the journal as an appendix to your essay.

3. You no doubt have had to make some fairly significant decision within the last few days or weeks. Reflect carefully on the thought processes you went through in arriving at your decision. In this intrapersonal argumentation (arguing with yourself), what factors were more important than others in making your final conclusion?

4. Attend some debate on campus or in the community (or watch one on television) and summarize in an essay the use of reasoning and

evidence by each side as they developed their case and responded to their opponents. If a formal debate is unavailable, visit some city council meeting, faculty committee meeting, legislative committee meeting, or some staff meeting where you work, and report on the role of reason and evidence in the verbal interaction which took place.

5. Discuss the quotation in this chapter from Pericles. Can you think of situations, actual past events, or hypothetical cases in which his advice may not hold up? In the light of these objections, can you still defend his position?

2 Ethical Responsibility

Importance of Ethics in Communication
Ethical Guidelines: Obligations Toward the Immediate
   Audience
Ethical Obligations Toward Others Not in the Immediate
   Audience
Sources for Ethical Guidelines
Summary
Exercises

IMPORTANCE OF ETHICS IN COMMUNICATION

Legal Speech

Most of us are aware that some communication is illegal. In the presence of a third party we cannot make statements about someone that are false and injurious to his or her reputation. This would constitute a defamatory statement, whether in written form (libel) or in spoken form (slander), and would be subject to court action. A convicted slanderer could be subject to the payment of a heavy financial reparation, or could receive even harsher punishment. Robert O'Neil, in his book entitled *Free Speech: Responsible Communication Under Law,* clarifies additional legal categories. "Even if the exposures are true and accurate, and thus clearly not defamatory [truth takes precedence even if it works a hardship on someone], the law of some states affords limited redress to the victim" who charges that an "invasion of privacy" has occurred; that is, his "name, physical likeness, reputation, or some intimate detail of his private life [has been used] for commercial profit without his consent."[1] Also, in a situation where a speaker can be proved to have intentionally caused "mental distress" to someone (not necessarily in the presence of a third party) through "humiliation, the practical joke, or...terror tactics,"[2] the speaker may be liable to court action.

Ethical Speech in Interpersonal Communication

Speakers who are concerned about living up to the highest moral standards direct their attention far above the legal levels of "mental distress," "invasion of privacy," and "slander." They are concerned not merely with what they can legally get away with but with what they ought to say and do as humane and responsible human beings. To do only what is "legal" is to stop at the elementary school level of moral development. Just as learning to read involves a lifelong process of advancement and refinement, to live life on an appropriate human level means one goes on and on to new levels of ethical commitment.

By the very act of oral communication the speaker enters into the mind and being of at least one other person, a fact which, to any sensitive individual, automatically raises ethical considerations. Richard Johannesen, one of the leading scholars in the field of ethics in communication, has put it well: "Potential ethical issues are inherent in any instance of communication between humans to the degree that the communication involves possible influence on other humans and to the degree that the communicator consciously chooses specific ends sought and communicative means used to achieve those ends."[3] What ought a person to say and what ought to be left unsaid in each speaking situation? Thomas Nilsen, who has contributed much provocative material in this area, has reminded us of the endless situations in which ethical implications may be present:

> ...a failure to speak when someone needs encouragement; a hasty response that suggests indifference; an arbitrary order that wounds someone's ego; a seemingly innocent remark that hurts someone's pride; a

1. Robert M. O'Neil, *Free Speech: Responsible Communication Under Law* (Indianapolis: Bobbs-Merrill, 1966), p. 95.
2. O'Neil, p. 96.
3. Richard L. Johannesen, *Ethics in Human Communication* (Wayne, N.J.: Avery Publishing Group, 1978), pp. 11–12.

word of disapproval in a context that magnifies the disapprobation; gossip; a half-truth, or the full truth at the wrong time or place.[4]

Ethical Speech in a Public Setting

Ethical concerns become even more important when an oral communicator addresses a public gathering, for more people are being affected. In this day of mass communication a speaker's words have even greater potential for good or ill. As the world shrinks and our responsibilities expand, as communication between groups and nations proliferates, with increasingly momentous decisions hanging in the balance, with harmony and good faith tied not only to "getting along with one another" but to continuing to exist on this planet, it is obvious that the aspect of ethics in oral communication is more important than at any other time in history. During the last two decades increased concern for the ethical implications involved in speaking has clearly been evidenced by the growth of significant literature in articles and books not only by scholars in the field of communication but also by philosophers, social psychologists, political scientists, anthropologists, and public officials.

Clarification of Terms

We should warn ourselves at this early state of the oversimplified polarity involved in our terms "ethical" and "unethical." We need to realize that we are dealing here with something on a continuum, that any given act is to be measured on a scale rather than labeled and placed into one of two pigeonholes. Therefore, while we use the two extreme terms of "ethical" and "unethical" for the sake of quick and easy communication, we need to realize that by the latter, for instance, we mean "that which is less than what it ought to be on the ethical scale." Instead of writing those fourteen words, or their equivalent, each time, we simply say "unethical."

Our emphasis in this chapter is on dynamic and flexible ethical *guidelines*, not dogmatic and static rules or mandatory prescriptions. We conceive of these ethical guidelines as strong moral commitments that pull us in a healthy direction, jostling with all the other factors, inherent in any given situation, that are trying to pull us in other, less healthy directions.

4. Thomas R. Nilsen, *Ethics of Speech Communication* (2d ed.; Indianapolis: Bobbs-Merrill, 1974), p. 11.

For example, suppose you have a chance to secure a good-paying job in a store, but it involves working on Sunday as well as selling merchandise in which you have little interest. What moral considerations will push and pull at you during your decision-making about whether to take the job? You owe it to yourself and family to secure a good income. You owe it to yourself and family and church to leave Sunday free for religious observances and for recreation. You owe it to yourself to sell merchandise that would be more interesting. You owe it to the store manager to accept, for the manager is having difficulty finding personnel and is, moreover, a family friend.

Likewise, a speaker may be confronted with difficult moral decisions. Suppose a candidate for political office is given some information about an opponent who is allegedly involved in a scandal. Should this information be used in tomorrow's speech? The candidate's campaign managers think so—and loyalty to the party dictates doing whatever is necessary to win the election. The candidate's family think not—and their feelings ought to be respected. The candidate's church may frown on it, but friends at the health club think it would be a good idea—and one shouldn't let one's friends down. Could one live with one's conscience if the information was used? How influential would the desire to win, fear of retaliation, or commitment to truth and justice be? What would happen to the opponent's reputation? With all of these pressures, the speaker needs to have firm commitments to ethical guidelines in order to see clearly the ethical issues and possible consequences and thus be able make the most humane decision. A ski towrope brings us to the heights, where we can get a clearer view. But just as the skier must voluntarily grasp the towline for it to have any effect, so must a speaker willfully grasp ethical guidelines.

Hopes and Preview

It is hoped that this chapter can aid you to grasp helpful moral guidelines more habitually and securely. The area of ethics is so nebulous and controversial that it is quite impossible to set down any simple blueprint of what is or is not ethical in every situation. But it is hoped that this discussion may bring out some helpful emphases that will enable you to become not only a more effective arguer but a more ethical one. At the same time, it is hoped that developing a keen moral sensitivity will not inhibit legitimate vigor and boldness in speaking out on the problems and issues faced in contemporary life.

This chapter will survey eight ethical guidelines that will help you fulfill more adequately your moral obligations toward your immediate audience, your circle of acquaintances, society in general, and yourself. Finally, the chapter will discuss what seem to be the sources for ethical standards for the arguer.

ETHICAL GUIDELINES: OBLIGATIONS TOWARD THE IMMEDIATE AUDIENCE

Ethical concerns of the speaker are mainly related to the immediate audience, for they are the human beings likely to be the most affected. You need to recognize your moral obligations toward your auditors regardless of the brevity of the remarks. What ought to be the major moral guidelines, the dominant ethical "pulls" operating on you as you try to fulfill these obligations? Any categorization would of necessity be rather arbitrary. But perhaps for the sake of analysis we could indicate that the speaker who would be highly ethical is the one who has a firm commitment to, and serves conscientiously, the following: (1) accuracy, (2) completeness, (3) relevance, (4) openness, (5) understandability, (6) reason, (7) social utility, and (8) benevolence.

Accuracy

Perhaps the first thing that comes to mind about ethics in argumentation is that communicators ought to be honest. They ought not to lie, they ought to tell the *truth*. This is the alpha, and for some people the omega, of the matter. But in order to understand this commitment more clearly we ought to recognize the dual elements in truth, that is, (a) *accuracy* and (b) *completeness*. Much mischief and needless haggling often occur when these two elements are not clearly separated.

For example, some individuals and doctrinaire groups have asserted that "religion is the opiate of the people" in that it has, like a drug, made people insensitive to problems of this world by teaching the devotees to think about life after death. Religious people have quickly countered, "But that's not *true!*" and then have taken on the impossible task of explaining away the numerous incontrovertible facts, both historical and contemporary, demonstrating that some branches of some religious groups have indeed played that kind of a role. But the original accusation obviously could be effectively countered on the ground of being *incomplete*. That is, more numerous instances might be cited wherein religion, far from being a drug, has been stimulant, an innovator, a pioneer, a corrector of social injustices. Witness the many hospitals, schools, colleges, homes for the aged, social work agencies, camping facilities, and so on, which were originally pioneered by religious groups and which now, in many instances, have finally been supported by an awakened secular society. Thus, when talking about "truth," it is important to look separately at accuracy and completeness.

Deliberately giving inaccurate information is hardly to be condoned. Reporting that your team has won five games when in reality it has won only three, announcing that a political opponent favors abolishing the income tax when you know that to be not so, or contending that you are a college graduate when you are not can be rather quickly seen as unethical communication.

Deliberately citing something out of context is unfortunately done on occasion, such as asserting that Candidate M is a very excitable person (and hence unworthy to be elected), for you saw a demonstration of that characteristic yesterday, but neglecting to mention that this occurred at the football stadium where the candidate's alma mater was playing. Quoting someone out of context is another form of deception. For example, if someone says, "When we receive the necessary federal support, expected in about twelve months, we ought to build a second school immediately." But if the quote reports the person as saying, "We ought to build a second school immediately," the point would be seriously distorted.

Likewise, quoting out of *time* context is just as misleading. For example, suppose a Republican candidate for governor is quoted accurately as having said: "The Democratic Party offers the most enlightened program and leadership for our state." But no mention is made of the fact that this was said thirty years ago when that individual held different political views, and the candidates and issues were different. In the international sphere, where the balance of power results in nations being "friends" in one generation and "enemies" in the next, serious misrepresentation of public officials' current attitudes results when they are quoted out of time context. During the 1950s, for example, when the United States was intent on containing Communist Russia, some officials had their pro-Russian statements of the early 1940s, when Russia and the United States were allies in the war against Hitler, used against them to show that they were supposedly "soft on Communism" and hence unreliable policymakers.

Also, sometimes speakers distort by going beyond the facts. The problem of juvenile delinquency, for instance, may be grossly exaggerated in the hope of getting some action by the city council. Unethical speakers may also spread excessive fear by predicting unusually dire consequences if the problem is unresolved, or they may generate unwarranted hope of a glorious utopia if the problem is handled as they urge. Ethical communicators would certainly try to avoid such emotion-laden exaggerations and try to give their auditors a more accurate portrayal. Furthermore, some speakers have been known to exaggerate their own "expertness," that is, they mislead the audience by pretending to be more knowledgeable, or to be more "in the know," than they really are.

Sometimes, of course, speakers may give inaccurate information or present a distorted view of their subject matter unintentionally. Is this unethical? Suppose speakers repeat information they have read, not knowing it was inaccurate, or simply give the wrong information by mistake. Some people might assert that speakers have an obligation to be carefully prepared, to ensure that such slips would not occur, that they have an obligation to be accurate, regardless of their intentions. While this may be a healthy rigor to submit oneself to, this would really be more a matter of intellectual, rather than moral, failure, at least in my opinion. In this chapter we are concerned with *intentional* acts, willfully and purposefully committed in order to mislead the listener, however slightly.

Another factor related to the ethics of accuracy is that misleading associations are sometimes created by unethical communicators. To link a person or idea or product with another person, idea, or product may induce unwarranted deprecation or prestige. To make such a linkage a spurious one with the intent to mislead rather than to clarify touches on the ethical dimension. The use of "common ground" by speakers to show a genuine identity with their listeners is quite appropriate in an effort to gain acceptance, but to suggest such a common bond when none really exists or when the connection is very faint is to mislead the audience. For instance, a speaker who is a college graduate may quite legitimately refer to college experiences when attempting to identify with a college audience. But if that person was speaking to a group of farmers and had no significant linkage with them, to pretend that a link did exist by bringing in all kinds of artificial, common-ground items would be questionable indeed. Also, the "transfer" device, when used to transfer the prestige from some person or institution to the speaker when that linkage is not true, or is artificial at best, would mislead. For example, to link directly or indirectly some public official to "communism," or some other current "evil" group or concept, when such an identification is false, would do a serious injustice to that official and would mislead the audience. Likewise, to try to transfer the prestige of, for example, the legal profession to yourself by mentioning your lawyer friends or your cousin who is a judge would be an inaccurate portrayal of your real relationship with the legal profession and hence mislead your audience.

Completeness

The second aspect of truth is *completeness*. A person may utter perfectly accurate statements, but the message may suffer from lack of completeness and hence be "untruthful." A speaker may pretend to be covering all the major points, but may intentionally omit some, thus giving the audience a warped view, and failing to fulfill their democratic right to know all the relevant points necessary if they are to make wise decisions. This process of distortion, whereby a person intentionally selects only those factors that bolster his or her position and omits or barely mentions those that tend to weaken the opposing case, is sometimes labeled "card-stacking." If entered into openly, so that the audience is aware that your statements represent only one side of the issue (such as a lawyer defending her client, a debater presenting his case, or a speaker prefacing remarks with such an admission), then of course no ethical problem is present.

Incompleteness may result not only from the presentation of a carefully prepared, slanted, single point of view, but also from simple, inadequate preparation. In other words, you should not pretend to be fully informed, but should openly admit that there may be some aspects of the problem that you have not as yet been able to study.

The speaker's sources of information, purposes, and affiliations   You should be completely open with your audience about the sources of your information, your purposes, and your affiliations. The sources of your information may be very crucial to an audience trying to evaluate your statements, so you should not hide your sources or falsify their origins. Thus, you would be wise to use sources of which you would not be ashamed. Time and circumstances obviously dictate that listing all sources, much like a bibliography at the end of a research paper, would hardly be expected. But the point here is that you should not be incomplete in your presentation by hiding sources if they are particularly relevant or if the audience asks for them. The same applies to mentioning the dates of the sources. For example, college enrollment figures of 1930 may have little bearing and in fact may distort the picture when discussing current college problems. Your audience has a right to know the dates of your material.

Likewise, you should not deceive your listeners as to your purposes. To pretend to be giving merely an informative survey to a topic when you really are attempting to persuade them, and perhaps to obtain a financial contribution, would be ethically questionable.

Furthermore, you ought to be complete by not hiding your true affiliations if relevant or if the listeners ask for them. To know that a speaker advocating higher wages for teachers is a member of the teaching profession, or that a speaker who is lashing out at desegregated schools is a member of the Ku Klux Klan would be highly relevant to the audience evaluating their statements. For these speakers to hide their affiliations would be highly unethical.

Authorship   Another relevant concern that ought to be discussed in connection with speakers' obligations to be completely open with their audience is the vexing issue of "ghostwriting." Do speakers have an obligation to tell their audience who helped them write their speech? Some scholars feel that ghostwriting is unethical. Most scholars, however, would not agree; they would assert that it is taken for granted that public speakers assume the responsibility for whatever they say. We might say, for instance, that when public speakers utter their statements, they are saying *chiefly* not, "This is something I have created all by myself" but, "This is what I believe, this is what I shall take responsibility for."

Of course, a much different situation exists in a classroom setting, for the speeches that students are assigned to create and deliver are expected to be theirs and theirs alone, since they are in a *training situation.* Any help they receive in composition will be quite improper and unethical, for when they stand in front of the class they are saying primarily, "This is something which *I* have created, on which you people will be grading me."

My position, then, is that ghostwriting is not unethical, except in speech training situations. Our busy men and women of affairs—university presidents, business executives, government officials—need some assistance in constructing speeches, for our society calls on them to speak not only frequently but also on an incredible variety of topics. But speakers must assume the responsibility for their statements. A doctor has nurses, technicians, and interns to assist in getting instruments, operating room, and patient ready for an operation. But the doctor performs, and takes the responsibility for, the operation. A speaking situation is admittedly somewhat different from this analogy in that speech and speaker are more an integral part of one another, so that we are concerned with a person as well as a product, but the difference is one of degree and not of kind.

Exceptions to Accuracy and Completeness

The alert student no doubt has already mentally formulated numerous exceptions to the ethical guidelines of completeness and accuracy so far discussed. Since the nagging question of "exceptions to the rule" is going to continue to trouble us throughout this chapter, perhaps it would be wise to discuss it at this point.

One may be thinking of the doctor who communicates less than complete or accurate information in order to serve the best interests of the patient, or of the parent who at a given moment tells a "white lie" in order to protect a child from abnormal fear. At times government officials have felt it necessary (in order, according to them, to unite the country, subdue exaggerated anxiety, reduce apathy, give impetus to a war effort, or negotiate with foreign powers) to withhold information, or give incomplete, misleading, or even outright false information. If officials deem this necessary, they should note the warning of a sensitive Dag Hammarskjold:

> The most dangerous of all moral dilemmas: when we are obliged to conceal truth in order to help the truth to be victorious. If this should at any time become our duty in the role assigned us by fate, how strait must be our path at all times if we are not to perish.[5]

These exceptions do not make the general ethic of truth-telling less virtuous or binding. They simply illustrate that humans have to decide in any situation where two or more values are struggling for precedence which one is to accept a subordinate position. We must recognize that multiple values are operating with various priorities in virtually every

5. *Markings*, trans. Leif Sjoberg and W.H. Auden (New York: Alfred A. Knopf, 1964), p. 147. For an insightful brief discussion of what is meant by "telling the truth," see Dietrich Bonhoeffer, *Ethics*, Eberhard Bethge (ed.), (New York: Macmillan 1965), pp. 363–72.

human act. Thus, the doctor and parent may decide that in a given instance compassion for patient and child takes precedence over telling the truth. The government official may decide that fulfilling the obligation to protect the nation takes precedence over telling the truth. It is not necessarily "going back on one's principles." It is not hypocrisy. It is deciding which value takes priority in a particular situation.

Suppose I were to assert that one "ought to be kind to animals," and also that "parents ought to protect their children from harm." These values usually exist peaceably side by side throughout most of our lives with little or no conflict. But if a mad dog was threatening to harm one of my children, I would not hesitate to harm that animal, giving precedence to protecting my child. There is no abandonment of principle here, merely a question of priorities. A member of the Society for the Prevention of Cruelty to Animals or a pacifist may establish different priorities in that instance, or may be less quick to define the situation as one in which the child was threatened. I would continue to voice commitment to both values without a sense of hypocrisy, nor should such an experience reduce my commitment to either.

Some individuals and groups establish a predetermined, rigid, non-changing hierarchy of values that keeps at the top the one value to which they are most firmly committed. For instance, a pacifist would be an example of one who keeps at the top of the hierarchy the commitment to peace and nonviolence, regardless of the problem. Regardless of the decision-making crisis involved, the pacifist would not permit any value, such as "freedom" or "liberty," to take precedence over peace. Some people place "law and order" at the top of their hierarchy of values, whereas many in society contend that where "justice" and "equality of opportunity" have been seriously neglected, these values ought to take precedence. This is at the heart of much of the contemporary social and political ferment.

Advocates of "relativistic" ethics sometimes give the impression that since "absolute" ethical norms are occasionally abrogated, they therefore are really inoperative and unimportant, and hence should not command intense commitment. For some people the game of "exception-finding" weakens commitment, which it surely ought not to do. Eating hot dogs at a football game with your mittens on should not lessen your commitment to the general guideline to wash your hands before eating!

In many instances the distinction between the two values may not be so sharp and clear. For instance, where does devotion to "human rights" end and "property rights" begin? "Public good" and "private gain" may sometimes be difficult to distinguish. Where does devotion to "being liberal in human affairs, but conservative in financial affairs" lead you when you have to decide whether public employees should be granted an increase in salary?

Before leaving this discussion of the need for flexibility in the midst of firm commitments, it should be noted that in no way should you get the impression that all values are created equal and therefore it makes little difference which value a person is attached to. It means, to the contrary, that speakers have to engage in an agonizing search within their own consciences about which value is to take precedence in each situation.

Relevance

In addition to accuracy and completeness, the value of relevance commands the commitment of the speaker who would be as highly ethical as possible. Just as you should not omit information that is crucially important to the subject being discussed, so you should not include irrelevant material purposely to deceive, mislead, or distract the audience. A common method is the *ad hominem* technique, whereby speakers purposely direct their arguments "to the individual" rather than to the issues. For example, instead of discussing the stand that a political opponent takes on the major campaign issues, the speaker below the optimum ethical ceiling talks about the opponent's divorce, awkward gait, and habit of talking very rapidly (implying untrustworthiness). Bringing in unrelated material, stories, or anecdotes intended to stall for time or to distract the audience away from the subject is certainly unethical, even if it is interesting and humorous. After entertaining an audience for a disproportionate amount of time, this kind of speaker will usually feign surprise that so much time has elapsed, and then announce that he or she will have to rush on and hit only the high spots. The inevitable result is incomplete coverage of the subject, in addition to presenting the irrelevant.

Openness

The speaker who would be ethical is also conscientiously guided by openness. Since a basic cornerstone in democracy is the people's "right to know" all necessary information needed to make intelligent decisions, any specific audience is thus entitled to a balanced and objective presentation, unless it is clear that it is the intention and task of the speaker to present only one side of an issue (such as a lawyer in court). Do not pretend to be doing justice to all sides of a question when you really are not. Show in attitude and demeanor as well as words that, in all justice to the complexity of the subject, other points of view have a right to be held and expressed, and, indeed, may prove to be more efficacious than your own. Meaningful alternatives should be thoughtfully and fairly given to the audience. Obviously the severe time restrictions on public speeches do not permit extensive treatment of all options. Indeed, even if an attempt were made to do so, it probably would result in a necessary oversimplification, which may be worse for the audience than listening to a more thorough presentation of one point of view. It may create an *illusion* that both sides have been thoroughly and fairly presented. But speakers should at least indicate what some other options might be. They should demonstrate their faith in the democratic ethic of the "free marketplace of ideas." That is, all thoughts on a given subject, regardless of how "offbeat" or obnoxious they may be, have a right to be held and expressed, and that through a free interchange, truth will emerge more surely (although it is not guaranteed!) than if any idea had been suppressed.

Just as in a vegetable market, where people are free to display their produce and buyers are free to choose what they desire, so it is in the open and free marketplace of ideas. The assumption is, in both instances, that the good items will be selected and the bad ones will be rejected. To this democratic faith and ethic the responsible speakers in our society ought to be fully committed. If they are, then they will have less difficulty in treating all ideas with fairness and justice. Indeed, the speakers will welcome the audience to differ with them in a sincere desire to gain a clearer insight into the truth. This attitude of "creative interchange," to use a phrase of Henry Wieman's, whereby "the viewpoint of the other is integrated into [our] own perspective,...is the chief way in which error is corrected, knowledge expanded, values purged, insight deepened, and appreciative understanding established among individuals, groups, and peoples."[6]

Speakers should guard against the subtle and serious temptation that they need not be too careful in their remarks (selling a few bad vegetables), for other people (with their superior produce) will correct them anyway. What if those other people don't? If they do, what if they are ineffective? Thus, the free marketplace of ideas should in no way be

6. Henry N. Wieman, "Speech in the Existential Situation," *Quarterly Journal of Speech*, 47 (1961): 150.

construed as an opportunity to slacken in the care exerted in one's expressions.

Understandability

Ethical speakers have an obligation toward their audience to make their material *understandable*. Unscrupulous speakers may confuse their audience by intentionally talking above their heads in order to appear vastly superior to them, or to get them to "give up" trying to understand the subject, thereby winning acceptance by default. Oversimplification also distorts. The audience is led to believe they understand, but they really do not. Furthermore, clarity of expression that eliminates, or reduces to a minimum, ambiguity and vagueness should become an ethical concern.

But it should be noted that some teachers, philosophers, theologians, and other public speakers may, with the highest of ethical concerns in mind, purposely employ irony, ambiguity, vagueness, and other means of muddying the water in order to stimulate their audience to think. For instance, this type of indirect communication was utilized by the nineteenth century Danish philosopher Sören Kierkegaard, who sought to be intentionally ambiguous by combining jest with seriousness or by combining attack and defense, so that auditors, puzzled as to Kierkegaard's actual position, would have to think through their own religious commitments for themselves. In short, Kierkegaard dissembled his own position in order to force his listeners to pay attention and to work out their own decisions. He felt that this was the only way to awaken people out of their cozy religious illusions. Many teachers today feel this is necessary to counteract the "know-it-all" attitude of some students. Thus, the goal of this indirect communication is "not to clarify an idea...but to stimulate the recipient into independent activity."[7]

This special method of communication, however, is used only by a few sophisticated communicators, and even then perhaps only in specific isolated instances and situations. For most public communications it may be disastrous. For instance, a "tongue-in-cheek" letter to the editor, an ironic comment in a news conference, or a subtle allegorical speech could land the communicator into great difficulty. The exceptions indicated, therefore, need not reduce the ethical imperative of clarity and understandability. The audience has a right to be given understandable material.

7. Raymond E. Anderson, "Kierkegaard's Theory of Communication," *Speech Monographs*, 30 (1963): 7.

Reason

Those who have written on the importance of ethics in communication, especially in connection with persuasive discourse, have emphasized, and rightly so, that *logos* (appeal to logic) should have precedence over *pathos* (appeal to emotions). They contend that the deliberate use of nonrational-motive appeals designed to short-circuit the thinking process of the listeners is inherently unethical because such appeals violate our democratic ethic, which demands freedom of choice. It results in psychic coercion. Furthermore, it is asserted that the utilization of nonrational means to appeal to our subconscious drives is basically an invasion of our privacy and an unfair exploitation of our human weaknesses.

Most writers would agree, however, that to be ethical a speaker need not eliminate all emotional appeals (as some texts in earlier decades seemed to maintain), even if it were possible. After all, human beings are not fully rational creatures and need to be met on all levels of their being, including the emotional. It does mean, however, that emotional appeals should be only supplementary, to give impetus, to rational appeals, and that the bulk of the emphasis should be on the latter, where the auditor can be taken along in an open, unemotional, logical fashion. The respect for the dignity of your listener certainly is a major relevant commitment to bear in mind when planning to tap some of his or her deep drives and motives. Furthermore, to pretend that your presentation is based on logical foundation when it is not is another instance of subterfuge that cannot be condoned. When a speaker says, "Now, let's look at this from the standpoint of logic...," it does not necessarily mean that logic follows!

To conclude this section with a positive assertion then, we would emphasize that ethical communicators would want to present a speech that rested basically on the rigorous demands of rational procedure. That is, they would rely on systematic investigation and on reflective, logical thought, and would judiciously utilize emotional appeals with a sincere moral sensitivity to the well-being of the audience.

Even here, however, some modifying insights ought to be discussed. There may very well be times when complete dependence upon rational means might approach the unethical. For instance, if the attention of the listeners is not maintained, they might turn to a more interesting but less rational demogogue. Since driving the listeners away reduces their opportunity to hear all alternatives to the question at hand and thus reduces their freedom of choice, a speaker may be engaging in unethical behavior. Brembeck and Howell, pioneers in demonstrating ethical concerns in persuasion, emphasize that the "cult of reason" is on somewhat shaky ground. It is unrealistic, they assert, to assume that listeners are more rational than they really are, and by avoiding nonlogical means the persuader might well reduce his or her effectiveness, which would not fulfill the moral obligation to be effective in a given crisis.[8] One might also raise the question whether many in the audience are not in need of an emotional jolt in order to awaken them from apathy or insensitivity. For instance, coaches harangue their athletes, parents badger their children, evangelists excite their listeners, student leaders arouse lethargic fellow students, and social reformers stir their audiences for "good" ends.

But even after having noted, and to some degree acknowledged, the shortcomings of relying solely on a rational appeal (if, indeed, such a thing exists), we would still be able to come back to our original affirmation that an ethical speaker would conscientiously endeavor to rely primarily on the rational, with emotional appeals to be used only as a supplementary, not substitutive, agent.

Social Utility

The speaker who desires to be high on the ethical scale would want to serve not only the guidelines of accuracy, completeness, relevance, openness, understandability, and reason, but also social utility. Brembeck and Howell, leading advocates of social utility as a basic value, have defined it as "usefulness to the people affected,"[9] that is, that which fosters the survival of the group both immediately and in the long run. They suggest that the probable amount of social utility may be determined by engaging in a conscientious attempt to understand "the group members and their common interests, ways our persuasion may help or hurt the group, and favorable and adverse effects on individuals."[10] This rests to some degree upon the principle of utilitarianism crystallized by the early nineteenth century English philosopher, Jeremy Bentham. That is, the greatest good for the greatest number ought to be one's guide. Of course, it is difficult at times to judge accurately what is the best for the well-being of the greatest number in the short and long range. But a conscientious prediction based on a genuine concern for the welfare of the audience will usually come close to the mark.

8. Winston L. Brembeck and William S. Howell, *Persuasion: A Means of Social Influence* (2nd ed.; Englewood Cliffs, N.J.: Prentice-Hall, 1976), pp. 237–38.
9. Brembeck and Howell, p. 245. See also J. Michael Sproule, *Argument: Language and Its Influence* (New York: McGraw-Hill, 1980), pp. 292–93.
10. Brembeck and Howell, p. 245.

Benevolence

This leads us to the final ethical guideline, one which undergirds all of the previous seven. It is a genuine spirit of *benevolence* toward one's audience. Respecting the dignity of each individual in your audience, you should exhibit a high degree of tactfulness, for no one has the right to intentionally or unnecessarily hurt another person by words, any more than by physical means. That words can wound, and wound severely and for long duration, is something of which we are all probably painfully aware. Some people have carried with them for a lifetime the scars left by some tactless speaker. We should put ourselves in the listener's place and ask the age-old question, would we want a speaker to do to us what we are doing to our audience? Sensitive goodwill is imperative. Of course, benevolence, good intentions, and sincerity should not be substitutes or cover-ups for solid intellectual substance in our speeches. Indeed, "sincere" speakers have caused great mischief because of inadequate intellectual ballast. On the other hand I would guess that "intellectuals" have caused far more mischief because of a lack of genuine benevolence toward others.

ETHICAL OBLIGATIONS TOWARD OTHERS NOT IN THE IMMEDIATE AUDIENCE

Thus far our focus has been on speakers' ethical responsibilities toward their immediate audience, those who actually hear them. But we need to realize that as they speak they have a moral obligation also to primary and secondary groups, to society in general, and to themselves.

Obligations to Primary and Secondary Groups

An oral communicator's words affect not only the people listening but may affect directly or indirectly those primary and secondary groups with which he or she is associated. Primary groups would include family, relatives, close circle of friends, local clubs and organizations, or fellow employees, that is, the people with whom he or she is closely identified and with whom he or she carries on intimate, face-to-face communication. Secondary groups would be such affiliations as the American Medical Association, Republican Party, Congregational Church, AFL-CIO, and so on, where communication would rarely be intimate (unless he or she is an unusually active member on some administrative unit above the local group), but with which he or she would be identified, even if he or she were an inactive member. Unethical speakers bring shame and ill will to their primary and secondary groups, just as a young person convicted of stealing does. It is the "law of association," which cannot be denied or repealed. On the other hand the same "law" dictates that an ethical speaker brings prestige and goodwill to these groups. Thus, a speaker ought to be sensitive to this fact and should have their welfare in mind as well as the welfare of the immediate audience.

Obligations to Society

Furthermore, oral communicators have a moral responsibility toward society in general. Their remarks may injure or aid their fellow citizens by weakening or strengthening the fundamental values upon which the society is based. They may actually endanger the safety and security of the national community during some peril such as war. In our democratic setting we would emphasize that a speaker demonstrate commitment to the preservation and expansion of such values as the dignity of all individuals, equality of opportunity, and freedom of expression.

What if a person feels that certain values in society are not worthy ones, for example, segregation, Fascism, Communism, and so on? Is that person bound to adhere to them? To say that those cultural values that *do* exist *ought* to exist would be an untenable position and, at best, a slavish perpetuation of the status quo. This issue is far bigger than the immediate focus of this text, but the possible dilemma facing a speaker in such a situation ought not to go by unnoticed.

Obligations to Self

Finally, speakers have a very real moral responsibility toward themselves. They must respect themselves if they are to respect their audience. They must be concerned with their own dignity if they are to be sensitive to the dignity in others. Their own integrity must be guarded, whatever the cost, for it is with themselves that they must live each minute of each day. When they know that they have deceived their audience, or have been less than conscientious about the audience's welfare, or have fallen short of the ethical commitments discussed in this chapter, they are in danger of creating a considerable amount of inner anxiety, or, at the least, some very unpleasant memories. We all, literally and figuratively, see ourselves daily in a mirror, and must live with the image that we see. Speakers owe it to themselves to speak ethically in order to be at peace with themselves. One could do worse than repeat the ancient axiom: *To thine own self be true.*

SOURCES FOR ETHICAL GUIDELINES

From where do these ethical guidelines come? In what soil do the seeds germinate and spread their roots? Or from where *ought* these guidelines come? Why do we, or why ought we, urge commitment to accuracy, completeness, relevance, openness, understandability, reason, social utility, and benevolence? It would seem that, essentially, four sources might be cited: (1) within the individual, (2) the immediate social context, (3) ethical values of the nation, and (4) universal, religiously rooted ethical demands. These four are of course interrelated, but it may be helpful to analyze each separately.

The Individual as a Source

Some writers have insisted that the source of ethical standards simply ought to be oneself, that is, one's own concept of self-interest, since this is the way people supposedly *do* behave anyway. We know, for example, that some people are "honest" only because they know someone is able and willing to dispute them if they slip (for example, in parliamentary debate), or because they know of the ill effects (for example, a store-keeper knows the customer will not return). Howard Martin[11] feels that this "imperative of self-interest" is the only guideline really operating, and that out of a collision of competing self-interests comes a synthesis, a decision that can be called "right" or "wrong" that brings social stability and order.

B.J. Diggs[12] refutes this by asserting that "self-interest," after all, is based on *learned* rules and social norms: "Self-interest does not tell man how to act rightly; that is what rules are designed to do." Social rules and conventions, with their concern with "oughtness," supplement and mold an individual's natural inclinations. Diggs asserts that Martin's position, while it purports to be free of rules, is really one big rule: "Always promote your interest," which Diggs feels is really of very little help. He

11. Howard H. Martin, "Ethics and Persuasion: An Impertinent Rejoinder," *Quarterly Journal of Speech*, 51 (1965): 329–331.
12. B.J. Diggs, "Ethics and Persuasion: Author's Reply," *Quarterly Journal of Speech*, 51 (1965): 331–33.

ridicules Martin's "laissez-faire theory of persuasion, according to which, from self-interested competition, order miraculously emerges."

I agree with Diggs that to rely on this "imperative of self-interest" is far too limited to serve as a sole source of ethical guidelines. But we need to recognize that it exerts a powerful pull on all of us and perhaps we ought to channel it to higher levels of long-range self-interest. That is, a clerk may think it is in her self-interest (larger commission, elimination of surplus merchandise, experiencing the exhilaration of successfully persuading, etc.) to convince a customer to make a purchase. But whatever immediate gain, it would soon evaporate when the customer discovers that he has been sold a product much inferior to what it was purported to be. Thinking of self-interest in a longer view would certainly be important, but, in my opinion, focusing on oneself for the sole source of ethical behavior is far from sufficient.

The Social Context as a Source

A second suggestion is that the source of ethical standards is to be found in the immediate social context. For instance, what is right in a public speech, such as advocating energetically only one point of view, may not be right in a classroom setting. This approach suggests that universal, exact, and unchanging moral laws, while possibly desirable, simply do not operate in real life because of numerous qualifications and reservations. For instance, "Thou shalt not kill" is seriously modified by permitting and even advocating the taking of human life in certain situations under certain conditions. Hence, universal prescriptive rules are thought to be unrealistic sources for ethical standards, and a better source is supposedly the immediate social context. A person should observe the actual moral behavior of one's contemporaries; advice given on the degree of rightness or wrongness of a given persuasive act should take into account the concrete circumstances surrounding the immediate situation. One's guide should be in part the degree to which the society affected will be hurt or benefited both now and in the future. In this regard, however, it may be wise to keep in mind the admonition of one writer: "...to establish that *some* ethical criteria are situation-dependent does not establish that *all* are."[13]

13. Dennis Day, "The Ethics of Democratic Debate," *Central States Speech Journal*, 17 (1966): 11.

The Nation as a Source

Most efforts in recent years have been toward an advocacy of the nation, the political state, as a source of ethical standards. It is asserted that the ideals of one's nation—in our case, the ideals of democracy—ought to be the source from which a speaker acquires a useful system of ethical guidelines. For instance, Karl Wallace asserted that we ought to "look for the ethical basis of communication in the ideals of our own political society."[14] He developed some guidelines that have found their way into many oral communication texts. Wallace summarized four fundamental values of our United States democracy: (1) respect for the dignity and worth of an individual; (2) the rights of freedom of action, restrained only by law; (3) faith in the equality of opportunity; and (4) faith that every person is capable of understanding the nature of democracy (its goals, values, and procedures), and hence the necessity of freedom of press, speech, and assembly. Many other authors have also emphasized that our democratic national values ought to be the source of ethical standards in our oral discourse.

This emphasis, however, raises some fundamental questions. For instance, this approach seems to assume that a code of national values is relatively easy to clarify. But this may not be the case. Readers no doubt are aware of localities and regions in the United States where some of Wallace's values listed above are not subscribed to (to say nothing of not being practiced).

Furthermore, what happens when the values of a society are found to be undesirable in the light of more universal commitments? Suppression of opposing views in a totalitarian country would be glorified. Such practices as perjury would be justified if accepted in a certain society. What *is*, is not necessarily what *ought* to be. As. B.J. Diggs has written:

> ... the rules and standards in force in a society are *not* always the best. Some rules-in-force in some circumstances should even be disobeyed.[15]

In other words, we must recognize that while the majority *rules*, the majority may not be *right* in its ethical norms.

In addition, within certain international groupings such as the "Western democracies," are national differences really so great? Are there significantly different ethical standards in Detroit, in Toronto, in London? This emphasis on *national* values might lead to a very unhealthful and unwise provincialism.

14. "An Ethical Basis of Communication," *The Speech Teacher*, 4 (1955), 5.
15. B.J. Diggs, "Persuasion and Ethics." *Quarterly Journal of Speech*, 50 (1964): 370

Finally, although this emphasis is usually put forth as a "relativistic" ethic supposedly avoiding the alleged pitfalls of a universal, religiously oriented system of ethics, it nevertheless has characteristics of an absolutist ethic. It applies in a given country the defined national values in a prescriptive manner just as a religious code does on a universal basis. Reducing the geography involved and substituting a political for a religious base hardly changes the inherent characteristics of absolutism.

Thus, in my view, despite the many admitted advantages of using a nation's values as a source of ethical norms, to rely *solely* on a national, cultural source for one's ethical standards seems unwise. Surely it would be incomplete.

Universal Religious Ideals as a Source

Finally, a traditional source of ethics is a religiously rooted code aimed at universal application for all peoples. Most of the authors who have written on ethics in public speaking have revealed a reliance on the Judeo-Christian tradition as a source of ethical standards, but have done so only implicitly. In fact, there seems to be a studied attempt to avoid reference to that religious origin. But as they deplore the use of such things as deceit, distortion, falsification, misrepresentation, and obtaining personal gains at the expense of the group, it would seem that they are drawing upon the ancient Judeo-Christian heritage in which our culture is rooted. After all, the ancient prophets were proclaiming justice, equality, honesty, and purity long before our founders were here to "found" anything.

Therefore, I would wish to acknowledge more explicitly our debt to, and reliance on, this religious heritage as a source of ethical guidelines. Even though many of the ancient religious precepts are in the dogmatic form of authoritarian absolutes, of "commandments," and are cast in social and historical contexts quite different from ours, yet these values have guided human beings throughout many centuries and are still powerful and relevant. In this day it might be wise to remind ourselves that if we canot fully reach our ideals, the fault may not be in the ideals! People must live with some unattainable goals that pull them in healthy directions. Tension that may result from not living up to ethical standards is not necessarily bad. Mature people have learned to live with meaningful tension and have let it help guide them toward higher plateaus.

SUMMARY

Arguers who are conscientiously concerned with living up to the highest possible ethical standards of a moral human being will be setting their sights far above just "what they can get away with." In the preparation and delivery of your message you will want to commit yourself fully to the ethical guidelines of (1) accuracy, (2) completeness, (3) relevance, (4) openness, (5) understandability, (6) reason, (7) social utility, and (8) benevolence. You should realize that in any decision-making situation these values will be struggling for priority, with the inevitable result that one or more will take precedence over others for that moment. But you also should realize that this should in no way reduce your commitment to those values that are temporarily relegated to subordinate positions.

Exceptions to these general ethical guidelines, therefore, should not cause you to lessen your commitment to them. You should endeavor to see the wisdom and necessity of both flexibility and firm commitment. You should also be anxious to ensure that what you say will reflect favorably on the primary and secondary groups with which you will inevitably be identified. You also should desire to protect your own personal integrity, to be able to live with yourself, knowing that you have acted in a morally responsible fashion. You need to appreciate that the sources of your ethical standards are varied and interrelated. They spring from your own self-interest, from the immediate social context, from the mores and values of your community and nation, and from some long-standing religious ethic, which for most of us is the Judeo-Christian framework. You should realize that freedom of speech brings responsibility of speech. By the very act of communication you are invading the hallowed privacy of another human being, and as you tread on that sacred ground, you ought to walk humbly with your conscience.

EXERCISES

1. Discuss some current incident you have observed or read about in which the free marketplace of ideas seemed to be sharply circumscribed. It may be on the campus, in your home, in your community, or in some other setting. Analyze why you think the restrictions on expression occurred, and suggest ways in which it could have been corrected.

2. Write an essay on some ethical absolute (such as, "Thou shalt not tell a lie"), and indicate under what conditions it might be modified in practice. Comment on whether you feel this invalidates the absolute or not.

3. Prepare a speech centered around some value (persistence, courage, compassion, and so on). You may want to illustrate at some length by dwelling on some individual who embodied your chosen value. Feel free to employ irony or other indirect means to communicate your material in an interesting manner.

4. Some teachers would contend that they should not become involved with the ethical dimensions related to their subject matter, feeling that to do so is improper or ineffective or both. Write an essay in which you react one way or another to that contention.

5. Prepare a speech in which you defend as the best single source for ethical standards one of the four discussed (individual, social context, nation, or universal religious ideals).

3 Claim-Making

We humans are constantly making claims. Such as the one I just made, for instance. Close friends exchange claims frequently, children and parents hurl claims at each other daily, and employers and employees make numerous claims from their given perspectives. Advertisements flood us with their commercial claims on billboards, in magazines and newspapers, and on radio and television. In courtrooms, legislative chambers, board rooms, public debates, and educational debates claims are forcefully expressed. In short, we encounter claims in all areas of everyday life.

A helpful system in understanding and testing claim-making, whether it be informal or formal contexts, is that supplied by Stephen Toulmin. This contemporary philosopher's approach has become familiar in recent years to students of argumentation, for it has found its way into most textbooks.[1] The Toulmin structural model views the claim-making

---

1. For a recent book in argumentation, to which Toulmin has contributed as one of the authors, see Stephen Toulmin, Richard Rieke, and Allan Janik, *An Introduction to Reasoning* (New York: Macmillan, 1979), especially Chapters 2–7.

process as being composed of six fundamental elements: (1) claims, (2) data, (3) warrant, (4) backing, (5) qualifier, and (6) reservation. Some of these labels are modifications of Toulmin's actual terminology. The first three, (claim, data, and warrant), are the core elements, with the other three being more peripheral. All of course are interdependent, but we need to separate them for the sake of fuller understanding. Often one or more of the elements are not present in the flow of argumentation, so the audience has to supply them mentally. By our discussion of these elements we hope to become better able to note their presence or absence, and evaulate their power, in any formal debate or in everyday informal argumentation. The Toulmin nomenclature helps us to see argumentation more clearly in its actual usage in all areas of life.

This chapter will discuss the nature and types of claims, and two subsequent chapters will analyze claims when made within a problem-solution framework. Later chapters will discuss evidence, so that will not be dealt with very extensively here. The remainder of this chapter will discuss warrants, backing, qualifiers, and reservations. The chapter will conclude with a brief recognition of what options the audience has in responding to the claims of the arguer.

NATURE OF CLAIMS

A claim is an assertion which the arguer wants to be accepted by someone else, and which the arguer is presumably willing to support. It has two terms: that about which we are talking (the subject term), and what we say about it (the predicate term). For example, if we say, "Skiing is fun," skiing is the subject term, and what we say about it, that it is fun, is the predicate term.

A variety of synonyms are employed for the term "claim." In informal argumentation we speak of assertions, contentions, stands, positions, conclusions, theses, and proposals. For example, someone may *assert* that a certain movie is an excellent production. People may *contend* that a large university is better than a small one. What *stand* do people in Utah take on the curtailing of railroad service? Someone's *position* on vegetarianism is that it is a sensible approach to eating. Her *conclusion* was that the dress really did not look very attractive. It was George's *thesis* that military preparations only produce less security. The mayor's *proposal* is to alleviate the parking problem with the construction of three municipal parking ramps.

In formal argumentation contexts, such as a legislative, public, or educational debate, or in a courtroom setting, we speak of resolutions, propositions, motions, bills, and indictments. For example, in an educational debate, the claim, the proposition, is framed in a formal resolution: "Resolved: That the United States should exert strong leadership in the Middle East." A member of a legislative committee presents a motion that salaries of members should be increased, and eventually that idea may become worded in the form of a specific bill. A prosecuting attorney presents an indictment, a claim that Mr. X is guilty of embezzlement of bank funds.

Whatever the label we happen to use in either formal or informal argumentation situations, it comes down to the same thing: someone is claiming something, and it is hoped that others will accept the claim.

Whether our claim is controversial or not depends on the attitude of the receiver, so claims are not inherently controversial. For instance, if the people to whom it is asserted that "skiing is fun" are avid skiers, there will be no controversy resulting from the claim. But if the audience is composed of people who feel that skiing is a very dangerous sport, then obviously the claim becomes controversial. With that understood, then, it is also important to indicate that a claim does, however, regardless of the audience, set the stage for potential controversy, as conflicting responses are implicitly invited. If a person says, "Vegetarianism is harmful to one's health," the claim-maker is opening the way for an opposing view to be expressed. In a normal debating situation, of course, the official proposition is indeed worded to ensure that controversy does result, for two sides are expected to be presented.

Claims may be either positive or negative, they may affirm or deny. For example, we may claim that "selling shoes is an interesting job," or we may claim that "selling shoes is not an interesting job." Debaters may assert that the United States should increase aid to a specified foreign country, or that the United States should not increase such aid.

A claim may be a single isolated assertion, or it may have multiple components, that is, it may be a chain of numerous arguments which are linked together to form a single overriding claim. For example, the claim, "Higher education is beneficial," includes numerous subclaims which build up to that final overall assertion, such as the following:

> Higher education is needed in order to qualify for a job.
> Higher education is an important way to become a well-adjusted citizen.
> Higher education is easily accessible to all who really want it.

Thus, a claim may be an intermediate statement as well as the final statement, it may serve as evidence for a further claim. Arguers obviously set their focus so as to limit their assertion and the supporting material to fit the time or space available in any given argumentative situation. An arguer working with the above subject matter, for instance, may decide that the situation will necessitate focusing only on, "Higher education is easily accessible to all who really want it."

> Claims may be in the past, present, or future tense.
> Past: She played poorly in last night's basketball game.
> Present: It's very windy outside.
> Future: He will be a great chemist some day.

Those claims which focus on the future are sometimes labeled predictive claims, for indeed that is what they do.

We of course make claims nonverbally as well as verbally. By our enthusiastic applause following a speech we communicate our claim that it was an effective presentation. The person in the audience who sits glumly with arms folded is making a different claim. In fact, everything we do can be interpreted as a nonverbal claim. For example, a person who enrolls in a university is saying that higher education is important, and the person who jogs daily is saying that jogging is important. Indeed, the claims may even go further than that and carry an implied assertion that other people ought to enroll in higher education or ought to engage in jogging.

We make many claims through pictorial means. The brochures put out by university public relations offices include campus scenes which, without captions, make the claim to prospective students that those universities are beautiful places. A speaker calling for housing improvements may have pictures depicting some run-down slum dwellings which make the silent but vivid claim that housing in that city is deplorable.

Then there is the indirect type of unstated claim which we often encounter in "goodwill" advertising, whereby some corporation, for example, sponsors a symphony concert on television or radio, with no direct advertising, only perhaps mentioning the name of the sponsor at the beginning and end of the program. Such goodwill advertising is of course making the claim that the corporation is a trustworthy one, is concerned with important cultural values, and is one whose product the audience should buy whenever the opportunity presents itself in the future.

But in this textbook we are not centrally concerned with such indirect, pictorial, or nonverbal claim-making, important as it may be. Here we are focusing on these claims which are verbalized, whether in a formal debate context or in some informal general argumentation situation.

TYPES OF CLAIMS

Various textbooks use slightly different categories and labels for distinguishing types of claims. For our purposes we will use the familiar standard groupings of factual claims, value claims, and policy claims. A claim states a conclusion about some fact or value, or advises action of some sort to be taken.

Factual claims

Factual claims assert that some fact exists (or does not exist) and it is assumed that it can be confirmed by objective data, that it can be verified by the receiver or someone else through their sensory powers of sight, touch, hearing, smell, or taste.

SIGHT: She is not wearing a red dress.
TOUCH: This sandpaper is really rough.
HEARING: The brakes on that car squeal.
SMELL: The odor in that tobacco warehouse is very pungent.
TASTE: This milk is sour.

Factual claims assert the occurrence (or nonoccurrence) of some event; or the existence (or nonexistence) or state of being of some person, institution, object, or idea.

OCCURRENCE OF SOME EVENT: Ten thousand people attended the boxing match last night.
EXISTENCE OF SOME PERSON: Sally is seated at the head table.
STATE OF BEING OF SOME PERSON: Donald is very excited about going to college next fall.
STATE OF BEING OF SOME INSTITUTION: The small family farm is decreasing in number.
STATE OF BEING OF SOME OBJECT: The huge oak tree down at the corner is in perfect condition.
STATE OF BEING OF SOME IDEA: The idea of husbands sharing housekeeping duties with their wives is increasingly being accepted.

Some claims of fact assert a cause-and-effect relationship. Consider the following examples:

Lowering the speed limit to 55 miles per hour has led to fewer accidents.

Studying late last night was not the cause of your headache today.

Television is causing an increase in juvenile violence.

These cause-and-effect claims, whether affirmations or denials, attempt to explain *why* something has, or has not, happened. Obviously such "facts" often are not very easily verified, so the student of argumentation needs to be particularly careful in using or evaluating such claims.

Claims of fact focusing on the past tense are central to courtroom argumentation, for the prosecution and defense assert that something did or did not occur in the past. The judge or jury have to decide whether the accused party is indeed guilty or innocent of having done some past act.

Ms. X did rob that bank.

Ms. X did not rob that bank.

Legislative committee hearings also focus to a great degree on the past.

The energy program cost $10,000,000 last year.

During the past decade, car accidents have doubled in the nation.

Much of our everyday argumentation also includes factual claims about the past:

But you promised yesterday that you would help me with my math.

Much of our factual claim-making is directed toward some future time. Some examples of such predictive claims are as follows:

The United States will not have enough oil by the year 1990.

He will get A's in all his classes this term.

Value Claims

Value claims render a judgment (give an opinion) on some person, institution, idea, place, object, or event.

PERSON: She is an excellent doctor.
INSTITUTION: We have an outmoded curriculum in our high school.
IDEA: Democracy is a precious way of life.
PLACE: I really like our dorm.

OBJECT: I think his hairdo is weird!

EVENT: The hockey game yesterday was the roughest one I've ever seen!

Some standard, some set of values, is brought to bear in the making of such claims. Value claims may touch on a host of standards: degree of goodness, usefulness, attractiveness, rightness, worthiness, effectiveness, timeliness, appropriateness, expertise, wisdom, or virtue. Unlike claims of fact, value claims cannot be verified by objective data, for what is considered attractive by one person may be thought to be "weird" by another. What makes an excellent doctor? One person may insist on a quiet bedside manner, whereas another person may think that to be a minor factor. What one person thinks is an outmoded curriculum, another person may regard as a fine, time-tested curriculum which ought to remain. By definition, value claims involve the application of some set of values, which may or may not be shared by others. As students of argumentation, we need to be highly attuned to our set of values and to the likely set of values possessed by those with whom we interact.

Value claims usually call for adherence only to a belief and are not a call to action, but the latter may often be implied. For example, if it is asserted that "she is an excellent doctor," this may carry the implied suggestion that the audience should go to her when in need of medical attention. But, basically, a value claim is asking one's audience to accept only the judgment uttered.

Policy Claims

A policy claim asserts that something should, or should not, be done by someone about something. It proposes that some course of action should or should not be taken. It usually calls for a change in the status quo.

> Student and faculty advisers should be assigned to each member of tbe Board of Regents.
> The United States should not send its grain to country X.
> Reporters should be barred from athletic locker rooms.

The key word in policy claims is the auxiliary verb *should*, which is linked with some action verb. The term should implies that the action *could* be taken, not that it necessarily *will* be taken. This is the standard position taken by college debaters as they begin the presentation of their case, and it is understood by opponents and judges that the affirmative team has the burden of demonstrating only that the recommended policy should be adopted, not that it will be.

If policy claims are analyzed closely, it will be noted that they incorporate both questions of fact and value, so that a policy claim really includes all of the things which have been said about claims of fact and value. Of course, the related claims of fact and value may often be unstated, may only be implied. Suppose it is asserted that "students should engage in a program of jogging." This no doubt involves a subclaim that there is need for such a program, that facts suggest that students have physical and mental problems which are in need of alleviation. It no doubt involves a subclaim that jogging is good. It implicitly predicts that if jogging is engaged in, students will enjoy a state of physical and mental well-being which will be better than what they now experience.

Policy claims are those usually used in educational debate, for students thus get experience in grappling with facts and values as well as with the feasibility and desirability of implementing a particular course of action. Students gain experience in dealing with real problem-solving situations. In educational debate the claim is of course phrased in formal fashion: "Resolved: That the income tax should be reduced."

In our everyday informal argumentation, too, of course, we are constantly encountering policy claims. A dorm roommate pleads, "Let's go to a movie tonight." Put in a more formal framework, it says, "We should go to a movie tonight." A student warns, "Don't take any classes from old Professor X," and a father commands his young daughter, "Wear your raincoat when you go out."

The specific policy advocated is usually put forth as the best possible means to achieve some specific objective. The objective may be only implied ("You should get a haircut"), or it may be explicit, "You should get a haircut if you want to attract the opposite sex." The objective of the policy claim "Students should engage in a routine of jogging" would be made explicit if "in order to avoid mental depression" is added.

It should also be noted that policy claims may be personal or collective in that they may call for a single person to do something or they may call on some collective entity to do something:

PERSONAL: You should get a haircut.
COLLECTIVE: The United States should reduce the income tax.

CLAIMS IN A FORMAL DEBATE

Selecting a Proposition

Those people who are responsible for selecting a proposition for some public or educational debate need to keep in mind a number of guidelines. First, the proposition should be timely and significant. It should be worth the time and effort which the debaters will put in it, and worth the time of the audience to come to hear it. Second, the proposition should be controversial enough to produce a meaningful debate. Much should be able to be said on both sides of the issue, with neither side having 100 percent of the truth. In other words, the subject should be debatable. Third, the proposition should focus on just one central idea; it should avoid having multiple major components. For example, consider the following proposition: "The University should abolish out-of-state tuition, and should actively recruit more foreign students." This contains really two major issues, which, while related, are distinctly separate and should be considered in two separate debate propositions, so that each could be explored without being distracted by the other. Finally, the proposition should be well adapted to the participants, to the audience, and to the occasion. The debaters should be knowledgeable on the subject or be able and willing to become knowledgeable on it. The subject should be of interest and concern to the audience, and should be relevant to, and appropriate for, the occasion.

Phrasing a Proposition

Phrasing a proposition carefully and appropriately is as important as choosing the subject. We need to phrase our claims carefully in all our argumentation, even in everyday exchanges, but especially when wording a formal proposition for a public or educational debate. The object is to phrase the central essence of the issue, no more and no less.

A number of suggestions should be kept in mind. First, the proposition should be in the form of a complete, declarative sentence. "Our Middle East Policy" would be inadequate and should be expressed as a specific proposal: "The United States should increase its military aid to friendly nations in the Middle East." Second, the proposition should be a simple sentence; avoid complex or compound constructions. Third, the wording should be clear and understandable. Fourth, the wording should be as neutral as possible; that is, avoid terms with emotional overtones. Do not let a particular bias have an advantage. "The United States should not establish the undemocratic system of compulsory military conscription" reflects an obvious anticonscription stance. That which is supposed to be debated (whether conscription is undemocratic) is already included in the phrasing of the proposition. Finally, the proposition should be phrased so as to set up an appropriately narrow focus, so that the debaters can deal with it in the time available for research and presentation.

Defining Terms

But even with careful phrasing of a proposition, the terms, especially the key terms, still need to be explicitly defined at the beginning of the debate to ensure that the participants are talking about the same thing. Especially important is defining technical terms or new terms, or terms which are to be used in a special sense in the debate. Failure to define clearly often results in the debaters going in diverse directions and not really clashing on the central issues. Certainly that often happens in our everyday informal argumentation, whereby needless controversy is generated by participants carrying different definitions in their minds. In a formal debate it is the duty of the first affirmative speaker to define the key terms in the proposition, and to do so clearly and reasonably, avoiding unique or tricky definitions which are designed to confuse the opponent rather than to clarify the issues. Unless there is a general agreement on the definition of terms, it would be difficult to achieve any meaningful debate. It should also be mentioned that the participants listening to the definition should realize their responsibility to listen carefully and accurately. Thus, in order to avoid misunderstandings, to increase the likelihood of better analysis of the issues, and to reduce lengthy, fruitless wrangling, it is necessary to have definitions of key terms explicitly and clearly stated.

DATA AND WARRANTS

The making of claims is intimately intertwined with data and warrants. In the Toulmin system of analysis, data and warrants are the other indispensable elements, along with claims, in an argument. The following example will illustrate these components. Suppose a classmate confidently asserts, "Our basketball team will definitely win tomorrow night." If her contention is accepted by the listener, then the matter probably is dropped, but the listener may say, "What makes you think so?" The response might be, "Coach Henderson said we would." Again, if the listener accepted that comment, the matter would end, but the listener might say, "So what?" This would push the original claim-maker to assert, "Coach Henderson's really on top of things."

Reconstructing and rephrasing the flow of the argument, we can see the three elements:

CLAIM: Our basketball team will definitely win tomorrow night.
DATA: Coach Henderson said we would win.
WARRANT: Coach Henderson's opinion is worthy of belief.

Data

Data, or evidence, is that substance which supports the claim. It may be some authority, as in the above example, it may be statistics, it may be an analogy, some specific instance, or some other form of evidence. Later chapters will explore more fully the realm of evidence; here we will only cite its role in the Toulmin format. If a claim is immediately accepted, then of course the arguer has no need to supply supporting data. If the response to "Our team will win tomorrow night" is "I agree," then there is no need to marshal supporting evidence. But if the listener should challenge the claim, then the arguer must come forth with data to bolster the claim. In short, the role of data is to support the claim, to indicate why the claim-makers feel their assertions are justified. The data may be uttered together with the claim ("Our team will win tonight because Coach Henderson says so"), or they may be expressed only if the audience requests them.

Warrants

The warrant indicates why we can make such a claim on such a piece of evidence. The warrant links together the data and claim, it serves as a bridge, it enables us to move from our evidence to the claim. It justifies, permits, warrants, the leap from data to claim. The warrant may be some principle or some substantive item. In our example above, "Coach Henderson's opinion is worthy of belief," is that which permits us to link together the data and claim. It is usually in the warrant that the clashes take place between arguers, and the above example illustrates that now the stage may well be set for the two participants to argue about the merits of Coach Henderson's opinion. The original claim will stand or crumble depending upon how the warrant holds up.

Additional examples will illustrate the close relationship of claim, data, and warrant.

CLAIM: The University of Minnesota should lower its tuition for out-of-state students.

DATA: The University of Wisconsin lowered its tuition with good results.

WARRANT: The University of Minnesota and the University of Wisconsin are similar in essential ways.

In such an analogy the implied or asserted similarity between the two schools is what permits the claim-maker to move from the evidence to the claim.

CLAIM: I guess it's quite clear that city hall is riddled with corruption.

DATA: Two aldermen were found guilty of bribery last month.

WARRANT: If some city officials are guilty of wrongdoing, there probably are more of them.

In this generalizing from some instances to a whole group, the warrant is the principle which enables the claim to be made on the basis of the evidence.

Thus, it is clear that it is important that the arguer should select warrants which the audience is likely to accept. For instance, returning to our first example, if the audience does not think very highly of Coach Henderson, then the warrant would be weak, and the arguer would be wise to shift tactics from arguing from Henderson's authority to someone else's opinion who is more respected, or to argue from factual information about the two teams. Of course, it goes without saying that one's warrant should be one in which the arguer, as well as the audience, also believes, so if the claim-maker actually does not think much of Coach Henderson's opinion, then it would be unwise to select that as the warrant.

Usually the warrant is unstated in the flow of argumentation, both in formal and informal contexts, so it becomes necessary for the listeners to discover and phrase the warrant in their own mind. An alert audience does so quickly and accurately, and we should join their ranks.

BACKING, QUALIFIERS, AND RESERVATIONS

Backing, qualifiers, and reservations are peripheral, secondary elements in Toulmin's system. While they are not essential, they nevertheless usually play a very important role in the unfolding and analysis of an argument.

Backing

Support for the warrant is called backing. If the audience accepts the warrant, then there is no need to back it up, but suppose someone in the above example were to question, "What makes you think Coach Henderson's opinion is any good?" Then the claim-maker would need to provide backing, that is, additional data or another premise which would strengthen the acceptability of the warrant. It might take the following form:

CLAIM: Our basketball team will definitely win tomorrow night.
DATA: Coach Henderson said we would win.
WARRANT: Coach Henderson's opinion is worthy of belief.
BACKING: He has accurately predicted the outcome of the last ten games.

This would be bringing in concrete data to back up the warrant. Another option would be to provide a general principle or premise, such as, "Coaches usually know the likelihood of their team's chances to win." In either instance the warrant has been bolstered, supported, backed up, and its reliability is enhanced. Backing, then, adds to the justification of the warrant. It answers the skeptic who wants to know why the warrant should be accepted.

Backing, like the warrant, is often unstated and has to be supplied by the alert listener. If the audience in the above example knew of Coach Henderson's past record of accurate predictions, then the backing would not be necessary; but if the audience was uninformed of his past accomplishments or was unlikely to accept the warrant, then the backing would need to be expressed. Terms such as *for, since,* or *because* usually introduce backing. In the above example it would be expressed: "Coach Henderson's opinion is worthy of belief, for he has accurately predicted the outcome of the last ten games."

By strengthening the warrant, backing provides indirect support for the original claim. Actually, a whole new claim-data-warrant chain is begun by supplying the backing, with "he has accurately predicted the outcome of the last ten games" being a factual claim which if challenged will have to be supported by specific data and a new warrant.

Qualifiers

Our original claim in the above example contained a specific qualifier, which perhaps the reader overlooked or has already forgotten. The claim was, "Our basketball team will definitely win tomorrow night." The term *definitely* indicates the degree of confidence that the claim-maker has in her assertion. The claim might have been that the team *probably* would win, or *perhaps*, or *certainly*, or some other type of qualifying term. We might say, "I'm 95 percent sure that this is the right road to take." We are not saying that the road definitely is the right one, but we are indicating the degre to which we think so, we are indicating the strength with which we want to make our claim. We admit that we are not 100 percent sure that this is the right road to take. Other terms which facilitate making some qualification of the claim would be *almost, maybe, possibly, sometimes*, or *virtually*. Qualifers permit us to adjust our claims to the reality of any given situation as we see it, to enable us to assert that which we can actually defend if challenged. Qualifers limit the extent of the claim, they indicate that universality is not part of the claim.

Qualifers can of course be used appropriately as an honest and sensitive way to try to communicate our precise degree of confidence in our claim. For example, when discussing causes and effects for something we need to use qualifiers, for in the social and political area, unlike the natural sciences, causes and effects are often only guesses. We have to honestly recognize that a return of compulsory military service will only *probably* bring increased security. Qualifiers may be used unethically as an evasion tactic designed to hedge and obscure our real position on something. Advertisers make heavy use of qualifiers in their claims. We consumers usually overlook them. For example: "Virtually all doctors recommend this medication" may be the commercial claim, but we blur out the *virtually* and carry in our mind only the core claim, which is precisely what the advertiser hopes we will do.

Reservations

Much of our claim-making involves some kind of reservation, that is, a statement of certain conditions under which the claim will not operate. Consider the following examples:

Our team will win *unless our star forward is injured*.
I'll come for you at 7. P.M., *unless my car doesn't start*.
You should tell terminally ill people the truth of their condition, *unless it would create extreme hopelessness in them*.

The underlined dependent clauses assert the circumstances under which the claim in the independent clauses will not materialize. Reservations cancel out the claim, cause the claim to be retracted. Reservations limit the area, reduce the force, of the claim.

Reservations can provide both healthy flexibility and unhealthy hedging in our claim-making. Since many situations in life are uncertain and ever-changing, we need to alert our audience to the possibility of circumstances under which the claim cannot be realized. For instance, in an example above, a young man could be thought to be honestly alerting his girl friend that in case his car did not start, he could not pick her up. But a reservation could also be a questionable hedging, setting up some contrived condition to enable the claim-maker to escape from the confines of the claim.

As claim-makers, we need to state clearly our intended reservations, to remind both ourselves and our audience of factors that may cancel out our central claim. As auditors, we need to be sure we do not overlook the reservation, to listen carefully to the reservations which are made, and remember them. After the passage of time we often forget what the reservation was, thus often leading to unfortunate misunderstanding and ill will. For instance, to extend one of the above examples, suppose someone is reprimanded for having told a terminally ill person the truth about her condition:

Ms. A: Why did you tell Carolyn the truth about her terminally ill condition?

Mr. B: But you told me to.

Ms. A: I told you to, unless it would give her a feeling of hopelessness, and that is just what has happened.

Mr. B: I don't remember you mentioning that.

Ms. A: Oh, but I did...

RESPONSES TO CLAIMS

The person to whom a claim is directed has several potential options as to how to respond.[2] The degree of wisdom and appropriateness of each

2. For a fuller discussion of choices, see Richard E. Crable, *Argumentation as Communication* (Columbus, Ohio: Charles E. Merrill, 1976), pp. 102–19.

response is of course dependent on each situation in which the claims are made, so no particular response is to be considered better than any other.

Some responses create conditions in which further argumentation is unnecessary or unlikely, thus terminating the interchange on that claim. First, the receiver of the claim might *accept* it ("You're right, we should go out to eat tonight"). In this case the claim-maker need not present any supporting data, for agreement is already achieved. Second, the person might *reject* the claim ("I simply can't go out to eat tonight"). Assuming that the rejection is total and firm, this also terminates any further discussion on the original claim. Third, the person might *ignore* the claim, which may result from a belief that the claim was not seriously made, or from an unwillingness to deal with it. If the receiver exits from the scene or if the claim-maker does not press her assertion, no argument occurs. It is possible, of course, that the claim-maker may repeat her claim in an effort to eliminate being ignored. In many instances, as we all can probably attest to, it is more frustrating to have one's claims ignored than to have them rejected.

Other responses set the stage for further argumentation. First, the receiver might *modify* the claim, that is, render a partial acceptance (or partial rejection, whichever way you look at it), such as, "Perhaps we should go out to eat, but not tonight." In this instance the central core claim is accepted, but it is modified as to when it should be acted upon. Second, the receiver might *request* additional information or reasons why agreement should be given. "How much will it cost?" "Where do you plan to go?" "Will it be awfully crowded?" "How will we get there?" "Why should I go?" This response forces the claim-maker to provide supporting material, and opens up the communicative exchange, for better or for worse depending upon the situation. For centuries parents have had to cope with the "why" response of their small children, and people in government, industry, and education have also had to try to handle this type of response from sensitive critics. College debaters certainly have had to scramble to deal with the penetrating requests of their opponents. Third, the receiver might *challenge* the claim ("Oh, you always want to go out to eat"). This of course forces the claim-maker into a defensive role immediately and stimulates an exchange, sometimes fruitful and sometimes not. Finally, the person might *counter* the claim ("Instead of going to a restaurant, why don't we go to an early movie?"). To the college debater the presentation of a counterplan to the one suggested by the opposition is a response fairly often employed.

The original claim-maker has the same options open to her as she reacts to the original receiver's responses, so the circular transactional interchange might involve many back and forth claims and responses. Obviously, the responses by both parties might include more than one of the above options, as some of them might well blend together or be followed quickly by a second type of response. For example, an initial agreement might suddenly be followed by a countering suggestion.

SUMMARY

Claims may be controversial or noncontroversial, positive or negative, isolated or intertwined, and may focus on the past, present, or future. Three basic types of claims are factual, value, and policy claims. Factual claims assert that some fact, some event, some state of being of a person, institution, object, or idea exists or does not exist. It can be verified by someone through sensory powers. Value claims render a judgment on some person, institution, idea, place, object, or event, and cannot be verified by objective data, for people may well have differing standards of goodness, attractiveness, or whatever the quality is that is being judged. Policy claims assert that something should, or should not, be done by someone about something. It proposes that some course of action should or should not be taken, and, in so doing, includes factual and value considerations. When working with claims in a formal debate context, it is important to select the proposition wisely, phrase it carefully, and define clearly the key terms.

A helpful system of analysis of claim-making is the Toulmin model, which is composed of the primary elements of claim, data, and warrant, and the secondary elements of backing, qualifiers, and reservations. Data or evidence is that substance which supports the claim; the warrant links together the claim and data, it is the justification for making the claim based on the data. Support for the warrant is called backing. Qualifiers are terms or phrases which indicate the degree of certainty the claim-maker has in the claim. Reservations are statements which indicate the conditions under which the claim will not operate. The diagram on the following page summarizes the six Toulmin elements and depicts their interrelationships.

The person to whom a claim is directed has several options as to how to respond. If the claim is accepted, rejected, or ignored, then further argumentation is unnecessary. But further interaction is stimulated if the receiver modifies the claim, requests more information, challenges the claim, or presents a counterclaim.

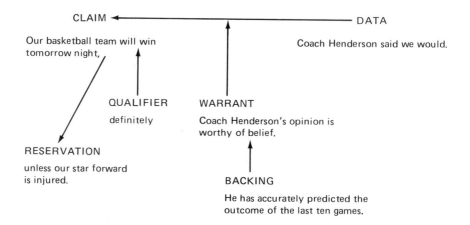

Coach Henderson said our basketball team will definitely win tomorrow night, unless our star forward is injured.

CLAIM ◄─────────────────────────── DATA

Our basketball team will win tomorrow night,

Coach Henderson said we would.

QUALIFIER

definitely

WARRANT

Coach Henderson's opinion is worthy of belief.

RESERVATION

unless our star forward is injured.

BACKING

He has accurately predicted the outcome of the last ten games.

EXERCISES

1. Turn in a list of the claims that you make over a period of three days. Categorize them as claims of fact, value, and policy. In a concise 300-word essay discuss your findings. Are you surprised at the number or types of claims? What accounts for your claim-making? Were some claims more sound than others?

2. Study advertisements in magazines or newspapers, noting the claims they are making. Bring the advertisements to class and share your observations in an informal class discussion. Comment on the degree of soundness of the claims.

3. Listen to debates by your college's debating squad, and for one of the speakers list the claims and data. Supply some of the warrants which link them together. Comment on the quality of the claims, data, and warrants. Have three classmates attend the event with you, and have each similarly analyze the other speakers. The four of you might then form a panel to present your observations to the rest of the class. Summarize your analysis in a 500-word essay.

4. Construct a five-minute speech in which you advocate some policy claim on a subject of concern to you. Support it with the best possible evidence available.

5. Study some written advocacy, such as editorials, letters to the editor, an essay in an opinion magazine, or a published speech in *Vital Speeches* or elsewhere. List all the qualifiers and the reservations. In a 400-word essay concisely discuss the significance of what you discover.

4 Claims: Analyzing Problems

The Nature of the Problem
The Villain
The Victim
Allies
Prediction
Summary
Exercises

Many, if not most, of the claims made by people are in the context of asserting that some problem exists. Often the person also will go on to assert or imply some solution. At the heart of argumentation is the careful exploration of what is involved in problems and their solutions. Seldom do people take the time to engage in rigorous systematic inquiry. These next two chapters will suggest some systematic questioning which will aid one in analyzing more insightfully and thoroughly any claims made within a problem-solution framework. To devote two full chapters to this is to demonstrate that the author agrees with Professor Otis Walter when he recently lamented that textbooks in speech communication have not focused fully enough on problem-solving.[1] These chapters, it is hoped, will stretch our vision to see many facets of problems and solutions which otherwise would remain in darkness. The term "heuristic" is used to refer to such a set of systematic questions, to such a systematic inquiry, so these next two chapters will present a problem-solution heuristic which will make students better evaluators of argu-

1. Otis M. Walter, *Speaking Intelligently: Communication for Problem Solving* (New York: Macmillan, 1976), pp. ix–x.

mentative claims made by others and more effective and responsible makers of claims.

In making claims about a problem, people are concerned with (1) the nature of the problem, (2) the cause of the problem, (3) the victims, (4) those allies who see the problem in the same light as the claim-maker, and (5) the prediction of what will occur. This chapter will explore questions fundamental to the eventual making of claims in these five areas.

THE NATURE OF THE PROBLEM[2]

A more accurate and complete view of the nature of the problem is possible if it is analyzed by exploring five elements: (1) substantive dimension, (2) spatial dimension, (3) temporal dimension, (4) quantitative dimension, and (5) qualitative dimension.

Substantive Dimension

Commission or omission? Is the problem a situation in which something is done which ought to be stopped or modified, or something which is not being done which ought to be done? The problem of course could well include elements of both, but one or the other is probably of more significance.

Television, for instance, is accused of having too many programs characterized by violence and mediocrity, and critics clamor for the elimination or alteration of such programs. Likewise, television is criticized for not having more programs with higher cultural content. The industry is accused of overlooking the wishes of many of the populace, of serious sins of omission in programming. Elected public officials may be accused of accepting bribes or of voting the wrong way on a given bill. On the other hand they may be accused of sins of omission, such as doing nothing about helping the unemployed or failing to supervise adequately their staffs. The problem may be one of employers mistreating their employees, or it may be that employers simply ignore the employees and their needs. Students might be unprepared for a class discussion because they read the wrong chapter (sin of commission) or they read nothing (sin of omission).

2. This section is based on J. Vernon Jensen, "A Heuristic for the Analysis of the Nature and Extent of a Problem," *The Journal of Creative Behavior*, 12 (1978): 168–180. Used by permission.

Attitude or deed?   The problem, says the teacher, is that the students have the wrong attitude toward their subject. On the other hand the teacher may accuse students of disrupting the class. Whether harboring an unhealthy attitude or perpetrating some disruptive act, the students have generated a problem for the teacher. The wise teacher knows that focusing on the visible action of a troublesome student may do little good to improve things if the real nature of the problem is an unhealthy attitude which somehow needs to be identified and modified.

The fundamental problem in racial discrimination may be cited as the attitude of one race that it is superior to other races and deserves preferential treatment. Or the problem might focus on the specific deed, that some races are excluded from housing in a particular suburb. In talking about social problems, students of argumentation need to see clearly whether the nature of the problem is primarily in the realm of attitudes and ideas, or in the realm of deeds. Obviously, both may be present and intertwined, but in any given situation one probably takes on greater prominence and urgency than the other.

Ends or means?   Is the problem one of some substance or of some procedure? Are students faced with the problem that their library has an inadequate supply of books or are they contending with a faulty delivery system; so that the problem is simply one of getting at the available books? Is the problem one of an inhumane administration, or is it inadequate lines of communication through which students might air grievances? If the problem is predominantly faulty lines of communication, to try to force the president to resign (and leave faulty lines of communication) would bring little if any improvement. Of course, it can be primarily both, thus necessitating dealing with both. The problem in health care might be the inadequate and incompetent medical attention given by doctors in health clinics. Perhaps the problem is not with the quality of medical expertise but with the difficulty of getting into the doctor's office; that is, appointments are available only in the distant future, lengthy delays occur in the waiting room, faulty record-keeping exists, or there is a shortage of nursing staff to process patients.

Active or passive?   Is the problem viewed as an active threat to the security and fundamental well-being of certain people, or is it merely an inactive, bothersome obstacle? If the former, then it has to be defended against and counterattacked. If the latter, then it merely has to be removed or circumvented. If the problem is an active threat, an arguer probably would need to discuss it with greater concern and urgency, and call for a more massive and concerted effort against it than if it were merely an inactive obstacle. For instance, does Nation A perceive Nation B to be a danger or merely an obnoxious neighbor? If the former, foreign and military policies would be quite different compared to the second. Students may view their antagonistic roommates as real threats to their ability to study, or they may be viewed as just harmless individuals who do not cause too much concern.

Spatial Dimension

Local or distant?   Public communicators sometimes talk of problems which are nearby: the inadequate park system, lack of downtown parking facilities, the polluted water in a local lake. But sometimes the public is told of problems in distant lands: starvation, racial segregation, drought, armed conflict, or lack of freedom. If indeed the problem is only a local one, the facts and implications drawn from the facts are, of course, mainly local. But decisions on local problems possibly may affect some neighboring community. Identification of the cause of water pollution, for instance, may stimulate other communities to study their water supply as well. Problems in distant lands, we need hardly remind ourselves in this jet age, have a way of affecting us in our own communities. As students shiver with sweaters and coats in their cool classrooms, they do not need to be reminded that "distant" conflicts in oil-producing areas have affected their daily habits and comfort. The degree of relationship between a given problem in a distant land and our community may be difficult to assess, but nevertheless it is important in most instances to be clear as to just *where* the problem, in its most crucial aspects, actually is.

Particular location(s) within a location?   When it comes to pinpointing a local problem, it may well be present only in one or more specific areas in the community. Thus the traffic congestion problem may well be a problem only in one or two fairly small, but significant, areas of the city. Rather than being a universal campus problem, overcrowding may occur only in certain rooms in specified buildings on campus, such as the Student Union building, in the library, or in certain classroom buildings.

Isolated or widespread?   The degree of linkage of a problem in one locality with related problems in other areas is important in many instances to establish clearly. For instance, a distant earthquake may be more isolated in its destruction and implications than a serious crop failure, which may fan out its repercussions in many other areas of considerable distance from it. That is, it may cause other areas to send emergency foodstuffs, it may alter prices drastically, it may rearrange established trade channels, or it may generate in some distant university the study of similar agricultural conditions. Misery loves company, and if students realize that problems in student government at their university are not unique but are also being experienced in many other universities, they somehow can take comfort and hope. It is helpful to ascertain whether the problem is, indeed, uniquely local, or whether it has repercussions for many other areas as well.

Is the problem part of a larger problem? Is it merely a local manifestation of a larger problem? Is the student unrest part of a general dissatisfaction with national policies and with higher education in general across the nation, or is the student unrest an isolated phenomenon on a particular campus strictly generated by local dissatisfaction, such as the high price of tuition and fees?

Temporal Dimension

Long-standing or recent?   Has the problem existed for a long time or is it a recent phenomenon? For example, juvenile delinquency has occurred ever since there were juveniles. It does give perspective and balance and perhaps even sanity to frustrated adults to realize that their children and the kids in the neighborhood are behaving exactly the way youth has always behaved, for centuries![3] But specific behavior by today's children, influenced by modern inventions such as cars and television, obviously is a contemporary phenomenon.

Then there is the type of problem which has really been present for ages, but was never recognized before as a problem. Lake pollution and pollution in general might be such an example. When lake property was plentiful, few people worried about pollution, but now states and counties are enacting and enforcing very precise regulations about deposit of wastes in lakes, and other strictures vis-à-vis building and use of lakes.

Present or impending?   Is the problem with us today, or, if certain practices continue and spread, are we moving toward the problem? Is the problem with us, or is it around the corner?

3. Aristotle's insightful and concise characterization of youthful behavior, for example, spans the centuries and still carries a contemporary familiarity (*Rhetoric*, 1389a).

For instance, high school dropouts are cited as future problems, for without schooling they will be lost in the world of tomorrow. The dangers of overpopulation may not exist in a given nation today, but that nation is warned that if present rates of population growth continue, then future generations will surely suffer from overpopulation. A small unattended campfire can become a massive forest fire.

Constant or ebb-and-flow?   Some problems come and go, depending on the time of day, week, month, or year. City buses are overwhelmed with passengers during the morning and evening hours when people are going to and from work. But other hours of the day the buses may be virtually empty as they go on their scheduled rounds.

Legislators are told that a given university is incredibly crowded with students, so a committee decides to visit the campus. They arrive at 10:30 A.M. when most students are in classrooms and virtually no one is visible on campus. The legislators feel they have been misled. But if they see that same campus between 10:50 and 11:00 A.M., as the hordes of students go to and from buildings, quite a different scene presents itself. If the legislators visit classrooms in the morning, they might find them all occupied and filled. If the investigators visited these same classrooms in the late afternoon, they might find many empty or sparsely filled classrooms. The problem thus manifests itself during certain times of the day. Likewise, long lines of students would be visible during registration week, but not during other weeks.

Quantitative Dimension

Singular or multiple?   Is the problem a single item or is it many? Are the workers in a factory discontented only with low wages, or are other elements, such as working conditions, hours of work, safety aspects, lunchroom facilities, parking arrangements, and general attitude of management, also integral aspects of the problem? Furthermore, all of these aspects are not necessarily equal in seriousness, and this relative weighting needs to be realized. For instance, perhaps the general paternalistic, insensitive attitude of management is at the top of the list and could be equated with three of the other aspects. That is, obnoxious attitude of management = poor parking + poor lunchroom facilities + poor pension plan.

Many or few people?   While this is closely related to the previous category, it is slightly different in that it focuses on the mass, on head-counting, on determing how many units are part of the problem. So if the claim is made that the workers of a given factory are discontented, it is necessary to know how many workers are so inclined. If the number is large (and "large" itself is relative), the situation is more serious than if the number is small. If only ten people out of a community of ten thousand think the park system is poor, then it probably is not to be defined as a community problem, but if one thousand people think it is, then almost by definition it is. This is the central function of the many poll-taking agencies—to try to determine, through sampling procedures, how many people feel a certain way about certain issues. If a high percentage think something is an issue, then it is an issue!

General or specific?   Does the problem apply to a general group of some type or only to specific individuals or subgroups within the larger general category? For instance, is the problem of outdoor advertising a universal, general problem, or is it only the scenery-affecting highway advertising and not the metropolitan advertising which is a problem? Perhaps the problem is only with smaller, "fly-by-night," gypsy advertising groups which flood our highways with advertisements, and not the big outdoor advertising agencies, which concentrate only in the cities. Arguers may want to specify that they are complaining about only the irresponsible student, not all students, only the medical quacks, not the whole medical profession, or only the price-gouging manufacturer, not all manufacturers. This will help not only to focus more clearly on the real problem but also will win the arguers more allies and reduce the intensity of the opposition. For instance, once doctors realize that a critic is not complaining about whole profession, they may even cooperate in combating the quacks.

Affluence or scarcity?   Is the problem of a shortage of something, such as a lack of education, lack of technical know-how, lack of natural resources, lack of food? Or is the problem one of too much of something: too many cars, too many people, oversupply of wheat, excessive smoke, too many empty bottles? The industrialized, developed nations suffer mainly from the latter, from problems of affluence. They are perplexed about how to distribute their food surplus, where to park their many cars, where and how to dispose of enormous amounts of refuse, and how to recapture the clean air overrun by armies of belching factory chimneys and auto exhaust systems. The underdeveloped countries might well hope for some of those problems, but instead they are confronted with problems of undersupply, such as lack of food, lack of electricity, lack of adequate transportation, and lack of bottles! Wealthy individuals have the problem of how to invest their money, whereas low income people have the problem of how to obtain the necessities of life. The overweight person has the "problem" of too much food; the starving individual has the problem of too little food. One football coach may have the problem of choosing eleven starters from a large number of excellent candidates, whereas another coach may have the problem of finding eleven people capable of taking to the field.

Qualitative Dimension

What values are being violated?   We now arrive at one of the most crucial steps in the analysis of problem-events, that is, ascertaining what values are being violated. Up to this point we have basically been concerned with the question: "What is?" That is, what are the facts? But that doesn't constitute a problem. A problem means that a value is being violated, something is other than what it ought to be. A problem is not merely "What is?" but "What is *wrong*?" And something is wrong when some value is being adversely affected. To desire change is to hold that something now existing is less desirable than it ought to be, that some value is not being realized fully enough. Violation of some value causes a dissonance, a disequalibrium in us, a tension, an uneasiness calling for the problem to be solved so that a feeling of equilibrium, of balance, can return. What value or values are being maligned? Does the problem-event violate morality, intelligence, justice, equality, humaneness, respectfulness, cleanliness, or orderliness?

Consider the value of cleanliness. A mother scolds her son day in and day out—perhaps for years—for not keeping his room clean. To him, as long as he can walk around in the room without stumbling over clothes or other objects, the room *is* clean. He keeps muttering, "What's wrong with my room the way it is? What's the problem?" As far as he is concerned, he is violating no standard of cleanliness. But his *mother's* standard of cleanliness is clearly being violated. They would both agree on the facts. That is, the bed spread is wrinkled; clothes are on the bed, not on hangers; clothes which have been worn for two weeks are in a pile in the corner; considerable dust is on the shelves; and numerous unorganized items are on top of the bureau. To his mother these facts say something is wrong. To him these facts do not communicate the same message. The son and mother have different values of cleanliness, and hence tension grows between them.

Two professors may agree on the fact that in a classroom with fifty seats there are fifty-five students, so some have to sit on the floor or stand. To one professor this is an instance of terribly overcrowded conditions, and to him it is a real problem. But the other professor doesn't think it is a problem at all. In fact, she may like to have a room filled to capacity, for it may give the group a better feeling of togetherness, and students seem to discuss more effectively than they would in a room half filled. So it again is a question of values, not of facts. It is a question of one's relation to, attitude toward, the facts.

People can look at the same facts from varying perspectives which causes one person to view the behavior as a problem, while a second person would not see it as such. Much literature exists on the teenage problem—all written of course by adult authors! Adults find it difficult to keep up with the abundant energy of youth, have forgotten the youthful, insatiable desire to experiment, have become desensitized to the openness and curiosity still so fresh in youth, and view the youthful carefree attitude as lack of responsibility. All of these attitudes and behaviors of youth create a problem, a difficulty in adjustment for adults, and hence they even write books about it. If teenagers wrote books, they no doubt would have much to say about the "adult problem," that is, that adults are lethargic, fear experimentation, lack openness and curiosity, and are somewhat neurotic in tending to responsibilities.

Thus, seeing and analyzing a problem depends upon alert, clear perception, but also upon a sensitive and clear commitment to a value system. Also, of course, students of argumentation have to struggle with the realization that some values are more important than others, especially in given contexts.

To what degree are the values being violated? If punctuality is a worthy value, and if someone is five minutes late or thirty minutes late for an appointment, it makes quite a difference in terms of how seriously the value of punctuality has been violated. If being considerate of roommates is a value to be honored, and Student A irritates her roommate slightly with occasional late hours of study or greatly with endless chattering, the value is violated more significantly in the latter instance. So the problem-event involves not only what value is being violated, but how seriously it is being violated.

Proper or improper values? A final consideration in the area of value violation is the question of whether or not the value itself is a proper one to hold. In other words, getting to the rootage, the question asks about the wisdom of holding to the specific values. For instance, is the value of pleasing a roommate a value worth adhering to in all situations? Perhaps some other value (diligent studying, hence the necessity to stay up late) takes precedence. This leads to the fundamental process of attempting to determine one's value system, and to determine priorities of values in each situation. To get much further into this discussion would be highly significant and interesting, but would divert us from the additional concerns that need to be analyzed here. But students of argumentation are hereby alerted to this fundamental and rather horrendous task of carefully determining their own values, particularly crucial at this stage in their lives. Rational and humane individuals will commit themselves to civilized and beneficient values.

THE VILLAIN

While endeavoring to define the nature and extent of any given problem, arguers also are probably concurrently searching for the villain—the who (or the what) that is the cause of the situation. Why did the problem-event occur? The importance of a villain, a devil figure, is indeed fundamental in argumentation. To create focus and understanding, to generate interest, and marshal support, a rhetorician must create a clear devil figure against which the rhetor is fighting. Indeed, it is true, as often asserted, that any campaign or speech or program needs a devil figure, for an audience needs to see what they are supposed to be against as well as what they are for.

Who is responsible for the problem?   This is a central question which springs immediately to mind whenever a problem-event presents itself. A car is parked in a person's driveway so she can't get out. Who did it? Who is the villain? Who is the enemy—opponent—adversary? Perhaps it is a *what* instead of a *who*, in that some inanimate force or object did it. Perhaps someone had fotgotten to set the brakes when parking and the car rolled down to block the driveway. Gravity was the villain! This suggests two considerations. One, that the villain, the cause, may be animate or inanimate—a person or a thing. Second, the villain may have multiple heads. That is, more than one agent may have caused the problem-event, in this case a careless person *and* the force of gravity.

Students of argumentation need to avoid bringing a ready-made villain to their analysis. We all have a tendency to assume we know the cause of a situation, and merely select and arrange the facts to confirm our preconceived notions as to who or what the villain is. Leaders in student government, for instance, automatically assume that few applications for openings in student government positions and student-faculty committees means that students are apathetic. That is, apathy is seen as the villain, and presumably something has to be set in motion to slay that dread beast. The true cause, however, may be merely that the students, far from being apathetic, are overly zealous, but about their studies, their work, and other interests—which does not leave them time for channeling efforts into student government. We all tend to feel that everybody should be interested in the same things we are, and if they are not, if they direct their time and energy in other directions, we say they are apathetic, disinterested, lazy.

Personal or impersonal?   Most social problems with which an arguer is dealing are caused by some person or persons. A human being usually is a major part of the whole causal factor. Lazy employees do shoddy work and cause their employers a problem. Parents cause problems by not letting their children use the family car. If a car does not start on a subzero day, is it because last week the garage mechanic did something improperly? Is it merely because of the extremely low temperature? Perhaps both are involved. Often a significant cause is an impersonal factor, such as the forces of nature, or a declining market for a given product, or a general social trend against a particular political party. Broad economic, social, moral trends may be the significant villain rather than individuals or groups of people.

First, second, or third person?   When the villain is identified as a person or group of people, is the villain in the first, second, or third person? Almost always, it is in the third person. That is, we point the accusing finger at "them." "They" are to blame for the sorry mess. The "system," the "administration," the "faculty" are the villains. If there is a gasoline shortage, *they* (filling station operators, the suppliers, the importers, the producers—somebody "out there") are to blame. We are rather slow to accuse ourselves and say, "*I* am, or *we* are, to blame." People overlook that they may be partially to blame for the gasoline shortage by driving their cars much more and much faster than they really need to. It is uncomfortable to accuse ourselves.

We are also rather slow to put the villain in the second person. For instance, we might hesitate to accuse the filling station operator from whom we buy our gas: "*You* are to blame, for you aren't vigorous enough in ensuring adequate supply." It is awkward to accuse someone in our immediate audience. It is usually far easier to accuse some stranger, someone who is absent.

Insider or outsider? Occasionally, the cause of disturbance in a particular part of town may be persons residing in that locality, but sometimes, indeed, perhaps most often, the troublemakers are labeled as outsiders. Southerners blamed civil rights agitators from the North for disturbances in their communities. It is most often "those hoodlums" from the other side of the tracks or "nonstudents" making trouble on campus, or teenagers from the big city robbing the stores in the neighboring small towns. People like to think the villain is an outsider, that their children, their neighborhood, would not do such dastardly deeds. It somehow salves the ego to think that outsiders are causing the problem. Since we are so quick to blame outsiders, we may need to pay particular attention to whether or not we are deluding ourselves on that score. At any rate, clearly establishing whether the villain is an outsider or an insider may be helpful in analyzing the causal factor.

Single or multiple? When looking for the person or persons who are responsible for a problem-event, the arguer must probe carefully and thoroughly. For example, suppose the claim is made that the reason the food at Restaurant X is so bad is because the cook is inefficient. The cook is the supposed villain. Perhaps the real culprit is the owner, who does not budget enough money for the cook to buy good food. Students of argumentation need to avoid the temptation of claiming they have found the villain until they have probed the situation fully and carefully. Perhaps both the cook and the owner are to blame, the former for lack of ability and the latter for lack of financial investment. But wait, perhaps a third party enters the picture in the form of the supplier of food. Perhaps the supplier is guilty of providing inferior produce. So the villain is really a three-headed one, and it is important to uncover all three if anything worthwhile is to be accomplished in the way of a solution. To clamor for the cook's resignation would overlook the other two heads, and may well have little if any effect as well as being unfair to the cook.

An important guideline to remember is that if only one cause has been found for a serious social problem, all the villains probably have not been uncovered. One cause per problem is highly unlikely! In the social sciences, unlike the physical sciences, it frequently is difficult to establish a clear singular cause for any given problem. Usually multiple causes are operating, and in difficult to assess combinations.

Primary or secondary?   When multiple villains are involved, some kind of priority listing which distinguishes the more important from the least important causes must be determined. All causes are not equal. Some are vastly more significant than others, and these variations must be determined. If to identify and expose the major culprits is all that is necessary in a given situation, then of course one can ignore the lesser villains. If, indeed, the cook is so thoroughly incompetent that no matter how much money the owner budgets, and no matter how excellent the raw material from the supplier, the cook would still turn out tasteless and unattractive dishes, then the cook no doubt is the primary cause; and the elimination of the cook would no doubt greatly improve, if not totally solve, the problem. However, one of the other two agents could be more important, in which case a different list of priorities of causes, a different list of solutions to offer would emerge.

Remote or precipitating?   The cook is seen as the immediate pre-cipitating cause, and therefore is quickly blamed for the bad food. That is, the cook has prepared the food, and it was judged to be unsatisfac-tory. The more remote causes are not immediately in view; they played their role in an earlier stage not witnessed.

Likewise, the police are always confronted with precipitating causes of social unrest and have to deal with them, while more remote and perhaps more important causes lurk behind the scenes and never are properly identified or dealt with by the police or the community in general. For example, suppose a disgruntled group of citizens stage a protest rally which results in scuffles and sufficient violence to warrant police involvement. But the causes behind the protest rally in the first place—perhaps unemployment, inadequate housing, or some highly unpopular decision by the city council—are more important causes. But being remote both spatially and temporally, they are not identified or dealt with—and certainly not by the police, whose job usually is limited to dealing with immediate, palpable, present, precipitating causal agents.

Alert students of argumentation need to avoid the temptation to overlook that which is not immediately visible, they must go back in time and discover the links in the chain which set off the problem-event. They must not focus only on the last link in the chain.

Motivation What motivates the villains to do the things they do? Why do they cause trouble for others? Students of argumentation have to probe this thoughtfully and carefully, realizing that this is a nebulous, elusive, even sacrosanct area, and one in which few answers, if any, may be found. Certainly, the admonition should immediately be made that arguers should avoid making any assertion whatsoever about motivation until they have studied it sensitively and carefully. Even then, claims must be made with great tentativeness so that the claim-makers do not mislead their audience or unfairly malign the villain.

It is extremely difficult to believe the villain's own statement of his motivation, for he may not really know. He may be unconsciously misleading himself and his audience, or he may be doing it purposely.

We tend to ascribe the worst possible motivations to the villains and thus often are guilty of exaggeration or brazen inaccuracy. Are they dishonest, deceitful, ignorant, uninformed, lazy, inconsistent, insincere, forgetful, confused, timid, or heartless? Are they motivated by evil intent—by injustice or lack of mercy—or is it a case of misdirected "good" motivation? For example, suppose a national official says she is concerned about the security of the country and thus directs employees to spy on other governmental employees and to discover the source of leakage of secret information to the press. This evil act is supposedly prompted by good motives. The highway planner who puts a freeway through a residential part of a city is motivated by the desire to arrange for quick, easy, and safe transportation. But to the homeowners who will have to move, he is the villain who is oblivious to the harm he is bringing to many citizens. This illustrates that things are done within limited spheres. While they may be good within that sphere (that is, the highway planner is fulfilling his job, with its specific objective of arranging for good transportation), the ripple effect from proposals extends beyond the original limited domain. In this case it extends into housing, care for the aged or other disadvantaged people, or to owners of small businesses who are forced out of business. That action, good in its limited domain, is evil in the light of these other considerations. Hence the person responsible becomes the villain. Much mischief is done by people who feel they are doing it for good ends—they have good motives. Furthermore, the examples should illustrate that it may not be very simple to separate right from wrong in complicated contexts. This is not to suggest reducing commitment to one's values, but to admit that complex contexts exist.

Students of argumentation, then, need to shy away from ascribing motivation. They certainly should not ignore it, but should be hesitant to claim they have fathomed it. The villain's method, tactics, and amount of information may more safely and more fairly be questioned than his aims, honesty, sincerity, or motives.

Relation of the villain to the malcondition If the villains are profiting in some way from the problem-event, then their action is viewed as being even more despicable. For example, if an absentee landlord gets an exorbitant income from rentals in her substandard houses, then this makes her action worse (at least it appears worse) than if she could demonstrate that she was only breaking even, or at least making no large profit. When it is revealed that oil companies are reaping huge profits during the time that citizens are called upon to make energy-saving sacrifices, then the oil companies appear far more of a villain than if they were making only a small profit.

THE VICTIM

Who are the victims? The victims need to be identified as precisely as possible. Often those who claim to be the victims are not really affected too adversely, and often those who suffer the most (or will in the future) are silent in their suffering. Sometimes the undue complainers need to be muffled, and the quiet sufferers need to be bolstered. But above and beyond that kind of moral contribution is the fundamental intellectual contribution of accurately identifying the real victims of a problem-event so that we can come up with the most relevant and desirable solution.

Is it the immediate audience? It is wise to clarify for one's immediate audience just exactly how the problem affects them, if it does. The importance of any communication transaction often hinges on the relationship of the audience to the subject being discussed. Sometimes the relationship is obvious, as it would be if a student was discussing the high cost of a university education with a group of university students, or if a speaker was addressing an audience of women on the problem of

discrimination against women in today's society. But even if the relationship is obviously clear, it may still need to be more comprehensively,
more accurately, and more compellingly brought home to the audience.
Situations in which the audience does not initially see how the problem
directly affects them gives the arguer the obvious task of making that
clear.

Arguers might be wise to clarify their relationship to the problem at
the same time. Thus they might establish a common ground with the
audience if they could demonstrate that they are suffering in the same
way the audience is, and it would improve their ethos with the audience
by clearly and openly declaring any vested interest which they may or
may not have in the subject. Thus arguers become either disinterested
parties with no axe to grind or open advocates who have fearlessly and
honestly laid their cards on the table for all to see.

The immediate audience in some situations may not be directly
affected by the problem-event, but perhaps it can be demonstrated that
their friends and others for whom they have concern may be directly
affected. Sometimes people respond even more energetically on behalf
of others because they do not have to contend with any guilt feelings
about doing something only for themselves.

Occasionally, the victims are succeeding generations, some people in
the future rather than the present generation. The problem may be an
impending one, such as overpopulation or depletion of natural resources, which will strike with full fury only in the future. It is
admittedly more difficult to stir an audience over such a problem, but
altruism, desire for well-being for one's offspring, and concern for
humanity and life in general may well help to convince the audience
that, indeed, the subject demands their immediate and concerned
attention.

The victims may be institutions rather than individuals. Of course, if
institutions suffer, then individuals related to those institutions will,
obviously, also suffer, so one can hardly separate them. It could be
demonstrated perhaps that the problem of freeway construction will
cause the removal of many churches, and that those institutions will
simply disappear. It may be contended that if certain practices continue,
such as the growing use of spying and secrecy in government, that the
institution of a free democratic society will be destroyed.

Qualities of the victim   Alert students of argumentation will try to
ascertain what qualities the victim is depicted as possessing and which

are being exploited or damaged. If the victims are sensitive, lovable, intelligent, humane, brave, skilled, and attractive, somehow the deed against them seems to be worse than if they are insensitive, ignorant, inhumane, unlovable, cowardly, unskilled, and unattractive.

Victims of armed conflicts are of course emphasized in news media and other accounts. Usually it is highlighted that women, children, and the aged are among the victims. Why does that generate more sympathy? For the obvious reason that these are relatively defenseless, innocent, harmless nonparticipants. In the "rules" of warfare, to kill or maim middle-aged men is not so reprehensible an act, for they are supposed to be able to defend themselves (and are trained and equipped to do so), they are identified (with uniforms), and are participants who possess great potential to be killers if given the chance.

To kidnap a child seems more reprehensible because the victim is defenseless and has a life unfulfilled. Will women's liberation reduce the emotional reaction to women being injured in society? Pregnant women, children, and hospital patients are perhaps the ultimate innocent victims. Concern for children and pregnant women may be related to people's desire for immortality, to ensure that they and their descendants will live on.

To justify harmful action against someone, it often is emphasized that the victims are unworthy anyway. Hence for them to be injured is not so reprehensible. They are, after all, *only* dirty capitalists, greedy landlords, violent revolutionaries or a mean parent. This dehumanizing of victims, attempting to make them subhuman, is something to be alert to when analyzing, and something to avoid when presenting material.

Public communicators often assert that they are speaking for victims who cannot speak for themselves. This aims at the double-barreled emphasis of pity for the victim and prestige for the speaker. For example, the anti-abortion advocate claims to be speaking in behalf of the unborn fetus, which cannot, obviously, speak for itself. Lawyers defending some poor, illiterate clients likewise claim to be speaking for those who cannot speak for themselves. Political figures often claim to be speaking for the elderly, who cannot adequately speak for themselves.

Relation of victim to villain   Any given problem takes on a greater coloration of dastardliness if the victim has in the past treated the villain well. Tenants who have been prompt in rent payments, responsible, and clean—in other words, who have treated their villainous landlord well—somehow, constitute a greater problem than tenants who have been irresponsible, untidy, and in arrears in their rent payments. Teenagers who treat their parents well but who suffer from parental maltreatment would get more sympathy than disorderly teenagers getting the same parental treatment. Thus, the relationship between the villain and the victim plays a role in defining the seriousness of the problem. The higher the ethos of the victim and the lower the ethos of the villain, the greater the problem. An employer that fires, for whatever reason, employees who have given good service for many years creates a greater problem than the same employer that fires recently hired employees, who have not developed such a close and responsible relationship.

ALLIES

Who also recognizes the problem?   Arguers realize that the credibility of their message increases if they clarify for their audience that other people see a given situation in the same light as they do—that they have allies. A nation with good allies is significantly strengthened. Arguers with good allies are also significantly strengthened.

Quantity   If advocates can demonstrate that a large segment of the population has the same views as they do, then their case becomes that much stronger. Through informal or formal polls or through whatever means possible, advocates need to discover how many people support their view. If a Gallup poll shows that 75 percent of the people in the United States feel that professional sports are overemphasized in our society, and this is what an arguer is trying to communicate to an audience, then this demonstrates that the majority of the citizenry is with the arguer. To obtain such a majority vote carries great weight in this land, where the individual and the common man are highly valued.

Experts or laymen   But it is also important to know whether one's allies are experts in the field or laymen. After all, ten skilled carpenters are better than ten unskilled ones for a carpentry job. If an economic issue is being discussed and reputable economists can be cited, if in discussing medical issues an advocate can have leading medical authorities in her corner, and if in discussing an educational problem, an advocate quotes from important educators, those advocates will be strengthening their presentation. By such argument from authority, advocates strengthen their case—provided their audience accepts the authorities.

But occasionally this argument from authority takes a reverse twist: experts are not trusted, and the nonexpert—the "common man"—a folk hero in America, actually stimulates more respect. His great common sense is viewed as enabling him to see the issue at hand more clearly than the expert. The latter also may have a vested interest in the topic, and may have only theoretical and not practical expertise. Furthermore, she may lack humaneness—all brain and no heart.

Current or past   Are the allies currently living or are they drawn from the recent or distant past? Is reliance placed on a contemporary expert economist, or some famous economist of the nineteenth century? For general testimony on general subjects, past authorities of course carry much weight, for their expertise has been verified by the passage of time. But if the subject demands a contemporary view, then some famous authority of the distant past may be a weak or irrelevant authority.

Principles as allies   One's allies can be intangible principles as well as people. That is, advocates may assert or imply that "Reason" is on their side. They may say that all reasonable people can see that an oil shortage exists. They may claim "Humaneness" as an ally when they assert that "to overlook the plight of the migrant worker is to lack humaneness." Occasionally, the advocate may personify values and treat them as if they were indeed people on his side in his effort to make a problem compelling. In the name of "Civilization" we are beckoned to see the inequalities suffered by many or we are told that "Decency looks down from her throne and demands that we see the problems in the slums." Indeed, some advocates even claim that God is their ally, their copilot, their co-worker.

While it is commendable to stretch for such principled allies, one certainly ought to do so with considerable humility, and at least be willing to realize that people who see the problem differently may also claim the same allies. While we want to get close to such allies, we ought not to assume that we are closer than we really are.

PREDICTION

What will happen to the villain, the victim, and the problem? The area of effects is a fundamental element in any rhetorical situation. Effects involve arguers in the future. They are inevitably forced into the role of predictor. Advocates during their presentation are wondering what the cumulative effect will be at the conclusion of the message, so even immediate effects—the immediate future—are on their minds. But the longer range effects—the near and more distant future—are also central to advocates. They implicitly or explicitly predict. That is, they assert or suggest what will happen if their audience ignores the problem about which they are speaking, and they assert or suggest what will happen if the audience sees the problem as presented. "If the problem of unemployment is not recognized and corrected, then the country will experience 10 percent unemployment by the year 1990," or, "If we recognize the problem of drug addiction and take measures to control it, then we will rescue tens of thousands of our young people from an aimless, and suffering life, and we will create a healthier and more productive society." Also, we sometimes are bombarded by vague threats (sometimes purposely vague) such as, "You haven't seen the last of me!" or, "I'll get even with you!" (if we don't attend to the problem). It implies that the problem will worsen, but just how is unclear.

Predictions sometimes stimulate exaggeration, and sound, ethical arguers keep their predictions as unemotional and as realistic as possible. To threaten, to conjure up fearful images, to frighten—or, on the other hand, to promise an unrealistic paradise, to claim the unclaimable—is to do injustices to the audience, to the subject, and to oneself. An expert and trustworthy student of argumentation consciously tries to predict as accurately as it is humanly possible to predict.

Predicting is of course only guessing, but sound guessing and unsound guessing may be miles apart. Students of argumentation are expected to make sound, "educated" guesses. They are expected to be wise predictors.

SUMMARY

This chapter has suggested some systematic questions which serve as generators of claims dealing with a problem. We have probed the nature of the problem by looking at its substantive, spatial, temporal, quantitative, and qualitiative dimensions. We have suggested a heuristic for better understanding the cause of the problem (the villain) as well as the victim. Finally, we have briefly focused on allies (those who see the problem as we do) and on the step of prediction, which is always present implicitly if not explicitly in making claims about a problem.

EXERCISES

1. Keep a log of your daily problems for five days, noting the nature of the problems and the causes of them. Who are the villains? Members of your family? Dormitory residents? Your roommate? The cooks in the cafeteria? Teachers? Bus drivers? Classmates who raise the curve? Classmates you distract your attention? Administrative officials? Clerks? Competitors for the attention of your girl friend/boy friend? Write a concise paragraph on selected villains, constructing an eventual 500-word essay.

2. Attend a movie, or see one on television, and report on the portrayal of the villain and the victim. Summarize your observations in a 500-word essay, and share your analysis in a class discussion. If possible, a group of four or five students should see the same movie, so they can share their impressions with the rest of the class.

3. Study a speech in *Vital Speeches*, or some other source, and note the allies claimed by the speaker. Who are they? How many are there? Are they experts or laymen? Are they contemporary or past? Does the speaker claim to have certain personified principles on his or her side? Present your findings in a 500-word essay.

4. Analyze some speech or essay in which you focus only on how the victim is discussed, using as many of the factors discussed in this chapter as are relevant. Note any emotional language which may be employed. Share your analysis in an oral report to the class.

5. Read some editorial or some letter-to-the-editor in your metropolitan or campus newspaper. What is the nature of the problem discussed? Who or what is the villain and who is the victim? Present your analysis in an informal oral report to the class. A group of four or five could read the same item and share their reactions with the class.

5 Claims: Proposing Solutions

We all need to suspend judgment and open to view as many solutions as possible to the problem with which we are grappling. Most of us do a great injustice to the problem, to ourselves, and to society by bringing ready-made solutions to a problem situation or by not being able or willing to explore all possible types of solutions. This chapter, it is hoped, will broaden our perspectives, will open up many new windows through which we can see considerations which will enable us to choose ultimately the very best solution possible, and thus make the wisest of claims.

THE NATURE OF SOLUTIONS

Substantive Dimension

Procedural or substantive?   Suggesting a way, a method, a means for solving something is offering a procedural solution. Presenting a definite substance, a definite commodity, is offering a substantive solution.

Suppose two aspirants for the office of mayor, Candidate A and

Candidate B, are discussing the traffic problem. Mr. A says if he becomes mayor, he will promise that three large parking ramps will be built in needed areas. Ms. B promises that she will appoint a committee of experts to study the traffic problem and come up with its solution. Candidate A was promising a substantive solution; Candidate B was promising a vehicle, a means of proceeding, but the ultimate solution will not be known until the committee submits its report. Candidate A, on the other hand, presented the voters with some product, some substance.

Attitude or act?   If Maythee solves the problem of the tension with her roommate by more tolerantly viewing habit of staying up late, by trying to understand more clearly why she does it, and by trying to realize that it really is not so harmful as she originally thought, then the changed attitude is the "solution." If Maythee really does not alter her attitude, if she still feels the same, but solves the problem by moving to another room, the solution is an act.

Repair or replace?   The solution might aim at replacing something, or it might repair, mend, reform, readjust, or modify the status quo. Should the old school be remodeled or torn down to make way for a new structure? If one's car gives constant trouble, it can be repaired or exchanged for a different car. If a political-economic system is not working well in a certain country, its citizens may seek to improve it or seek to replace it with another system—which is the difference between reform and revolt.

Needless to say, to revolt—to replace something—is the line of action taken only when conditions are deemed to be beyond reform, beyond repairing. This of course is a value judgment. Bruce may think his car is repairable but his brother may think it is beyond reform and needs to be exchanged. Citizen A thinks the capitalistic system needs to be overthrown through revolution, whereas Citizen B thinks only reform is needed.

Known or unknown?   Will the solution be known or unknown to the audience? Will the cure be something old or someting new? A doctor may prescribe a familiar medicine for an ailment, and the patient may be satisfied because she knows the prescription has worked in the past. On the other hand the doctor may prescribe a new drug which has just been placed on the market. It is supposed to be more powerful, have fewer side effects, and cost less, so the patient should be well pleased with it. But the patient may prefer her previous known medicine, for there is security in the known.

A cover-up or open-up?   We probably need no reminders that people may attempt to solve something by covering it up, by hiding it from the view of other people. To "sweep it under the rug" is a familiar idiom depicting the cover-up as a solution.

A massive industry owes its success to the desire of people to cover up body odor with deodorant and perfume. If we have left our room in a mess, we keep the door closed so no one can see it. A damaged wall we cover up with a picture.

A cover-up solution is frequently intended as a temporary one, but may eventually become permanent. We close the door until we have time to clean up the room, and we intend to repair the damaged wall soon.

But it should be acknowledged that a cover-up solution can be quite an appropriate type of solution. An unsightly backyard filled with junk might be solved for the neighbors by building a fence, so it can no longer be seen by them.

Voluntary or mandatory?   When the government sets up its plan to conserve energy, it may include both elements. Citizens may be requested to voluntarily lower their thermostats, but may be required by law to reduce driving speed on the highway to 55 miles per hour. A nation may decide to provide for its defense through a volunteer army or through mandatory conscription.

The advantages and disadvantages of both are quite familiar. A voluntary plan increases the likelihood of a better attitude, and it protects the value of individual freedom. But it also increases the possibility of noncompliance, and reduces the possibility for planning. A mandatory system increases compliance, honors equality of treatment for all, makes possible better planning, and increases the likelihood that the task will be accomplished. But it can create sullen attitudes and angry nonconformists.

Normal or emergency?   In times of stress, danger, or sudden confrontation with a problem a solution may be justified as being an abnormal procedure necessitated by the emergency. Nations declare an emergency if threatened by invasion, and that permits the government to rule with special emergency powers, proposing courses of action without legislative scrutiny. When faced with a flood, a community may institute solutions which it would never dream of doing in normal times. For instance, bulldozers may be ordered to tear up people's yards in order to build a hasty earthen dam to hold out the water. Normally, anyone trespassing across those same yards would be severely reprimanded.

Spatial Dimension

Local or distant?   Is the solution a local, homemade solution, or is it a solution created in some distant place, Washington, D.C., for instance? If University Z proposes to solve the faculty-student tension on its campus with a series of student-faculty committees which are unique and which grow out of the experience and conditions of that particular campus, then they would be creating a local, homemade solution.

Particular location within a location?   An advocate may have occasion to suggest a solution which is aimed at a particular spot within the general locality. To improve the food service situation on her campus, Irene may suggest that of the five food service centers, A should hire more students in order to speed up service, B needs a larger eating area, C needs more variety in food, whereas D and E are adequate as is.

Advance or withdrawal?   A solution may call for a sort of advancement toward the enemy, an attack against the problem creator. On the other hand a solution could be a retreat, a "strategic withdrawal," to avoid clashing with the enemy at that place and time.

The military metaphor brings to mind military examples. The plan of a nation to meet growing tensions along its border with a neighboring country may be an increased marshaling of men and equipment right at the border to confront the enemy eyeball to eyeball. Or the plan may be to withdraw men and equipment from the border area to a strategic location from which they could spring if needed, but which would reduce or eliminate any charge of provocation.

If tension exists between parents and children, or between students and teacher, sometimes the best solution may be to have the two sides discuss openly their respective points of view and grievances. In other situations the best solution may be to have the antagonists back away from each other and let separation and passage of time help to heal the tension.

Temporal Dimension

Preventive or curative?   Frequently an arguer will want to propose solutions which are primarily designed to forestall, to prevent, a problem from occurring. Ski resort owners work toward making the ski slopes safe in order to prevent serious mishaps, and homeowners remove snow from their roofs to prevent ice build-up and eventual leakage. Conscientious parents try to develop values in their children so that they will not become teenage delinquents, and communities set up preventive crime bureaus. An experienced machine operator lubricates his machine conscientiously to prevent strategic parts from wearing out.

Immediate or long range?   For some types of problems an immediate solution is mandatory. In fact, if it cannot be done immediately, then it is really no solution. Timing can be crucial. Get to a doctor (solution) immediately when cancer is suspected. To go later may be no solution at all, for the disease will have won. A town threatened by a flooding river needs to build the dike by next Monday before the water crests. Students need to study before the exam on Friday.

Temporary or permanent?   Is the solution meant to be permanent or only temporary? This would make considerable difference in the type of appeal to one's audience. For instance, an arguer may propose that the problem of underemployment of minority group members in specified department stores in the community should be attacked immediately with a temporary quota system. That is, the number of minority members employed should match the number in the community, so that a community with a minority population of 10 percent should reflect a work force of 10 percent in the department stores. But the arguer may then go on to assert that once the proper percentage has been reached and maintained for a certain length of time, say, three years, then the quota system should be terminated, on the assumption that once the breakthrough has been made, equality of employment opportunities will continue.

By clarifying that a plan is temporary, designed only to meet an urgent, immediate problem, and that there may even be a specified termination time, the plan may be accepted more readily. People are understandably hesitant to saddle themselves with permanent solutions. Permanent is forever, and forever is a long time. People also, however, are very wary of so-called temporary arrangements which seem to continue endlessly.

Constant or ebb-and-flow?   Is the solution one which has a built-in time rhythm, an ebb-and-flow to meet the same daily, weekly, monthly, or seasonal rhythm of the problem? This of course would be a special kind of solution for a special kind of problem. It might take the form of extra buses, regular or minibuses, operating during morning and evening rush hours to meet the enormous demand during those hours, which are then reduced to match the lower need during other hours.

Forward to Utopia or back to Eden?   Is the solution presented as a step forward to a "bright new day," or is it portrayed as going back to the "good old days"? The first strategy ties in with the appeal of "progress," of going ahead into promising lands. The latter strategy, the rhetoric of "restoration," appeals to the notion of returning to a former time of glory, of well-being, before corruption, high inflation, war, or permissiveness ruined the wonderful state of affairs—before the fall of Adam and Eve ruined the Garden of Eden.

Quantitative Dimension

Singular or multiple?   An arguer might come up with a solution which has a single aspect to it. For instance, suppose Don suggests that to meet the growing interest in tennis the city government should allocate a special grant of $50,000 to improve the tennis program. He has one concrete proposal. But suppose he advocates some other specific things as well. In addition to the $50,000 special grant, he urges the city government, through its recreation department, to put lights on all existing courts, to supply all-weather nets for all courts, and to operate an extensive tennis instructional program throughout the year. His Solution (with a capital "S") has, then, four specific parts to it, so while he might speak of his plan in the singular, he really means those four aspects.

It is extremely important to realize that a single solution is seldom adequate for a single problem. A single solution is an illusion too often accepted by too many poeple. Just as more than one cause is usually at the root of a problem, so multiple components are needed to solve it.

Partial or complete?   Perhaps the most one can hope for in many situations is to get only part of one's ideal solution accepted. For instance, the problem of protection against airplane hijackers might be met by increased rigid inspection of passengers prior to boarding; placing security officers on all flights; making death, or life imprisonment, the punishment for the guilty; and establishing international coordination through the United Nations. Because of the complex negotiations needed for establishing United Nations involvement, that point may have to wait for the future. Because of the high cost involved, the inspection of passengers prior to boarding cannot be appreciably increased at this time. So the advocate is left with only a partial solution: the remaining two points. One accepts these partial solutions, and works for the future achievement of the other two points.

Expansion or contraction?   Is the solution the type which is calling for addition or subtraction, expansion or retrenchment? For example, as an industry grows in size, more employees are needed, thus more facilities for the employees are needed, more outlets are needed for the increased production, and more salesmen are needed to move the goods.

Recent years have seen numerous problems arising in all kinds of institutions calling for retrenchment of programs and staff, calling for subtraction of personnel and goods and services. They may be needed, but they cannot be afforded given the financial plight. How does an institution decide which employees to subtract? This is a problem agonized over by numerous universities, for instance. One solution might be to trim the staff by a certain percentage, say, 10 percent. Perhaps the plan is to release the people hired last. Perhaps the plan is to release those connected with programs which have the smallest enrollment and appeal. Perhaps the plan is to release no one but to cut everyone's salary by 10 percent. Perhaps the troublemakers will be the first to go, or those who are employed part time.

Qualitative Dimension

What values are being supported by the proposed solution?   As was stated in the previous chapter, a problem is by definition something which is wrong. It thus involves values. Likewise, a solution, something which rights the wrong, inherently is enmeshed in values. For any solution to be suggested means that it is rehabilitating, returning to or creating a value structure which was absent while the conditions were described as a problem. If one's solution calls for a municipal low-income housing project to increase the amount of acceptable housing available for the citizenry, especially those on small incomes, then that solution carries imbedded in it the values of equality of housing opportunities, cleanliness, good health standards, aesthetics, and, perhaps, racial equality.

What motivates the "hero"?   The question "Why?" is behind any solution, just as it is behind any problem. What motivates the person—the hero—who proposes the solution, the antidote, to the villain and his evil works? This is obviously related to the whole area of values. But motivation is a complex and mysterious business, primarily because human beings are complex and mysterious.

Advocates propose plans ostensibly for the "good" of someone other than themselves. But there also is usually an element involved which does good for the advocate, too. That is, Ann may propose sending food to starving children not only to help them but because it makes her feel good, it fulfills an inner desire to help others, and it may get her notoriety and prestige. All of these motivations are intertwined, and to rate them as to which is the most powerful would be difficult indeed, if not impossible.

Survival or enrichment?   A solution may be in attempting to come to grips with a situation in which a people are on the brink of extermination unless something is done. Thus an arguer may suggest sending massive food supplies to a nation faced with a devastating famine in order to keep its people alive. On the other hand an arguer may recommend sending mass communication experts to a nation to help it get its own television industry started so that the nation may enjoy the pleasures of television and enable its citizens to enrich their lives.

Mild or severe?   To minister effectively to the seriousness of the problem the solution will have to be at the same level of intensity. If there have been an unusually large number of drownings at a particular swimming area, a drastic solution is called for. Additional lifeguards and instituting other important safety measures may be the answer. On the other hand if it is a swimming area which has had no serious problems in the past, and there is no reason to believe that any will arise, then one's proposal need be only a mild one, calling for minimal lifeguard supervision.

FEASIBILITY OF SOLUTIONS

At times arguers need to be willing to accept less-than-ideal solutions if they have to. Tanya may want to go to the moon one day, but is it possible? People make decisions, in large part, based on the practicality, the feasibility, of the proposal. Their desires have to bend to fit what can realistically be put into practice. Solutions to social or personal problems have to measure up to the demands of feasibility criteria in order to be accepted.

At the same time it is hoped that an undue emphasis is not placed on feasibility, for it can deaden imagination and creativity with a devastating effect. An employee, for example, comes up with an exciting but expensive suggestion for improving production; the owner simply asks where the money is coming from. The sickening silence indicates that the dreaming has ceased, the imagination has been stifled. Respect feasibility, but do not worship it.

Transition Dimension

Can the solution be implemented without unreasonable effort?
Human beings, by nature, want to conserve energy. Their own. When someone advocates a solution to some problem, the audience and other interested parties quickly want to know how much effort they and others will have to exert to put the proposed plan into operation. An advocate of a proposal will have to convince the audience that the amount of energy demanded (1) is not great, (2) may be great initially, but then will taper off, (3) is considerable, but the objective is worth it, or (4) that someone else will handle whatever effort will be needed. All the varied and unique elements of the specific circumstance will have to determine which line of argument would be the appropriate one.

Can the solution be put into operation quickly?　In many situations a solution is simply not acceptable if it cannot be shown that it will be put into operation quickly. A military commander constructs a plan to send reinforcements into an embattled area. They are to move immediately or it will be too late.

Can the solution be put into operation without cutting ties with the

status quo? It usually is important to demonstrate how one's solution is linked with the existing situation. It is generally effective to propose something which is both "new" and "old." Nations are more likely to join some international association if they are assured that they will not have to give up their sovereignty. By showing how one's plan is linked with the present and past, an advocate is less likely to alienate people, especially those who have an investment of time, money, ego, and effort in their present organization.

Is an existing mechanism available? To be able to demonstrate that a means—a person, organization, or system—already exists through which one's solution may be put into operation is to possess a strong appeal. Many states are debating various new plans for coping with the energy crisis, and one recurring issue is whether the state should set up a new agency to be devoted entirely to energy matters or whether the state should handle energy matters through existing agencies.

To handle one's new plan through existing agencies carries the appeal that the machinery exists, with all that that suggests, such as trained personnel, tried and tested procedures, and immediate implementation. It suggests that the new plan will move quickly and smoothly and effectively into operation. But the situation may call for a break with the status quo machinery if the problem is so massive, urgent, and significant that it demands a whole new mechanism, or if the status quo machinery is deemed inappropraite or ineffective, even dangerous, and that a new mechanism is needed.

Is there an existing precedent? In legal circles, of course, precedent is crucial to any court decision. But decision-making in many other areas likewise rests heavily on precedent. Even personal relationships rely heavily upon it. Suppose parents announce a new plan to allow their teenage daughter to have the family car only one day every two weeks. She immediately protests, saying that they had let her older brother have the car at least three days a week. The precedent had been set, the new plan violates her expectation that the former practice would be continued in her case as well. Plans which violate some precedent frequently run into similar objections.

Will transition to future modification be easy? Not only is it important to convince one's audience that one's plan is easily put into operation but an arguer should also convince them that it is relatively easy to administer and alter once it is put into operation. Assurance that resources and personnel will continue to be available is important. Also it may be wise to give assurance that suggested procedures will be maintained unless better techniques are discovered. Demonstrate that the plan can be enforced efficiently. If the plan needs to be amended, give assurance that this can easily be done. Virtually all constitutions of organizations include a statement on how amendments to the constitution can be made. This merely recognizes the obvious fact that human institutions are not perfect and will probably have to be modified to some degree in the near or distant future.

Resource Availability Dimension

Is the cost prohibitive?   A bedrock consideration in any proposed solution is, "What will it cost?" This giant doorman blocks the entryway to virtually every plan put forward for anything. Money sets rigid limits to plans. If arguers can satisfy their audience that the cost of their plan is not "out of this world," that it is within reach, then they have taken a major step toward gaining acceptance for their proposal. If they cannot demonstrate that their plan can be paid for, then they might as well forget it.

It is important to be certain not only that the money is available but that the necessary material and trained personnel are also available. If a nation pushes through an extensive, federally funded medical system but then discovers that doctors, clinics, and hospitals are in short supply, then the plan simply cannot function as it was supposed to. It should also be noted that the availability of money, material, and personnel is tied to other, existing or suggested plans. That is, will the suggested solution take resources away from current or projected programs? The cost of a solution is not evaluated in a vacuum. An excellent proposal to build a municipal swimming pool may take moves away from the city baseball program and cancel out the plans for other park equipment.

Ally Dimension

Is the plan supported by experts in the field?   Strength for one's proposed solution may come from drawing on the testimony of acknowledged experts in the field. An advocate of some plan for tax reform would cite taxation experts. Securing expert allies does not guarantee that one's point is right or will be accepted, but it does lend strength to one's contention. The degree of strength depends on how acceptable the authorities are in the minds of the audience.

Modern life imposes on us the need for relying on authorities. We cannot visit each trouble spot in the world, so we rely on foreign correspondents and news commentators. We cannot know everything about today's complicated machinery, so we rely on repairmen. We need the expert opinion of those in a position to know, at least who know more than we do. Remember, however, that their statements are opinion, not fact. Doctors may give their diagnoses and prescriptions with an air of great assurance, but they may be trembling inside, for they know it is just their guess, their opinion. Despite their limitations, experts are valuable allies. They reinforce an advocate's contention that her plan is feasible. Without them, advocates would have a weaker case and a greater task.

Is the plan supported by important laymen?   Another category of authoritative allies to have in one's corner is well-known, revered laymen. They are not authorities in the field but they have much prestige because of accomplishments in other areas. For example, a respected clergyman or parent may be a very helpful ally for one's plan to help drug addicts.

We have been speaking of only individuals as expert and lay authorities, but we should hasten to include also groups, organizations, or institutions. For example, a sorority might pass a resolution supporting one's plan for reform of student government. Newspapers and magazines formulate editorial positions on social problems and political candidates. Organizations, such as the American Medical Association and the Farm Bureau, speak out on public issues relevant to their interests. What organizations say, then, in any kind of corporate statement, can be very helpful to arguers as they attempt to get their plan adopted.

The "voice of the people" is another form of ally. Any proposal in public life needs the support of majority opinion. Democratic societies have a common central thread: they operate on the concept that the majority should rule. The majority may not always be right, but they rule. If John can show that majority opinion in the community favors his plan to build a monorail transit system linking the airport, the metropolitan center, and the university, the likelihood that his plan will be adopted is enhanced.

The very fact the the majority voice is sometimes associated with rigidity, with outmoded status quo, with wrongheadedness means that sometimes the voice of a minority can be a significant and powerful ally in getting a proposal adopted. This is particulary true if it is a significant minority, such as a group of highly knowledgeable and respected "opinion leaders" in the community. They represent the "uncommon man," society's elite. Also, any group of citizens, elite or not, through tight organization can wield tremendous power, and often can decide questions as they see fit.

Are those who are directly affected one's allies? An advocate may have a plan for increasing access to membership in all fraternities and sororities to all students regardless of race, religion, or national origin. While it would be important to gather the opinion of the student body as a whole, it would be particularly important to obtain the opinion of current members of fraternities and sororities, who will be the most affected by the proposal.

Are personalized principles allies? Frequently, advocates assert or imply that they have important spiritual allies. That is, Justice, Reason, Humanity, Morality, God are on their side. They speak of them as they would speak of persons. We hear the claims that Humanity and Justice, for example, dictate that a given plan for ghetto rehabilitation should be accepted. In the name of Equality, girls ought to be able to participate in all athletic programs along with the boys. A natural concomitant is, of course, that when advocates claim to have Justice, Reason, or God in their corner, then those who are in opposition presumably have Injustice, Irrationality, and the Devil in their corner. This may lead to insufferable arrogance, at worst, or amusing naïveté, at best, on the part of the advocate. If advocates claim that their solution has some basic principles as allies, such a claim should be made with considerable humility and care.

Analogical Dimension

Have identical or similar plans been tried successfully elsewhere?
Whenever advocates present some plan, another question they inevitably encounter is, "Has this plan been successful anyplace else?" If city officials are thinking of arranging for an extensive bikeway network throughout the city, they will want to ascertain how such a proposal has worked in some other city. We feel the need to ascertain the experiences of someone, so that we might better predict what our experiences will be

if we adopt a similar course of action. Not to do so would be to ignore valuable experience. Not to do so condemns us to endless repetition of mistakes and zero progress. Civilization is built on the experience of others.

Another aspect of the procedure of comparison is raising the question of whether the proposed solution is too similar to something now in operation. In other words, does the plan needlessly and unwisely duplicate something already in existence? If university administrators propose to set up a committee to study the question of student expenses but discover that there already is a student-facutly committee working on that very subject, then the administrators would be unwise to duplicate those efforts by forming another committee.

Legal and Ethical Dimension

Is the plan legal?   For some solutions to social problems legality is of central concern. After all, one can hardly expect to claim that a solution is workable if its legality is seriously questioned. The police may wish to wiretap suspects in order to gain valuable information, but is it legal to do so? Admittedly, it might be efficient and in many cases extremely helpful in apprehending people involved in serious crimes against the community. But if the procedure is illegal, then one can hardly present it as a viable and feasible plan.

Is the plan ethical?   This may be even more difficult to answer than the question involving legality. But it is just as clear that if advocates wish to have their plan accepted as a viable, workable solution, they have to dispel any doubts as to its ethicality. Even though abortion may be declared legal, for example, many people still firmly believe that it is unethical.

DESIRABILITY OF THE SOLUTION

Once past the "feasibility" hurdle, one can look at the question of desirability. It must be clearly shown that the proposed solution fits the analyzed problem. In the phraseology of the debater, "The plan should fit the need." The plan brings distinct benefits to the victims, and appropriately deals with the villain.

These present tense assertions are really future tense predictions, for arguers are telling their audience what they *predict* will happen once their plan is put into operation. They assert that their solution has the capacity to solve the problem, to bring additional benefits, to overcome any objections brought against it, and to avoid creating any new problems. To visualize specifically, vividly, and concretely is to intensify the desire of the audience to accept one's plan.

Applicability to the Problem

Substantive dimension   If the problem is one of something left undone, then the solution should clearly show that that oversight is corrected. If an advocate pinpoints the problem as being one of men having the wrong attitude toward women, then the advocate needs to stress the creation of a different attitude before anything else can be accomplished in achieving equal employment rights for women. If the problem is that the library simply has too few books, then a solution which improves only the means to get at that inadequate supply hardly corrects the real problem. If a person succeeds in stopping the sobs of her close friend, she should not feel that by solving the visible, she has really solved the problem. She may need to spend more time counseling that person in order to determine what caused him to cry in the first place.

Spatial dimension   If an advocate is dealing with the traffic problem on his local university campus, then to present a plan which really does not fit that campus is hardly very wise. In probing the problem of lack of student participation in student government on her campus, an advocate discovers that it is a widespread problem in many universities, so she arranges for a conference of student leaders from many different institutions to seek solutions which might be common to many campuses.

Temporal dimension   If a problem is a long-standing one, advocates should approach it with that historical perspective in mind. Approaching juvenile delinquency, for example, one should know the long-standing nature of the problem and attempt to come up with wiser solutions.

It is important to distinguish clearly whether one's solution is for a present or impending problem. If for the latter, an arguer has the more difficult task of admitting the present situation is not particularly serious but that future implications are extremely serious, thus calling for strong measures now.

A problem which has an inherent ebb-and-flow rhythm to it needs a solution to match it. Thus a plan to ease the city's rush-hour congestion on buses, commuter trains, and subways might be to increase significantly the facilities used during these morning and late afternoon hours, and to reduce them during other hours.

If an arguer contends that the passage of time will automatically solve student riots, then with great stoicism she must endure the riots until they subside.

Quantitative dimension   If a problem was described as having multiple aspects, then the solution needs to take care of all of them, or, at the least, the most important ones. To satisfy the grievances of coal miners, it might be necessary not only to increase their wages but also to improve safety measures, ban forced overtime work, provide better facilities for showering, and improve health insurance coverage.

If the problem is complex, an arguer needs to provide a solution which at least makes an effort to touch and untangle the important intertwining strands. Counselors have learned that to help a mentally disturbed child they need to work with not only the child but also its parents, siblings, friends, and any other person who may be part of the problem.

In dealing with a problem of affluence, an advocate's task is essentially one of wisely distributing resources. One should not create new and perhaps worse problems in the process. By a program to curtail factory wastes, does one force the factory to cease operations, thus causing unemployment and depriving the consumer of a needed product?

Make sure the solution is massive enough. If one's plan will obtain more water for a community but still not enough, then the plan probably is not worth adopting.

Qualitative dimension   If the problem is one of enrichment rather than an issue of stark survival, then obviously one's approach to the solution would have less urgency, but, nevertheless, would communicate that enrichment is important in its own right.

If an advocate has designated a problem as primary, then she needs to approach it with urgency and thoroughness. In order to meet the problem of finding adequate time to study she may set up a plan of scheduling her time very precisely for each day of the week, because she feels that studying well is a primary concern for her.

Since in the analysis of a problem an advocate points out that something was wrong, that a value had been violated, in presenting the solution the advocate has to demonstrate that the damged value will be salvaged and fostered.

APPLICABILITY TO THE BENEFICIARIES

Who are the beneficiaries?   In addition to showing how the solution fits the problem an arguer needs to show how the solution ministers to the victims cited earlier. The arguer visualizes just how her plan will aid the victims of the status quo, how her plan will convert victims into beneficiaries.

If the immediate audience is to be considered part of the victims, the arguer should be sure to emphasize this specifically. The audience may have the general feeling that they are victims, but such a generalized feeling may be inadequate if the arguer wants to get his plan accepted.

The potential beneficiaries may not necessarily be the immediate audience but rather friends and others in the community and nation for whom the audience has concern, or even succeeding generations. If this is the case, then the same detailed visualization is needed plus a reasonable appeal to altruism or a related motivation.

The quantity of beneficiaries should of course match the quantity of victims. If the arguer demonstrated that 15,000 students suffered from excessive costs at her university, and her plan benefited only the 2,000 out-of-state students, then she probably had better rethink her plan.

What are the virtues of the beneficiaries?   Arguers would no doubt want to emphasize specifically in their visualization process that their plan will be reinforcing the commendable virtues of the beneficiaries. A plan seems to be more worthwhile and desirable if Henry can show that the people who will benefit from his family-farm preservation plan already possess the outstanding virtues of being hard-working, trustworthy, responsible, thrifty, efficient, and long-suffering.

How significantly are the beneficiaries affected?   This is of course specified throughout the above discussion, but it sometimes might be wise to add a summation of what the whole benefit will amount to. A gathering together of previous points into a sort of overview of significance might be helpful. The plan should bring benefits important enough to warrant the action called for. The victims should clearly be turned into beneficiaries.

Another important line of argument which often operates but seldom is mentioned out loud is this: "If you don't accept this plan, someone else will." And the "someone else" is usually specified or hinted to be some beneficiary less worthy than you, or even someone you despise. In other words, you should accept the proposed plan or some unworthy beneficiary will get it. Some, perhaps far too many, marriages are entered into with that kind of motivation. Suppose Mary is undecided about whether to accept Jim's proposal of marriage, but she knows that if she does not grab him, some other girl (naturally not so worthy as she) will move in. Stuart has a chance for some overtime hours at his place of employment. He is not too anxious to accept them, but he knows that if he does not, his unfriendly colleague will get them.

APPLICABILITY TO THE VILLAIN

How does the plan cope with the villain? Although we are more concerned with how the plan helps the victims of the problem, we also are interested in how the villains will be put in their place by the proposed solution.

Arguers will again want to remind their audience explicitly and clearly just who the villain is. By so doing they will be able to visualize more vividly just how the new solution will take care of that evil agent. If multiple villains exist, arguers need to be sure to show how their plan takes care of all of them. One cannot solve a problem by letting three out of four thieves go free.

Does the solution take care of the remote as well as the precipitating agents? Does the plan both restore order in a riot situation (precipitating cause) and get at the remote, or underlying, causes for the riot?

Does the solution get at the motivation which prompted the villain to act as he did? Little is to be gained from a solution which assumes that the university administrators (the villains) acted out of malice toward students, when really ignorance of the facts rather than malice played the major role. Thus, the solution needs to be something which provides the administration with necessary information rather than something which accuses them of ill will.

Just as the evil deed seems worse when the victims possess many virtues, so the harm done to the villain by a new plan is tempered by the assertion that she was unworthy anyway. If the plan makes absentee landlords go bankrupt, that fact is softened by the claim that they had it coming to them, as they are greedy people. They deserve some financial setbacks. A solution calls for elimination of 10 percent of the faculty, and if one assumes that the 10 percent are merely inefficient deadwood anyway, they don't deserve to be kept on the payroll.

Also, another line of argument is that advocates might be able to assert that their plan will not hurt the villains too much, or that the plan will actually aid the villains in the long run. That is, the villains may come to see things in a new light, they may become converted, or their initial losses will be averaged out over the long pull. Evil landlords, for instance, may actually be better off getting rid of their old substandard apartments and investing their money in better housing, or use their money in other, more healthful ways, which is worth the gamble.

PREDICTION: DIRE RESULTS IF PLAN IS NOT ADOPTED

At the very minimum, if the proposed solution is not accepted, then the evils of the status quo remain uncorrected. Usually, it is also contended that these evils will multiply and intensify if uncorrected. We explicitly or implicitly assert that the consequences will be disastrous, or too horrible to contemplate.

In most informal argumentation situations, people offer threats (implied or explicit) of various kinds, to be put into operation if their wishes, their plans, are not accepted. We announce, for example, that if our friends do not want to see the same movie we do, then we do not want to keep their company.

Occasionally, advocates are vague in predicting what the ill effects will be if their plan is not accepted. The teacher says, "You'd better not get caught cheating on the exam." This leaves unsaid just what the ill effect will be, and might be more of a threat than mentioning the specific punishment. Suppose the punishment the instructor has in mind is that she will give the student an "F" on the exam; whereas the student might be visualizing possible expulsion from college. The father might say to his children, "You'd better behave, because next time I won't use only words." This makes clear what will not be done, but still leaves uncertain just what he *will* do. The imagination of the children probably magnifies the punishment. Other familiar, ambiguous threat statements include: "You'll regret it"; "You'll wish you hadn't;" "You'll be sorry"; and "It will have tremendous repercussions."

Arguers should be judicious and reasonable when suggesting ill effects, because of their obligation to the audience, their intellectual obligation to the truth, and their obligation to themselves. Advocates should not give themselves a bad name by becoming fearmongers.

SUMMARY

In formal or informal argumentation, claim-making is frequently cast in the context of proposing solutions to stipulated problems. This chapter analyzed a comprehensive heuristic which should create helpful options for the person engaged in putting forth solutions (propositions, plans, proposals). In making claims about the nature of solutions an arguer can focus on various dimensions—substantive, spatial, temporal, quantitative, and qualitative. When making claims about the feasibility of proposals an advocate can make assertions about (1) aspects of transition from the status quo; (2) resource availability (money, material, personnel); (3) allies; (4) where the proposal has been utilized successfully; and (5) how that proposal meets legal and ethical standards. When arguers make claims about the desirability of a proposal, they can (1) assert that it applies directly and beneficially to the problems cited; (2) clarify the proposal's applicability to the beneficiaries; (3) indicate its applicability to the original villain; and (4) predict dire results if the proposal is not adopted.

EXERCISES

1. Using some healthy introspection, analyze a current or recent personal problem you have had with either friends, family, fellow workers, employers, teachers, or classmates. Relate in a brief oral or written report how you solved the problem, describing the solution using the dimensions discussed in this chapter.

2. Divide the class into groups of five students: have some groups present a problem (real or hypothetical), and other groups solve it as quickly and as imaginatively as possible. It should be an exercise in nimbly discovering as many solutions as possible. When finished, note which factors discussed in this chapter were used and which ones were not.

3. Develop a persuasive case for some proposition related to something in this chapter. For example, you might contend that society should be focusing more on preventive rather than curative solutions to problems. Present your case in a 500-word paper or a five-minute speech.

4. Select a problem in your community or on your campus and develop a solution using the heuristic of this chapter to guide you as much as possible. Arrange your solution in an outline form which resembles the outline of this chapter.

5. Listen to newscasts on radio or television and notice how much time is spent on problems in society and how much time on solutions. Do the same thing with your metropolitan or campus newspaper (the front page or some section or the whole paper), noticing the amount of space devoted to problems and the amount of space devoted to solutions. Also note the relative degree of emphasizing, of highlighting of problems and solutions; that is, note the role of headlines, of placement, of photographs, or tone of voice, which may put additional focus on the problem or solution.

6 Evidence: Classifying and Gathering

Classification of Evidence
Gathering Evidence
Summary
Exercises

Evidence is the data, the raw material which supports claims, and which thus are an integral part of the argumentation process. Arguers gather evidence, and then, through reasoning, link the evidence to claims for the purpose of increasing the likelihood of winning acceptance by the audience. As one author has recently put it:

> ... obtaining and using ... evidence increases the explicit connection between our own arguments and the real world. ... Evidence helps us to make a personal conclusion more "real" by showing that it is not just the product of one fevered brain.[1]

A number of years ago, Waldo Braden wisely admonished us: "Many debates are won before the speaking starts; they are won in the library, at the study table, and in conference with colleagues."[2] We seldom end up with all the evidence we would like for any given argumentative need, but in order to build the strongest possible case, and to build their inner confidence, arguers should diligently search for the best possible evidence that conditions permit.

Even more important, arguers should develop a firm commitment to being willing to be led by evidence. Rather than forcing evidence into

1. Sproule, *Argument*, p. 387.
2. Waldo W. Braden, "Research for Debate," in James H. McBath (ed.), *Argumentation and Debate*, p. 70.

our already formulated notions, we should be willing to modify our claims on the basis of what the evidence shows us. The following motto has been a handy, humorous warning for many collegiate debaters: "My mind is made up, don't bother me with the facts." We should keep an open mind. We should base our claims on the evidence.

We live in an age of information overload; that is, we are swamped with potential material, and we have the task of sifting and choosing. In contrast, centuries ago, with written resources so scarce, the problem was one of lack of information. Today we are bathed in information from the flood of books, magazines, and newspapers, and easy access to radio, television, and telephone. We have to learn how to select wisely, what to exclude as well as what to include.

This chapter will discuss the classification of evidence and the gathering of evidence. The next chapter will discuss types of evidence, evaluation of evidence, and general principles of strong evidence.

CLASSIFICATION OF EVIDENCE

Evidence has been categorized into a variety of classifications which help us to see its various dimensions. It can be classified according to whether it is (1) some tangible item or a statement by some person; (2) a firsthand or secondhand account; (3) preplanned or impromptu; (4) reluctantly or willingly given; (5) present or absent; and (6) directly or indirectly related to the claim being made.

Personal or real   Personal evidence is that which is given by a person, either fact or opinion. Facts are those statements about some phenomenon which presumably can be empirically verified by another person. For example, if Ms. A says: "There are 22 employees in Factory X next door." Mr. B. can check on it himself to verify it. Even if Ms. A were to say: "There are 22 employees in Factory X in Hong Kong," presumably someone could check on it for Mr. B. That is, a factual statement is open to empirical verification either by our own experience or someone else's. If Ms. A were to say: "There are a lot of lazy employees in Factory X," she would be giving an opinion, an evaluation of the employees, which is more difficult for another person to verify. Mr. B may personally observe those same workers and conclude that they are not lazy, that is, he would come to a different judgment, a different opinion. Which person's judgment is right? The soundness of an opinion rests on a host of factors which will be discussed later when we explore the type of evidence labeled "testimony." Opinion is indeed helpful when the facts cannot easily be observed directly, and opinions are capable of being projected into the past and into the future.

Real evidence possesses the power inherent in being palpable, something which arguees can touch, see, smell, or hear, that is, can experience directly with their senses. It would include such things as photographs, maps, clothing, fingerprints, weapons, handwriting samples, X-rays, and wounds. Instead of listening to a real estate salesperson describe a certain house ("It has fourteen rooms"—a fact— "and a beautiful view"—an opinion), potential buyers can go to the house and observe it for themselves. Instead of listening to the prosecuting attorney describe the murder weapon, the jury is shown the actual gun— "Exhibit A." Instead of reading what someone has to say about certain animals, students can go to a zoo and see for themselves. Suppose a person wished to support the claim, "You can get some good sized fish in this lake," by mentioning a large bass he caught a few weeks ago. To say that it was five pounds, four ounces would be meaningful only to a person who knows the significance of those statistics. To portray the size by gesture would also have limited effect. But to be able to point to the actual stuffed specimen hanging on the wall makes a compelling visual impact. Obviously, in many circumstances, it is not possible or wise to place real evidence in the presence of the arguees, so we then can be grateful for persons giving us facts and opinions.

In evaluating real evidence we have to ask about the authenticity of the object, at least silently, if not publicly. That is, can we be sure that the photograph has not been altered in some way? Is the murder weapon in the courtroom actually the one used? Can we be sure the tape or movie has not been edited in some way? Furthermore, is the item typical? Was the photograph of atrocities typical of conditions, even if it was authentic? When the motel clerk shows a person a beautiful, clean, bright room, is that really typical of the rooms in the motel, or is it a showpiece?

Primary or secondary   Evidence may be thought of as being either primary or secondary. Primary evidence is firsthand observation or experience, original data. The arguer goes to the original source of the evidence. For example, if people are discussing the merits of a certain bill recently passed in the legislature, they would be using primary evidence if they cite the bill itself. Persons reporting on an auto accident which they have personally observed would be giving primary, eyewitness accounts.

Persons reporting an accident on the basis of what others have told them, hearsay evidence, would be giving secondary versions; that is, some intermediary source was between them and the actual event. In fact, it might even be a third-hand or fourth-hand account, as the news finally reached the audience through multiple intermediaries. News shared with one's family around the evening dinner table about some event that occurred that day often may be such thirdhand or fourthhand versions of that event. Most people have probably played some version of the parlor game whereby some statement is whispered to a person who passes it along to another until the final person repeats the message aloud; usually it is far different from the original message, prompting a good laugh from all.

We usually assume and assert that primary evidence is better than secondary, for there is no intermediary source(s) to distort the information. As Newman and Newman have expressed it: "The greater a witness' personal observation of a matter to which he testifies, the higher his credibility."[3] But when the perceivers themselves do the reporting, we still have to worry about *their* competence and reliability rather than the accuracy and trustworthiness of multiple intermediaries. In courtrooms, in historical writings, and in other such situations primary evidence is greatly preferred, but in most informal general argumentation, secondary evidence often is and has to be used, for primary evidence may not be available and probably is not crucial. We should not deprecate secondary evidence just because it is misused occasionally, and of course we would want to check the intermediary reporters for accuracy and reliability if we can. In general, however, we should try to secure primary evidence if at all possible, and get in the habit of searching for original sources; at the very least, be aware that much of our evidence probably is secondary.

Prearranged or impromptu   At times, people attend an event with the intention of reporting their observations. Students attend class lectures with the intention of taking careful notes for review purposes prior to a future examination. A labor official collects evidence throughout the year to use at the annual negotiation sessions with management. Political figures prepare a public statement "for the

3. Robert P. Newman and Dale R. Newman, *Evidence* (Boston: Houghton Mifflin, 1969), p. 83.

record" in order to make their views known and for future reference. This prearranged or preappointed evidence is usually, then, created for a particular purpose. The federal government manufactures news and gives out news releases in order to explain and win adherence to its programs and policies. Legal documents, such as wills, deeds, and contracts, are created expressly for reference purposes at some later date.

At other times we are merely casual observers of evidence, and our impromptu reporting of it is thus less accurate, careful, or complete. Asked to relate what a public speaker said, we have difficulty repeating it, for we listened to the speech without realizing that we would be asked to repeat its content. People who were present when a robbery took place in a supermarket no doubt observed the event, but with no planning aforethought. Their testimony would be "accidental," "undesigned" evidence.

Neither prearranged nor impromptu evidence is inherently better than the other. The former may be more accurate, precise, and relevant, for it was gathered for a particular purpose; we ought not to feel that it is spurious because it was purposeful. Impromptu is likely to be less accurate, complete, or precise, but may carry the implication of being more honest and less slanted, for one's statements do not conform to some preplanned intention. The person had no hidden motives. But whether we use it or someone uses it on us, it is helpful to be aware of whether the evidence is prearranged or impromptu.

Reluctant or willing   When people testify against what would seem to be their own best interests, that testimony is thought of as reluctant evidence. For example, a teacher might testify to a legislative committee that salaries for teachers are quite adequate; an oil company executive might admit that oil profits are unusually high; and a real estate agent might admit that homes in an exclusive section of the city are not shown to minority clients. Sometimes such testimonies are made under pressure of careful questioning, and are made grudgingly.

Sometimes such reluctant testimony may carry considerable prestige, for it suggests that the persons testifying are honest and are speaking from conscience, regardless of the harm it may bring upon themselves. We respect a doctor who admits he made a wrong diagnosis (though we may not go to him again), or a baseball pitcher who says his team lost the game because he pitched so poorly, or a student who says she did poorly on an examination because she simply did not know the material well enough. "If they say so, it must be true" is our likely reaction to such testimony. They are not letting selfish personal interests cloud their views, we say. But at other times, such testimony may raise some doubts in the minds of the audience, for it is so much against human nature to testify against one's own best interests that the audience suspects the arguer of having some hidden reason for giving such damaging testimony.

Willing testimony is that which is given freeely and without any of the conditions connected to reluctant testimony. Since it is assumed that most testimony is given willingly, such evidence is seldom labeled as such.

Negative or positive   The significant absence of evidence is spoken of as negative evidence. To be silent in the presence of some accusation suggests that the person is guilty as accused, for if innocent, "she would have said something." If a student's signature did not appear on the attendance sheet, it testifies that she was absent, since one would expect her name to be signed if she was present. If her name was listed by the teacher on the roster of absentees, this would be positive evidence, but the term positive is seldom used, for it is rather redundant to so label all existing evidence. If an investigating committee fails to find any evidence of corruption in the mayor's office, this furthers the claim that the mayor is not guilty of wrongdoing. If there are no women in upper management in a particular corporation, it is negative evidence of sex discrimination.

Obviously, negative evidence has to be used carefully, for the accused party might have been too shocked by the accusation to respond, the mayor might have been extraordinarily clever in covering up the misdeeds, the corporation might have had three women vice-presidents whisked away (just recently) by rival corporations, and the student simply might have forgotten to sign the attendance sheet. While negative evidence is usually not so strong as positive evidence, the former does carry considerable weight in many instances, for it is unlikely to be contrived.

Direct or circumstantial   Factual evidence which is immediately verifiable and directly related to the precise claim being made is spoken of as direct evidence. Evidence which indirectly points toward some fact, which together with the accumulation of other such facts leads one to infer a claim, is spoken of as circumstantial evidence. In a courtroom a number of circumstances may be represented by the prosecuting attorney to back up her contention that the accused party is guilty of some crime. Each item is not directly related to that claim, but when put together, in accordance with the special rules of the court, the circumstances may convincingly point toward such a claim. Of course, the inference from the facts has to be sound. One usually seeks to secure direct evidence, for example, some witness who definitely saw the accused persom commit the crime; but in the absence of direct evidence, circumstantial evidence is not to be scorned. In general argumentation, circumstantial evidence is frequently and effectively used. It is perhaps best to have both direct and circumstantial evidence as supportive of each other.

GATHERING EVIDENCE

Where does one find evidence? The desire to secure it is commendable, but even better is knowing where to go to obtain it. The sources may be categorized as (1) written materials, (2) oral communication, and (3) personal observation, knowledge, and experience. Once we have found some evidence, we need to record it efficiently and file it in some meaningful manner.

Obtaining evidence from written sources   Libraries are rich storehouses of written materials, and most campuses and communities have excellent libraries for students to explore. Large universities usually have many departmental or college libraries in various locations on campus, in addition to the central library, but, unfortunately, many students fail to utilize these multiple resources. Likewise, large urban centers have many branch libraries in addition to the main library which can be very helpful. Also, increasingly sophisticated interlibrary loan systems bring the resources of distant libraries to the student. Alert students see to it that they familiarize themselves with all these opportunities.

Each main campus library no doubt has a detailed brochure explaining the various holdings in the library and how to gain access to them, so here we will only sketch the main types of sources to which a student might go.[4] Also, students should not hesitate to ask librarians for assistance, for they are more eager to help than most students probably realize.

1. General books are of course the main commodity of libraries, and virtually all students by now have learned how to use efficiently the author, subject, and title cards in the card catalog in order to secure the volumes desired. If the library has open stacks, students should immediately become familiar with them if they have not already done so. Finding one source via the call number and then looking at books surrounding that in the stacks will quickly bring to a student's attention many other volumes on that same subject. Students should get in the habit of frequently browsing in the stacks, and reading book reviews to keep informed of new publications. Students should remember that the material in most books probably is already two years old by the time the book is published, and that it takes additional time for the library to secure and catalog it.

2. Memoirs, autobiographies, diaries. An important special category of books may be those primary sources written by the individuals involved. Students may even have access to some unpublished materials, but the published diaries, memoirs, or autobiographies provide special insights into people which would greatly supplement and enrich such secondary accounts as biographies or other published works.

3. Reference books have an immense amount of excellent detailed data; often these are sources to which students would want to go early in their search, for such sources will give good basic information and will direct one to other sources. Students need to become familiar, then, with specialized and general encyclopedias (such as *Encyclopedia of the Social Sciences* and *Britannica*), biographical dictionaries (such as *Who's Who* and *Who's Who in American Education*), indexes to general periodicals (such as *Reader's Guide to Periodical Literature* for general types of magazines, and *International Index* for scholarly humanities and social science articles), indexes to periodicals in special fields (such as *Educational Index* and *Business Periodical Index*), indexes to newspapers (such as those of *The New York Times* and *Christian Science Monitor* Index), and almanacs, atlases, and dictionaries. A trip to the Reference Room of the library may well save students many hours of research time.

4. Documents of various kinds, probably housed in a separate room or

---

4. For a helpful survey of library research, see the chapter, "Finding the Facts," in Jacques Barzun and Henry F. Graff, *The Modern Researcher* (3rd ed.: New York: Harcourt, Brace, Jovanovich, 1977), pp. 51–82.

section of the library, are an incredibly valuable source of abundantly detailed and reliable information which too many students overlook. Many documents from municipal, county, state, and federal governmental agencies are available, as well as from international organizations. Legislative committee reports, legislative debates (such as the *Congressional Record*), and publications from numerous executive departments are highly significant materials. Students may want to write to some federal governmental agencies for specific documents, many of which are free or are available at a small price. Also, documents from nongovernmental institutions, such as the Ford Foundation, are sources that students might want to check.

5. Pamphlets published by various organizations and special interest groups can be a good source of concise data, both fact and opinion. AFL-CIO, chambers of commerce, Farm Bureau, American Legion, American Medical Association, and the National Education Association are some examples. They and others like them can place in one's hands an abundance of specific information related to the interests and concerns of the organization, slanted of course to reflect their viewpoints and to promote their programs.

6. Contemporary or from past years, learned journals or popular magazines, whatever the age or type, periodicals can be an extremely important source for students to examine. In addition to checking the various indexes to periodicals, students should get into the habit of browsing occasionally in the Periodical Room of their library, and gradually become familiar with the type of articles that appear in the various publications. For some magazines, of course, students do not need to go to the library, they may be subscribed to, or obtained from friends or relatives or read in the doctor's or dentist's office.

7. Newspapers may also be subscribed to, or secured at the library. The collections of newspapers, in print or on microfilm, in many libraries are a rich source of information; they bring students close to the time and the occasion of the subject with which students are concerned. While considerable inaccuracy and incompleteness exist in the dailies, they can still be very instructive. Students should not overlook newspapers from Great Britain, such as *The Times* (London) and *The Guardian* (Manchester), or other English-language newspapers from foreign countries; and of course if students can read foreign languages, they then have access to even more newspapers. Students will find their library's Newspaper Room a highly interesting and informative section with which to become familiar, and students should be sure to find out if their library keeps newspaper clipping files on current events.

8. Students may want to enter into correspondence with various ex-

perts, government officials, or officers of organizations, from whom they might receive letters which would be very informative. By asking precise, well-thought-out questions, students could get specific data from very authoritative sources. Many of the suggestions made below on interviewing would also apply here.

9. If it is well designed and carefully administered, a questionnaire can be very helpful in securing specific data from a large number of people. For example: An investigator wants to find out what students at a particular university think about some campus or community issue. It would be extremely difficult to interview hundreds of students, but the needed data could be secured rather efficiently from questionnaires, and it could be gathered in exact statistical form. The discussion on sampling procedures discussed below with statistics would be relevant here also.

Obtaining evidence from oral sources   While written material is usually the most heavily relied upon by arguers building formal cases, some form of oral communication is also extremely important as evidence for both formal and general argumentation. Written material obviously is more permanent, provides better verification, is easier to refer to in the future, and is always the same to all who consult it (except for varying interpretations by readers). Oral communication is transient, disappears the second it is uttered (unless it is recorded), and even if repeated (for example, a professor repeating a lecture), may well be slightly different each time. Whatever the potential weaknesses of oral materials, they also have much virtue, and should be utilized by the serious student of argumentation. The following may be used with great profit.

1. Instead of writing to people, students might interview them and get their oral responses to specific questions. Investigators may want to interview a famous economics professor on campus, the mayor of the community, an elderly immigrant about her early experiences, or the local star baseball player. It is very important to be thoroughly prepared before interviewing people if one wants to obtain maximum value from the effort. The more one knows about their background, achievements, experiences, and biases, the better one will be able to understand and interpret their remarks. One should know exactly what it is one wants to find out; one should prepare questions beforehand, but of course be flexible and extemporaneous in asking them in the conversation. Interrogators should focus on the person's area of expertise, for since information that would be difficult to secure elsewhere is what is desired, it would be a shame to waste

valuable time on general subjects (except in briefly aiding the informality and pleasantness of the interview).

One should come prepared to listen and accumulate information; time should not be wasted by arguing with what is being said. One should not impose too much on other people's time, so the interrogator should be brief, and, of course, punctual in arriving at the appointed time. The questioner should be tactful and appreciative. If it will not intrude in the proceedings and if the person consents, questioners might be able to tape record the interview, in which case it would be available for easy and accurate referral at a later time. If it is inappropriate to tape record, then one should take careful notes either during or immediately after the interview. Even if it is tape recorded, interrogators would want to jot down their impressions and other information as soon as possible. Also, one should be sure to document the date, place, time, setting, and interviewee for future reference.

2. Listening to speeches can be a helpful source of material. Students do not need to be reminded of the hundreds of lectures they will have listened to during their college days, and we certainly won't bring up how valuable they are! Regardless of what we may think of the lecture system in general or of specific lecturers, we would probably admit that in the long run we have gathered much information from that source. General public speeches often give us other kinds of concise and interesting material. Students may find it helpful to tape record some public presentation, or at least take appropriate notes. While peer pressure helps us take notes in the classroom, audience pressure makes us feel awkward about note-taking in public settings; we ought not to be concerned that we seem to be the only ones taking notes. After the speech, and certainly a week later, students will be glad they did take notes. Students may also secure from their library some recordings of past speeches by public officials; unfortunately these rich audio sources are often lying unused in many libraries.

3. Oral testimony by people before legislative committees, in courtrooms, or in a host of informal contexts is another helpful source of information.

4. We should not overlook the common mode of informal conversation, which can often render up some useful data, and often in a rather unsuspecting manner. In addition to serving as a good testing of evidence one has already gathered and a good test of one's thinking on the subject, it also can generate new data. Students should choose their conversationalists wisely, and it may be discovered that this is a richer source of information that one had ever realized.

5. Radio and television for decades have served as a very important source for information which is used eventually in formal and

informal argumentation. "We *are* going to have a tornado tonight, I heard it on the radio this morning!" "Iran really is experiencing unrest, I saw some of their riots on TV last night." These electronic media have brought oral communication from highly authoritative sources into our homes, and the material we gain from them finds its way as evidence into the everyday claims we and others make.

Obtaining evidence from personal observation, knowledge, and experience   People often overlook the obvious, and do not stop to think of themselves as possessors of valuable evidence on a given subject. If arguers are making claims about the inadequate bus service in their city, and they frequently ride on the bus, their experience certainly serves as evidence to substantiate their claims. If they are making claims about the beauty of the Rockies, having been there last year, their observations are certainly relevant. If people are making claims about life in Brazil, critics in the audience might support or refute some of the assertions based on some reading about Brazil which the critics had done last year. If someone makes some claims about a religious subject and critics in the audience have done a great deal of reading and thinking about it for many years, the critics certainly might bring forth their thoughts as evidence. If one hears that gas stations have long lines, one might get into one's car and go see for oneself. In short, one's current observations or experiences, and one's past knowledge and experiences, can be rich sources of evidence. Students should be introspective, or at least should not forget to look to themselves as a source for evidence. Of course, one has to apply the same tests, such as possible bias, that one applies to other sources of evidence, but that will be discussed later.

Summary of sources of evidence   To draw together these various sources that have been discussed, let us suppose that students were preparing an argumentative research paper defending the claim that drunken drivers ought to be given harsher punishment than they now receive. Students could take books on the general subject out of the library; go to the autobiography of some famous person who had been an alcoholic; check reference books; write to Alcoholics Anonymous for some of their literature; write to the State Departments of Highways and Law Enforcement; read some sociological journal articles on the subject; read articles in various general circulation magazines; see whether the library has a newspaper clipping file on the subject; write to some law enforcement and highway officials, some officers in Alcoholics Anonymous, some lawyers and judges, and some sociology experts. Students could construct and administer questionnaires to give to randomly selected students on campus, set up interviews with the above lawyers, judges, highway officials, and classmates, attend any speeches in the community which might touch on the subject, attend any relevant legislative committee meetings or court cases, engage in conversation with friends and acquaintances, and watch for any radio and television programs on the subject. Finally, students could recall their own experiences or the experiences of their friends with drunken drivers.

Recording evidence   Finding material is one thing, but it is quite another to record it systematically so that it can be used efficiently in the present or future. Researchers usually develop a system of taking notes on cards or slips of paper of four-by-six or three-by-five size. Many scholars prefer the four-by-six slips of paper, for they are large enough, but not too large, for most purposes, and can easily be filed. Some people prefer regular-size notebook paper. Students should choose what seems to serve them best. Facts, statistics, quotations, paraphrasings which one thinks will be useful should find their way into one's notes. Knowing what to record and what to omit is of course difficult; experience helps but never solves that puzzle, for in a sense, one cannot possibly know until enough data have been collected just what will be useful. One should be discriminating is all that can be suggested. One should expect to take more notes than one will use, and one should not become frustrated by having unused data lying around. It might be useful in the future, and working with it will no doubt strengthen one's understanding of the subject and increase one's confidence. Not using material immediately and directly does not mean it is wasted.

One's notes should be legible, accurate, neat, and complete. This sounds trite and simple. But after a few weeks have gone by, and students return to their notes, they often discover with much chagrin how these admonitions have been violated. One should be especially careful that quotations are accurate, and that any omitted words are indicated with ellipses (...), or four dots if it includes the end of the sentence or if more than one sentence is omitted. One should put only one subject on each note card, use only one side of the card, and put a subject label at the top. One should be sure to include the necessary documentation on each note card; for example, if it is a magazine article, one should include the name and date of the magazine, the author and title of the article, and the pages. One may need to refer to the material in the future, or may need to include that information in a footnote. Many students have wasted valuable time and generated needless frustration by omitting such documentation.

Basic to careful recording of evidence, is the construction of accurate and complete annotated bibliography cards. For an article this would include the items just mentioned; if it were a book, it would include the author, title of the book, publisher, place and date of publication. Then in a few sentences one should indicate what is in the source and indicate one's evaluation of the material. That is, one's notation should very briefly describe and evaluate the material.

Filing evidence   Developing an effective filing system is as important as developing the skill of finding material. Again, many students no doubt have experienced the frustration of knowing that they have some important data, but cannot remember where they put it.

Most university debaters develop a filing box which they carry into the debate with them, and pull out the indexed card to refute something the opposition asserted. Effective debaters use it with rapidity and skill; ineffective debaters fumble around and waste time. In setting up such a filing box, debaters should arrange the notes in some clear and meaningful fashion, and cross-index those instances where a subject card could relate to more than one topic. Once an abundance of material is gathered, debaters will then separate out those items which will be used in a debate tournament, that is, their "active" file, and leave the "reserve" file back in their room.

But filing material is relevant not only to the debater, for all students should develop a lifelong habit of keeping file folders on subjects related to their major fields of study or on controversial topics of interest to them. Into these labeled folders one may put research notes, outlines of speeches heard, newspaper and magazine clippings, ideas which have been generated on the subject, and any additional relevant information. It is a wonderful feeling and a tremendous time-saver to be able to go right to a labeled file folder and find one's accumulated data.

SUMMARY

It is of fundamental importance that students of argumentation secure a firm grasp of the role of evidence, that which supports the claims put forth. Evidence may be classified as personal or real, primary or secondary, prearranged or impromptu, reluctant or willing, negative or positive, and direct or circumstantial. Students need to widen their horizons as to the many sources to which they can turn in the search for evidence: the innumerable written sources, the many oral communication situations, and one's own personal observation, knowledge, and experience. In order to profit from one's labors in finding evidence, students need to know how to record it carefully and file it in a meaningful fashion.

EXERCISES

1. Take careful and complete notes of a specific classroom lecture or a public speech. Compare your notes with a classmate's and describe the similarities and differences. Suggest reasons for the differences. Share these insights in an informal discussion with the whole class.

2. Each student might be assigned a specific task in relation to library research, the results of which would be shared with the rest of the class in an informal discussion. For instance, students might be assigned to report on specific encyclopedias, dictionaries, and indexes, specific governmental and nongovernmental documents, specific newspapers, specific scholarly periodicals, and specific popular magazines.

3. Each student might be assigned to interview someone in the community, a public official or anyone knowledgeable on a certain subject. In an informal class discussion the students could share their experiences: what kind of advance preparation was made for the interview, how they conducted the interview, under what conditions, and with what results. How might the experiences have been more fruitful? Students should take notes on the ideas generated in the class discussion, and thus would build up a handy list of ideas for improving their procedures for future interviewing.

4. Analyze some speech or essay which advocates something and classify the evidence employed according to the categories discussed in this chapter. What was fact and what was opinion, and what was primary and what was secondary? Was any reluctant or negative evidence sensed? Was the evidence direct or circumstantial? Share your findings in an informal class discussion, and write a brief essay in which you summarize your findings.

5. Construct a five-minute speech in which you advocate a claim on any subject relevant to this chapter. For example, you might contend that primary evidence is more significant than secondary, that your library has a very weak or very strong collection of periodicals, or that your particular habit of note-taking and note-filing is one which other students should adopt.

7 Evidence: Types and Evaluation

Types of Evidence
Evaluating Evidence
General Principles of Strong Evidence
Summary
Exercises

This chapter will continue the exploration of the world of evidence. It is important for the student of argumentation to understand the varying types of evidence, and to have command over a number of basic questions which need to be asked when evaluating any piece of evidence. At the end of the chapter a number of general principles will be summarized which students of argumentation should find helpful to their concern that the strongest possible evidence be utilized in any given argumentation episode. Throughout the chapter it is well to keep in mind the admonition of Ehninger:

> Unless all the pertinent evidence bearing upon a point is given exactly the weight it deserves—neither more nor less—judgment is impaired and faulty beliefs or unwise actions result.[1]

TYPES OF EVIDENCE

The three most important types of evidence are specific instances, statistics, and testimony. But also significant are illustrations, compari-

1. Douglas Ehninger, *Influence, Belief, and Argument: An Introduction to Responsible Persuasion* (Glenview, Ill.: Scott, Foresman, 1974), p. 62.

sons and contrasts, definitions, restatement and repetition, imaginary dialogue, and cartoons.

Specific instances   Suppose a person says: "Many cities are experiencing a severe shortage of gasoline; look at Los Angeles, Minneapolis, Chicago, and Boston." She would be citing specific instances (examples) of what it is she is asserting. The specific cities mentioned would serve as evidence to support her opening claim. Just as many buildings are constructed brick-upon-brick, so are many claims constructed by utilizing numerous specific instances. This can be a highly effective means of support, especially if one's opposition is not able to counteract with other, specific instances.

Statistics   Statistics are a compact, numerical way to express specific instances, which results in a clear, detailed, factual presentation of information. Statistics might be expressed as raw data or as percentages. An example of the former would be to say, "Ten members of our class were absent today." If, for example there were fifty students in one's class, one could express the same information: "Twenty percent of our class were absent today."

If a student were to ask all fifty members of his class if they liked the class, and thirty were to say "no," and he reported that three fifths disliked the class, he would be using descriptive statistics. On the other hand, if he asked only a sample of the class, say five members, and three of them said "no," he could still say that that three fifths of the class disliked the class, but it would be inferential statistics; that is, he would be making an inference on the basis of only a sample instead of dealing with all of the group. Questions touching on the soundness of sampling procedures will be discussed later in the chapter.

Statistics have a strong appeal with their precision and sense of being "scientific." But the methods by which they are secured, and the care with which they are interpreted, are central to their soundness and will be discussed later. As we all know, statistics can, unfortunately, conceal and distort the truth, and confuse and bore the audience, if not used appropriately and responsibly.

Testimony   Since we cannot be everywhere at the same time, we have to rely on the statements, the "testimony," of other people who have been there. For example, a person may not be able to visit College X in some distant state, but she can ask a friend who has attended it to give her some facts and opinions about it. People cannot be experts in all things, so they have to rely on the testimony of those who are experts, that is, those who possess special training, knowledge, or experience in that field. For example, people seek a doctor's advice when they feel ill; they go to an auto mechanic when their car does not behave; they need a fingerprint expert to interpret the fingerprints submitted as evidence. The testimony of others, then, is an important kind of evidence. Testimony is especially important in "the realm of value disputes,"[2] in religion, politics, art, or any other area in which value judgments are likely to be at the heart of most assertions.

The testimony may be not only that of individuals but also the voices of organizations, institutions, and magazines. A church, a fraternity, an industrial firm, a monthly magazine, or a daily newspaper speak out, give testimony, on issues that affect them, and, of course, may have considerable influence. Historical figures are sometimes called upon to testify; and their prestige often seems to grow with each passing year. For example, how often has George Washington been called upon to testify that the United States ought to avoid entangling foreign alliances? The Constitution, religious scriptures, and other revered documents are also cited as testimony to support a claim. Even writers of fiction and some of their characters (for example, Mark Twain and his fictitious personages) are called upon to testify. The testimony of others, then, is an important kind of evidence. Arguers should seek more than one testifier, and should supplement them with other kinds of evidence as well.

Illustrations   An extended, more fully developed specific instance is an illustration. Instead of just mentioning Los Angeles as one specific city in which a gas shortage exists, one arguer may choose to give considerable details about the situation in Los Angeles: many stations closed, long lines waiting at those that are open, heated arguments and even violence, people late for work, low attendance at movies and churches, and department stores experiencing declining sales. Advertising often makes use of illustrations; for example, the used-car lot which informs radio listeners that they have a hundred and ten excellent buys, and then spends most of the commercial describing in detail one of those bargains. In other words, the advertiser illustrates, gives a fairly full picture of what one specific item is like.

2. Gerald R. Miller, "Evidence and Argument," in Miller and Thomas R. Nilsen (eds.), *Perspectives on Argumentation* (Chicago: Scott, Foresman, 1966), p. 46.

In addition to such real illustrations, an arguer might construct hypothetical illustrations, whereby she creates details of what some situation could reasonably be expected to be. The following might be her imaginary, hypothetical illustration of an ideal place to work: "Suppose the store where I work gave three weeks paid vacation every six months, paid ten dollars an hour, gave lots of opportunity for overtime, gave us a nice lounge area in which to relax during coffee breaks, and provided free uniforms? Wouldn't that be neat?"

Illustrations often can strengthen a claim by being detailed, vivid, concrete, in narrative form, dramatic, simple, and often humorous. They can be especially helpful in the early part of an oral presentation, for they catch the audience's attention quickly and the listeners find it easy to enter into the subject.

Imaginary dialogue   Another imaginative, vivid, and concrete method to support a claim is to construct an imaginary dialogue between two people, which would usually show both sides of a controversy but support the point of view the advocate wanted to put forth. For example, picture the following exchange:

CAB DRIVER: You'll really like this town. It's got some great hotels, good shopping malls, three nice lakes close by, big league baseball and soccer, and the temperature usually is just right. The other day one of the local baseball players said that this city has better restaurants than any other city of its size that he has been to. And he really gets around.

PASSENGER, WHO GOT IN AT THE AIRPORT: But I've heard that everything really costs a fortune.

CAB DRIVER: Oh, it's sort of rough, but certainly no worse than any other city of its size. You can find reasonable prices if you just take time to look for them.

Through this imaginary dialogue, which has specific instances, statistics, and testimony imbedded in it, the claim has been made and supported that a certain city is a pleasant place to be. Technically, an imaginary dialogue is not a separate type of evidence, it offers a special form into which other types of evidence may be expressed; but it often is discussed as a type of evidence, so it has been included here.

Comparison and contrast   An arguer might seek to make something more clear and evident by focusing on similarities or differences of two phenomena. Pearl might back her claim that City X is better than City Y by contrasting the two; the former has professional football, an excellent airport, and beautiful lakes, whereas City Y has none of those. Dick might support his claim that his university is an excellent one, just as prestigious University Z; they both have superior faculty, low teacher-student ratios, and stress the importance of excellence in teaching. The comparison might also be figurative, so that the university is compared to a beautiful oasis: they both have beautiful atmospheres, both are isolated from the undesirable life around them, and the products of each enrich the whole area of which they are a part. The process of comparing will be discussed more fully in the next chapter.

Definitions   An arguer might strengthen her claims by constructing clear and helpful definitions. Suppose Barbara asserts: "Freeways are really a blessing to modern transportation." But the person to whom she uttered such a statement is a foreign student whose country does not have freeways, and he asks her what they are. She proceeds to define them by indicating their major characteristics: wide, multiple lanes; one-way traffic; no cross traffic; widely separated access and exit points, and no traffic lights or other hindrances to maintaining a constant rate of speed. After she has defined a "freeway," her foreign student acquaintance will be more likely to accept her opening claim, or at least know what she is talking about.

Repetition and restatement   Advocates can sometimes strengthen their claim-making by repeating something exactly as it was originally stated. If someone contends that "the mayor is corrupt," she simply repeats that expression at various appropriate intervals in her presentation. Restatement is reasserting an idea but using different phrasing. So she might, through various phrasings, keep the mayor's corruption before the audience.

Repetition and restatement can often help in comprehension and retention, and can be especially helpful at transitional locations, and in internal and terminal summaries in an oral presentaion. But as a later chapter points out, we ought to be leary of repetition at times, as advertisers and political demagogues remind us continually.

Cartoons   These visual creations frequently and regularly appear in newspaper editorial pages and in magazines to give support to a point of view held by the editor, the owner of the publication, or the cartoonist. A cartoon has strength, for it catches the eye of the reader—and at times we may look only at the cartoons in a publication. Cartoons have humor, and are interesting with their frequent subtleness, exaggeration, and figurative language. The visual format and the narrative context help to support the claim being made.[3]

EVALUATING EVIDENCE

Evaluating specific instances

1. Are the instances representative? Suppose someone said, "The students in our section of the dorm are really hard drinkers. Look at old George and Herman; they're drunk almost every other night." Perhaps those two specific instances are not typical of the thirty people in that section of the dorm. Often, extreme cases of what it is people are talking about come to mind and tend to serve as misleading instances for the whole group.
2. Are there enough instances? If only George and Herman were cited out of a group of thirty, it might be reasonably pointed out that the number of instances was too small to substantiate the claim about the students in that section of the dorm.

Evaluating statistics

1. Have the statistics been collected accurately? Some professional poll-takers have gradually built up a basic reliability, and although they, too, may be wide of the mark, other sources might be far less reliable. The persons taking a poll, for example, might have suggested to the people participating in the survey the kinds of answers that were wanted, or might have recorded the responses in a careless manner. Those answering the questionnaire might have given false information, might have responded in a lighthearted vein, given answers they felt the questioner wanted, or answers they felt pressured to give. In other words, perhaps the interrogators have collected merely an impressive abundance of false and misleading statistical data.
2. If the statistics are inferential, that is, based on a sample population, has the sampling been representative and has it been numerous enough? If an interrogator wanted to find out, for example, how the students at her university felt about athletics in a university, and she went to the gymnasium to "randomly" ask students, she proba-

---

3. One of the first textbooks in argumentaion to deal with the importance of claim-making via cartoons is the recent volume by J. Michael Sproule, *Argument*, pp. 346–52.

bly would end up with a proathletic sample that would hardly be a representative cross-section of the student body. Likewise, if she asked only ten students, out of a student population of 15,000, she would not have a large enough sample to formulate a very accurate and meaningful statement about the attitudes of the students at her university.

3. Has the subject being examined been clearly defined? If an arguer is presenting figures on the number of unemployed people in his community, how does he define "unemployed"? Does he include students who are out of school in the summertime? Does he include people who are temporarily laid off for a week or so? Does he include people who are currently training for jobs? Does he include unemployable people, that is, those with serious physical or mental handicaps? Does he include those people who are unwilling to work? Does he include those who are greatly underemployed in terms of their qualifications? Does he include people who have regular jobs but who work no more than 25 hours a week? His figures on the number of unemployed people in his community obviously will reflect how he answers these questions; and since he might answer them quite differently from someone else taking a similar survey, the two surveys would present significantly different statistics.

4. Are the units being compared actually comparable? For example, suppose the following statistics are accurate: the United States spends five percent of its annual federal budget on education, whereas the Soviet Union spends 25 percent of its budget. Obviously, one concludes, the Russians have a higher regard for education. But then one is reminded that much of the education in the United States is run not by tax money but by private funding; whereas in Russia the only education is run by the government. Hence one is comparing apples and oranges, and certainly one cannot make the inference that the Soviet Union values education more than the United States, or even that as a society they are spending more on it.

5. Is the base of the percentage a reasonable base? Suppose the year 1975 saw the greatest amount of rainfall the state of Illinois has experienced, and an arguer uses that as the base year when saying that this year Illinois has had two percent less rainfall than in 1975. Thus, the current statistic on rainfall might not sound like much, but Illinois might actually have experienced the second highest rainfall in its history.

6. Does the base of the percentage remain constant? For example, suppose the college administration says it wants to treat its faculty equally this year and give them all seven percent salary increases. Is

that treating them all equally? The person with $10,000 would receive a $700 raise, while the person with $30,000 would receive a $2,100 raise. Since the bases from which the percentage is figured are widely different, the raises are vastly unequal.

7. Is the average clearly specified? That is, should one state the average being the mean, median, or mode? Suppose someone asked Bob what his average bowling score is. His last five times, he quickly recalls, resulted in scores of 210, 200, 130, 120, and 120. Being a mathematical whiz, he quickly adds them up, divides by the number of games, and says: "156." That is the arithmetic average, the mean. The median, the midpoint of a range of numbers—that is, there are an equal number of figures above and below it—would be 130. The mode, that is, the number occurring most frequently, would be 120. One can see, therefore, that in some situations the selected average could make quite a difference in the message conveyed.

To cite another example, suppose the five top executive officers of a company earned salaries of $200,000, $60,000, $30,000, $20,000, and $20,000. It is claimed that they do not need a raise this year because the average salary is $66,000 (the mean). But the lower paid executives point out that the average is only $30,000 (the median), or even $20,000 (the mode). Thus, one has to be careful that the average is clearly specified, and that it is the most meaningful and least misleading figure in the context of the claim which is being made.

8. Is the precision which is asserted rather meaningless in a certain context and perhaps intended to impress the arguee unreasonably? In short, sometimes an arguer may be overly precise. Decimals are occasionally used in this manner. For example, suppose the following assertion is made: "The number of students who are below the poverty level is 2,103.45." Round numbers would be more meaningful, and certainly would be more clear and memorable. Each arguer, of course, has to make a decision in each case whether it is more or less appropriate to use round figures.

9. Is the subject quantifiable? For example, suppose someone claims: "Wives who stay home are twenty percent happier than wives who work outside of the home." How can happiness be measured in such a precise quantitative way?

10. Do the statistics cover a sufficiently long period of time? Often, statistics are used to substantiate claims of trends. For example, suppose someone asserts that the price of potatoes is rising dramatically, that they cost twenty percent more than they did three months ago. The implication is that the price of potatoes will continue to rise at a similar rate. But perhaps those three months were prior to the

local harvest, and when the local produce is available, the price will drop sharply.

11. Is the arguer predicting beyond the figure? The above example also illustrates this, for the arguee is left with the implication that the increase of the past three months will continue in the months ahead. The arguer draws the line off the chart, so to speak, continuing the upward line.

12. Are the data statistically significant? Some statistics are expressed in ranges so that differences within that range are insignificant. For example, I.Q.'s of 115 and 120 are not significantly different, for they would be thought of as falling within a range, for instance of 110–130. In addition, some allowance of a margin for error normally would need to be taken into account, so a slight difference in figures would be insignificant.

13. If there is a visual presentation of the statistics, say, in some sort of graph, does the portrayal accurately and fairly present the information? For example, in a bar graph, using money bags instead of a bar illustration would introduce a dimension of width as well as height, and hence would distort the relationship depicted.

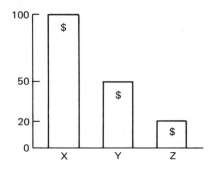 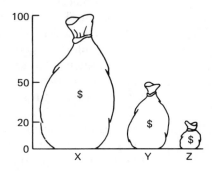

Evaluating testimony   Whether the testimony is expressed by experts or laypeople, there are some basic questions a student of argumentation would want to keep in mind when trying to determine how much weight she would give to their comments. In debate and other formal situations it is very important to distinguish between experts and nonexperts, but that is not so crucial in general argumentation.

1. Did the person have an opportunity to observe closely and carefully? Did she have enough time to observe the bank robber in order to verify the suspect? Was Mr. X in a foreign country long enough to make the judgments he is asserting?

2. Was the person physically and mentally capable of observing accurately? Does she have good eyesight? Was he sleepy, drunk, or ill? Was the person emotionally upset at the time? Is the person mentally retarded or physically handicapped in a significant way? Does she have good perceptive and memory powers? Does he have effective verbal ability?

3. Did conditions impede accurate observation? Was some obstruction in the way, such as a pillar, a dirty window, darkness, or a heavy rainfall?

4. Does the observer bring to the event preconceived expectations? When people observe their favorite football team, they see the things they want to see. They expect their team to do all the right things, and expect the opposing team to break rules and deserve penalties. They come with a purpose of seeing the good in their team and the bad in the opposition. This psychological mind set obviously affects the observations of most people, and needs to be noted.

5. Is the person biased? Does he stand to reap some personal gain? Even if he is biased, this does not completely negate his testimony, but a critic needs to keep the bias in mind. Whenever possible, one should seek the objective observer's testimony. Newspapers and magazines can communicate their bias in many subtle ways: the placement of a story, the headlines used, the choice of photographs, or the length of article. Seldom do people explicitly reveal what their bias is; members of the audience have to ferret it out for themselves.

6. Is the person of good moral character? Does she have a reputation for exaggerating, for making outlandish claims with little regard for their accuracy or their impact? What is her reputation for honesty? In short, is she trustworthy, and, hence, is her testimony worth considering seriously? Of course, one cannot let a single bad experience with that person govern one's attitude completely; after all, having exaggerated on one occasion does not make her untrustworthy forever.

7. Are there any factors in the reporting process which might affect the soundness of the person's testimony? Is the information being clearly reported? Is it being quoted out of context? Is the person afraid of giving bad news to the audience, and hence giving inaccurate testimony? For example, people occupying high positions in government, business, or education have to beware of advisers who report all news in the most favorable light, thus actually misleading their superiors. A student may not want to anger his professor, and hence reports that a research paper is "almost done"when in reality it is far from that stage.

While the above factors relate to any person giving testimony, whether an expert or a layperson, the following considerations are more applicable to experts.

1. Does the person have specific formal education and training in the field in which she is supposed to be an expert? Is the educational institution a reliable and prestigious one? Can it be verified that her degree has actually been obtained?

2. Is the person an expert in the subject field under investigation? That is, an expert in dentistry is not necessarily an expert on heart problems or farm policies. In this era of specialization, a person may not be an expert in the whole field which he represents; for example, a medical doctor may not know very much about certain specific diseases, and a foreign policy expert on Thailand may not know very much about Nigeria.

3. Is reference to the expert vague? Many times we are told that "economists," "industry spokesmen," "educators," or "doctors" back up certain points of view. While such vague references might be appropriate in some contexts, in far too many situations such general reference to expert opinion is hardly sufficient and may be an illegitimate extension of one expert to the whole group. Alert audiences would demand a more specific identification of the experts.

4. Is the expert highly regarded by other colleagues in the field? If other football coaches speak highly of Coach Y, then he gains strength as an authority. Occasionally, jealousy, personal dislike, or friendships result in misleading evaluations of colleagues. But, in general, receiving the backing of fellow experts is an important endorsement.

5. Is the testimony of the expert really relevant to this situation? Is it needed? Does having a person highly trained in meteorology to read the weather forecasts make it more authoritative?

6. Was she aware of the significance of her remarks? Occasionally, for instance, experts may express themselves in "off-the-record" situations and do not expect their remarks to be made public. If they knew their statements would go beyond the immediate setting, they would have expressed them differently.

Experts are of course only human, so it is not unusual that they might disagree, leaving us to choose between them. Two psychologists may have examined an accused person; one testifies that the accused is not mentally capable of standing trial, while the other psychologist asserts that the accused is capable. Which should one believe? One army general asserts that the nation's defenses are adequate, while another general contends that the defenses are woefully inadequate. Which general should one believe? In short, often we simply have to judge the judges.

It is good to utilize testimony, but it is wise not to rely only on that type of evidence. It ought to be supplemented with other types. And, of course, one should not rely on only a single authority.

Audience acceptability of the evidence

It should be explicitly reemphasized that while we are concerned with inherent strengths in evidence, which it is assumed would be accepted by the mythical universal audience (this will be more fully discussed in a later chapter), we always have to measure the strength of evidence in relation to the specific audience involved. An arguer should, as Thompson admonishes, "select and present the kind and the amount of evidence that will be the most persuasive with those listeners whose approval is critical to the objective of the speech."[4] Material which may be powerful with the universal audience may not mesh with some particular audience at some particular time. But while it is commonly asserted that evidence is strong only as it appeals to a particular audience, which denies that inherent strength in evidence exists, one should not abandon the emphasis that the strength of evidence should also be measured against the mythical universal audience. If this were not so, then why talk about seeking authorities who are generally reputable? We would only seek those authorities, even if they are known to be charlatans, who would impress a particular audience.

But certainly the crucial question in argumentation in action still is, Does the immediate audience understand and accept one's evidence? Is one's evidence instrumental in helping them adhere to one's claims? Specifically, the following questions need to be asked: Does the material coincide with the beliefs and motives of the audience? Is the evidence on an appropriate intellectual and technical level, so that the audience can grasp it easily? Will the audience know and respect the source of one's material?

GENERAL PRINCIPLES FOR STRONG EVIDENCE

What has been discussed in this chapter might be drawn together into the following general principles which should serve as helpful guidelines in seeking the very best evidence one can find in each situation.

4. Wayne N. Thompson, *Modern Argumentation and Debate: Principles and Practices* (New York: Harper & Row, 1971), p. 116.

Recency   Especially on contemporary social issues, the more recent the material, usually the more effective it will be. If the subject is a historical one, then of course older material closer to that time period might well be more valuable. But since most claim-making is concerned with contemporary issues, students of argumentation need to be alert to the importance of having recent data. Facts and events are constantly changing, so what might have been true yesterday, may no longer apply today. Recency ought to be respected, but not worshiped. One should not be trapped by the assumption that the most recent fact is always the best; recency simply means that that fact has passed one test of strong evidence with high marks. There are other tests to pass as well.

Clarity   Is the evidence presented in such a way as to be clear to this particular audience? What people cannot see, they cannot understand, and cannot accept. Hence, as has been stressed throughout this chapter, arguers need to strive constantly for clarity.

Accuracy   Is the material presented in an accurate fashion? As has been discussed, arguers should seek to ensure that they have accurate statistics and specific instances. They need to be sure they do not quote someone out of context, and that their paraphrasing is accurate. An efficient and responsible arguer will always be thoroughly committed to the goal of accuracy.

Sufficiency   In addition to accuracy, another fundamental component of truth is completeness, so arguers need to make sure that they have a sufficient amount of evidence backing up their claims. Total completeness is usually not possible in dealing with complex issues given the limited time or space constraints that people have to operate in, but at least arguers should keep in mind that a higher degree of completeness is more impressive and has more integrity than a low degree of completeness. One should always keep asking oneself, "Do I have enough evidence?" In practice, "enough" usually means the quantity sufficient to secure adherence from one's specific audience. Enough depends on the audience, on how controversial the subject is, and on whether or not there is opposing evidence to refute.

Representativeness   In selecting specific instances, a sample for a statistical survey, and in choosing testifiers, arguers should seek representativeness. At the very least, they should seek to avoid that which is obviously atypical. To be realistic, they may not have the ideal representative situations available, but at least they should be sensitive enough to omit selecting that which is obviously not typical.

Relevancy   Is the evidence directly related to the claim being made? The material may be impressive but somewhat peripheral to the issue at stake. Sometimes, of course, it is not always easy to determine just how relevant something is, but effective arguers usually can make a pretty good guess if they conscientiously try. It should be clear to the advocates and their audience just what the relevancy of the evidence is to the claim.

Internal consistency   Does an arguer make remarks which remain consistent during a presentation? "First you say that Ms. X is a good teacher, and now you say that she is disorganized and untrustworthy. How can you be so inconsistent?" We all no doubt have been challenged for being inconsistent with our previous remarks. This internal consistency may also extend over a period of time, so that we may be charged with failing to be consistent today with something we had said a week ago. Lack of consistency may be revealed through nonverbal cues as well as verbal. For example, picture the speaker who talks of the dangers of smoking, and then absentmindedly lights up a cigarette during the question period; or the pastor whose Sunday sermon on "kindness" is followed on Monday by brusquely chasing children off the church property. Internal consistency is needed if arguers are to develop and maintain respect and influence over their audiences.

External consistency   Is the material consistent externally, that is, consistent with other known evidence? "You say that Mr. X is a lousy baseball player, but everyone knows he was a star infielder in college and in the minor leagues." If five Senators visit a factory and four react very favorably to conditions there but one reacts very unfavorably, we may question the fifth Senator's lack of consistency with his four colleagues. (Of course, we may well question their lack of consistency with him, too!) An important test of evidence, then, is whether one's material is verified by other material.

Cumulativeness   Do the bits of evidence "add up"? Do they supplement each other, so as to contribute to building up a compelling and clear case for one's claim?

SUMMARY

The most important types of evidence are specific instances, statistics, and testimony, but also useful are illustrations, imaginary dialogue, comparison and contrast, definitions, repetition and restatement, and cartoons.

In evaluating specific instances, students of argumentation are concerned with whether the instances are representative and numerous enough. In evaluating statistics, students need to ask such questions as the following: Have the statistics been collected accurately? Has the sampling been handled appropriately? Has the subject being examined been clearly defined? Are the units being compared actually comparable? Is the base of the percentage a reasonable base? Does the base of the percentage remain constant? Is the average clearly specified as the mean, median, or mode? Is the preciseness misleading? Is the subject quantifiable? Do the statistics cover a sufficiently long period of time? Is the arguer predicting beyond the statistics? Are the data statistically significant? Are visual portrayals accurate?

In evaluating testimony, students likewise need to ask a number of questions: Did the reporter have an opportunity to observe carefully? Was the person physically and mentally capable of observing accurately? Did conditions impede accurate observation? Does the observer bring to the event preconceived expectations? Is the person biased? Is the person of good moral character? Are there any factors in the reporting process which might affect the soundness of the person's testimony? Does the person designated as an expert have specific formal education and training in the field? Is the person an expert in the subject under investigation? Is reference to the expert vague? Is the expert highly regarded by other colleagues in the field? Is the testimony of the expert really relevant to this situation? Was the person aware of the significance of her remarks?

While evidence is often tested as to how it would likely affect some mythical universal audience, arguers need to be constantly aware that the specific audience with which they are communicating is the one against whom they need to measure the strength of their evidence. A number of general principles for strong evidence emerge: recency, clarity, accuracy, sufficiency, representativeness, relevancy, internal and external consistency, and cumulativeness.

EXERCISES

1. Examine some essay or published speech which is mainly persuasive in nature and make a list of the various types of evidence used. In a 500-word essay evaluate the effectiveness of the advocate's use of evidence. Attach your list as an appendix to your paper.

2. Employing relevant questions discussed in this chapter, evaluate how some advocate in an essay or a published speech used statistics. Summarize your analysis in a 500-word paper.

3. Over a period of about two weeks collect some instances in which advocates have relied on vague references to expert testimony. For example, study advertisements, listen to sermons, to political speeches, to conversations, read editorials and letters-to-the-editor in campus and community newspapers, noting the vague references. Summarize your findings in a 500-word essay, and share your insights with the rest of the class in an informal discussion.

4. Develop a five-minute speech in which you advocate something relevant to material discussed in this chapter. For example, you might defend the proposition that the principle of recency is vastly over-emphasized in the mass media, or that the bias of an advocate can be determined in a variety of ways.

5. Construct a five-minute speech on any contemporary controversial issue in which you are interested. As you endeavor to win over the audience to your point of view, make an effort to include as many different types of evidence as you can. Make a list of your varying types of evidence, and turn it in to the instructor on the day that you speak in class.

8 Inductive Reasoning: Generalizing, Comparing, and Connecting

Nature of Inductive Reasoning
Improving One's Generalizing
Reasoning by Comparing
Reasoning by Connecting
Summary
Exercises

NATURE OF INDUCTIVE REASONING

Particulars to a Conclusion

Suppose Melvin arrives at the bus stop corner one morning to discover that the two people who usually wait with him are not there. He realizes that he is about three minutes later that morning. In panic he jumps to the conclusion that he has missed his bus. He has engaged in inductive reasoning, whether or not he is aware of it. He took particular bits of evidence (absent people and his tardiness) and moved to a conclusion. He quickly constructed a theory to account for the facts.

Induction is that form of argument which moves "from particulars to arrive at probable conclusions."[1] It is called the scientific form of reasoning, for that is the process of the laboratory, where scientists carefully examine test tubes or other particular items under investiga-

1. Ziegelmueller and Duase, *Argumentation*, p. 95.

tion, and then come to a conclusion. From a vast number of carefully controlled observations they build up to a conclusion. The scientific laboratory has no monopoly on induction, for all people engage in it many times a day in their daily activities. The opening illustration at the bus corner is a case in point. People seek to explain something, to make a single statement about many phenomena.

People may move from particulars to an encompassing statement about a single entity, be it a person, event, or state of affairs. In a court of law, for example, the prosecuting attorney gathers together multiple pieces of evidence which she contends point to the guilt of the person accused. The judge or jury weigh the evidence and decide whether it adds up to a verdict of guilty or not guilty. The politician campaigning for election lists his qualifications and his stands on issues, all designed to lead his audience to accept his claim about himself, which is that he is the best person for the position. When one's sister is silent, grumpy, and noncooperative, one hypothesizes that something is bothering her. The hypothesis may be right or it may be very wrong.

People may also move from particulars to a statement about a group, a whole class of entities. It is claimed that what is true of some members of a group is true for all or a proportion of that group. Suppose the first student that Trudy meets in her dormitory comes from a small town, and so do the second, third, and fourth students. She generalizes that the students in her dorm are all from small towns. If Gary has classes with four different professors who all give disorganized lectures, he concludes that the professors at his college are disorganized lecturers— or worse. If Julie visits a large city for the first time and observes people in various settings being constantly in a hurry, she generalizes that citizens of that city are always rushing around, or she may even extend her conclusion to state that people in all large cities are always in a hurry.

Whether people are constructing statements about a single item or a whole class, the process is the same, that is, they are going from particulars to a conclusion. They are constructing some statement which summarizes the facts. They claim that the particular items add up to some overarching conclusion.

Metaphorical images

Did the reader notice that in the foregoing discussion the author used various metaphors to try to describe the inductive process? Looking at those metaphors more closely will give us a clearer understanding of the inductive process. The three metaphors are arithmetic addition, jumping, and pointing.

It is very helpful to realize that inductive reasoning is akin to arithmetic—specifically, to the process of addition. When one was in elementary school, one's teacher no doubt frequently wrote a list of numbers on the blackboard and asked the student what the numbers added up to. If the given numbers were 5, 7, 10, and 3, the student would respond that they added up to 25. In a courtroom the prosecuting attorney presents the sixteen pieces of evidence she has gathered, and insists that they add up to the guilt of the suspect. In an above example, Trudy noted the large number of students from small towns in her dormitory, which she added up into a general statement about students in the dormitory. "So, what does it all add up to?" This is a question one may ask not only of the checkout clerk in a supermarket but also of one's classmate when the latter lists specific characteristics of his parents. It is understood, of course, that in arithmetic everyone adds up the numbers to the same answer, whereas in other areas, different people may well add up the same items and arrive at different answers.

In one of the episodes above, a person "jumped" to the conclusion that he had missed his bus. We speak of the inductive "leap." This figure of speech is central to, is the essential characteristic of, the inductive process, for it expresses clearly and vividly that a person is leaping from one ledge (known facts) over a chasm (the unknown) to the ledge on the other side (the conclusion). As Beardsley has expressed it: "What makes an argument inductive is that the conclusion takes a leap beyond the data that support it."[2] This metaphor dramatizes very well the lack of certainty in the inductive process, in contrast to the deductive process (to be discussed in the next chapter), whereby the conclusion necessarily follows from the premises.

The final metaphor is that which says the evidence "points" toward something—toward someone's guilt, or toward some generalization about students in a dormitory. That is, there is a sense of multiple strands converging, like multiple streams coming together to form a large river. The confluence of the many to form the one is a vivid image, helpful in depicting the inductive process, for indeed it is the many particulars converging to form a single statement.

It will be noted that these last two metaphors, pointing and leaping, are horizontal images, depicting movement along a horizontal plane.

2. Monroe C. Beardsley, *Thinking Straight* (4th ed.; Englewood Cliffs, N.J.: Prentice-Hall, 1975), p. 86.

The first metaphor, adding up, is the vertical image, which brings to mind a vertical list of numbers for which the claim-maker supplies the correct total at the bottom. Being aware of these fundamental horizontal and vertical dimensions may help students to see more clearly just what the metaphors are bringing to our attention and just what is involved in the inductive process.

Tentativeness

It becomes clear that students of argumentation need to realize that tentativeness is an inherent characteristic of the sound inductive process. They are dealing with probability. There is no certainty in one's inductive leaps; one is jumping into the unknown, hence one should readily acknowledge that one's conclusion is tentative. One's conclusions are approximations. They may well be altered if additional evidence is brought to one's attention, or if, through further analysis, one sees a new interpretation of the existing facts.

Pursuing one of the above examples, suppose that after Trudy met those three persons in her dormitory who came from small towns she next met a dozen people who were from large cities. This makes her realize that her first conclusion was erroneous. With the new evidence she now may be led to the conclusion that "many people in my dormitory are from large cities." Her first conclusion was tentative (as, indeed, is her second, pending a thorough survey), and she ought to be ready to alter her conclusions if new evidence so dictates. Often, laziness will make people slow in changing their decisions; often they are afraid others will think they are inconsistent or fickle. Often, especially if they made their first conclusion public, they are afraid to because it will show them up to be unsound thinkers. If Trudy already had told six people and had written to her parents that "the students in my dorm are all from small towns," she might be reluctant to announce her revised conclusion, as it would make her look hasty and foolish in her con-clusion-drawing.

At the heart of sound inductive reasoning, and mature scholarship, generally, is the recognition that we should be willing to be led to whatever conclusion the facts direct us, that early decisions may indeed be temporary, tentative, always open to modification. When people say, "Don't confuse me with the facts, my mind is made up!" they are demonstrating that they are unwilling or unable to live with the notion that conclusions are temporary.

Risk

All of this means that risk is involved in the inductive process, just as risk is involved in leaping over a deep chasm. People may fall in, or may land on an insecure ledge on the other side. Likewise, arguers may arrive at a weak, misleading, or totally incorrect conclusion. The doctor may add up the symptoms erroneously and treat the patient for the wrong disease. A coed may conclude that her boyfriend no longer likes her, only to discover later that she seriously misinterpreted his actions and attitudes.

Rewards

But tentativeness and risk should not paralyze people into inaction or apathy, for induction is also rewarding. Life becomes more manageable when people can construct summarizing statements about multiple facts, and can thus organize their thoughts and actions more wisely and efficiently. It permits people to predict with greater accuracy. For example, it is self-protecting to formulate a conclusion (assuming it is accurate) that a certain person is generally untrustworthy in certain situations. Life demands that people must act today, and to have at least some conclusion on which to operate until a better one is formulated permits them to meet life's demands.

IMPROVING ONE'S GENERALIZING

The following guidelines should help to improve one's ability to handle the inductive process of generalizing more effectively and responsibly.

Avoid hasty generalizing   One should not engage in the inductive process hastily, whether one is constructing a hypothesis or a generalization. One should be careful not to jump too quickly to one's conclusion, for one may jump the gorge before one has given enough time to consider the facts and the nature and implications of one's conclusion. As in many things which people do too hastily, they may have to backtrack, that is, jump back across the gorge to study the terrain more thoroughly before they make a new decision. Obviously this is often dangerous, at the least it is embarrassing, and one's ethos, one's dependability, is questioned by those with whom one is communicating.

In one example above, in which Melvin jumped to the conclusion that he had missed the bus, what likely followed? He probably would quickly run back home to call a friend for a ride, only to find out later that the bus actually was a few minutes late, and if he had waited, he would not have inconvenienced his friend and caused needless anxiety. He formulated his hypothesis too quickly. Often in inductive reasoning, haste makes waste, as in many other areas of life. In short, one should take one's time in formulating conclusions. Just as one needs to let time test one's relationship during a courtship period, lest one hastily gets married to the wrong person, so one needs to let time test one's conclusion, lest one gets stuck with the wrong claim from which it may be difficult to divorce oneself.

One more example will further illustrate. Suppose a coed's boy friend is twenty minutes late for a date, is unusually quiet, is not very affectionate, and is abrupt when he does speak. The girl concludes: "Oh, he doesn't love me anymore!" She decides to shop around for a new attachment. A couple of weeks later she discovers that her boy friend's parents were getting a divorce and it disturbed him greatly, thus accounting for his earlier behavior. Discovering this additional fact, she reevaluates, and comes to a different conclusion: "He does still love me; he is upset by parental discord." (Of course, the second conclusion may also be incorrect.)

Obtain Enough Instances

One should obtain enough instances before one formulates one's conclusion. The reader probably is immediately asking, "How much is *enough?*" One has to make an educated guess, based on the circumstances of each situation. It may depend on the audience; that is, how favorably inclined they are, how critical, or how knowledgeable. Generally, the more instances the better. Nine pieces of evidence may be sufficient to make a convincing presentation in one court case, but nineteen may be needed in another (especially if a different judge or jury are present). All someone may need is two episodes to convince him that his girl friend is untrustworthy.

In addition, alert students of argumentation obviously know that all facts are not created equal, that some are more important than others, so that two extremely minor episodes do not equal two major episodes in permitting one to move to one's conclusion. Thus, if Miguel's girl friend doesn't laugh at his jokes and is unusually quiet, this should not permit him to jump to the hypothesis that she no longer loves him. On the other hand, if he discovered that she went with someone else to a major school event, and told him bluntly that she wants nothing more to do with him, Miguel would have to conclude that she does not love him anymore. So one has to consider the seriousness or intensity of the facts as well as the quantity of facts but the starting point for testing the soundness of one's induction is to ask oneself, "Do I have enough instances?"

When generalizing about a group of some sort, if one actually is able to canvas each individual in the group before formulating one's conclusion, one ends up with *descriptive statistics*. That is, suppose one questions all thirty members in one's biology class, and they all say that they enjoy dissecting frogs. Thus one can generalize: "This biology class enjoys dissecting frogs." One has generalized about the group based on questioning each and every member of that group.

Most of the time, however, one is in no position to question each member of the group about whom one wants to generalize. A person running for state governor, for example, wants to know what the voters in her state think about various issues. It is impossible to ask each voter, so a sample of the voters has to be queried, and on the basis of that sample the candidate infers, makes an inductive leap to apply her conclusion to all the voters. Thus, she may conclude that most of the voters are in favor of abortion. In this case the candidate has utilized *inferential statistics*.

This raises the question about sampling procedures. One may follow a *ramdom* sampling procedure, whereby each item in the group has an equal chance to be selected. Choosing a straw from among ten offered would be a random selection. A *systematic* sampling procedure would be, for example, having the above thirty biology students count off by three's, and the questioner would select all the number two's for his sample, and base his conclusions on their responses to his question about dissecting frogs.

Actually, in some contexts people often can and do generalize on the basis of only one item. Such a procedure is *arguing from example*. Suppose the neighbor boy who goes the university is a hardworking, studious gentleman, so his neighbor generalizes that boys going to the university are hardworking, studious gentlemen.

Whether the particulars in an arguer's situation happen to be a single example or a multiple sample arrived at systematically or randomly, one needs to ask oneself whether one has enough items on which to base one's conclusions.

Accurate Quantifiers

Arguers need to select carefully an accurate quantifier in their conclusion. A quantifier in an *unlimited generalization* is "all." That is, one is making a claim about the whole group under consideration. Examples of unlimited generalizations would be: "*All* baseball players chew tobacco." "*All* dogs are lazy." "*All* trees provide good shade." A *limited generalization* makes a claim about only some proportion of the group, such as: "*Most* baseball players chew tobacco." "*Some* dogs are lazy." "*Many* trees provide good shade." Some other quanifiers would be "a few," "a majority," or "almost all," Quantifiers, then, make clear the quantity involved in one's claim, whether it is all or some proportion of the whole. When one is the claim-maker or is evaluating the claims of others, one needs to be alert to the quantifier employed.

The quantifiers "some" and "many" are especially troublesome, for they are ambiguous. The former implies less than 50 percent and "many" implies more than 50 percent, but in many contexts it is unclear just how much is involved when those quantifiers are used. For example, whereas "most" clearly indicates more than half, "many" could be more or less than half. "Many" frequently is used for unwarranted exaggeration and needs to be carefully watched; on the other hand it is also employed when arguers are being very careful not to use "most," when they are not sure whether more than half is warranted. At any rate, since "many" and "some" have such wide and unclear boundaries, one should be especially alert to their usage.

One of the most important considerations in connection with the use of quantifiers is their absence. That is, the absence of a quantifier usually implies the unlimited "all," and gives rise to numerous needless controversies. Suppose Joe has two professors who are frequently tardy in coming to class, and he thus expresses to a friend, "Professors here at the university sure are tardy." That implies that "all" professors at that university are tardy. His friend, perhaps, has not encountered any tardy professors, and she retorts, "What do you mean? None of my professors has ever been tardy!" Joe tries to defend himself, "Well, I didn't say *all* professors were tardy." She responds, "You sure implied it." Joe bellows, "I did not!" She follows, "Yes you did!" Some male chauvinist may proclaim, "Women expect men to open the door for them," thus, intentionally or unintentionally, implying "all" and setting the stage for a heated exchange. Parents often say, "Kids sure are thoughtless these days," and children often assert, "Grown-ups never listen to our side of it!" Although absent, the unlimited "all" is implied. In one's everyday conversations one should make a special effort to note how the absence of a quantifier implies "all," and note the difficulties it creates.

Avoid Exaggerating

Focusing on quantifiers leads one to another closely related admonition: avoid the temptation to exaggerate. All too easily people utter such contentions as: "Thousands of students were lounging on the campus grass yesterday"; or "Thousands of cars were stalled on the freeway during the snow storm"; or "A fantastic number of my classmates is cutting Physics 1002." One's exaggeration may be conscious or unconscious, or somewhere in between. Why does one do it? Usually it is not out of a desire to mislead one'a auditor; one usually does not intentionally want to tell an untruth. Admittedly, the truth may be stretched slightly. But why? Often it is for dramatic effect, to catch attention, to make one's assertion more vivid, or to communicate quickly that what one is saying is important. Or one does it for humorous effect: "The Yankees fumbled the ball all afternoon," instead of the accurate, "The Yankees made two errors." One may do it to inflate one's ego: "Hundreds of people at the meeting said they were going to vote for me," instead of the accurate, "One dozen people..." Sometimes one may exaggerate simply out of laziness in order to establish an accurate claim. Whatever the motivation, to be an accurate and responsible arguer one must hold in check the all too easy desire to exaggerate one's claims.

Select Typical Instances

Are the instances typical of the whole? This is a crucial question in the inductive process of generalizing. If the members of the class whom one selects are not representative of the class, one can hardly construct an accurate generalization about the class. Suppose an investigator asks ten of the thirty students in her class whether they enjoy playing softball, but she asks only those whom she knows are interested in athletics. Suppose all ten answer in the affirmative, and she then says, "My classmates enjoy softball." This generalization would no doubt be based on an atypical sample. If she questioned only honor students about their attitudes on curricular issues, she could hardly generalize about all the students at her university, for she would be dealing with a select, atypical portion of the whole student body. To find out what the student body felt on a given issue, one would have to make sure one had a typical, represent-ative portion of the student body. This is especially important when arguing from example, that is, where only one item forms the basis for a conclusion about some group. Is that hardworking, studious, gen-tlemanly boy next door typical of university students, so that his neighbor can generalize from that one example? Is that reckless, irresponsible, unkempt eighteen-year-old living next door typical of teenagers to warrant attaching those labels to the whole class of teenagers?

Account for All Facts

Does the conclusion account for all the facts? If some facts remain unaccounted for, the strength of the claim is accordingly reduced. The convincingness of the claim increases in proportion to its ability to account for all of the facts. To return to an earlier episode: Melvin is three minutes late for his bus in the morning, two people who usually wait at the corner with him are absent, *but* two people in the next block who usually catch the same bus are still waiting. Melvin's hypothesis that he has missed the bus does not account for the last fact. Why are they there? Without that third fact accounted for, his hypothesis would be weakened. In court cases a suspected bank robber is hoping to present one (or more) fact(s) which proves that she could not have committed the crime. The suspect hopes for that evidence which cancels out all the other circumstantial evidence presented and demonstrates that the prosecuting attorney's hypothesis, that the suspect robbed the bank, is false. An alert listener is always quick to query, "But how does that account for ... ?" The person making the original claim is thus challenged to show how, indeed, the claim does take into account all possible relevant facts. Occasionally, of course, a hypothesis may not necessarily crumble completely if one fact cannot be accounted for, but the hypothesis is at least weakened, even if only slightly. At least the quantifier may have to be modified. For example, the claim "*All* mothers are kind to their children" would have to be changed to "most" or "some" when one discovers one or more mothers who are not kind to their children. Thus, it is clear that students of argumentation need to search diligently for missing data, for relevant omissions, which could have a bearing on claims they make, or those made by others, if truth is to be better served.

Formulate Optional Hypotheses

One should not accept a hypothesis until one has thought of at least one alternative hypothesis with which to compare it. Just as one probably would not buy a pair of shoes unless one compared them with at least one other style, so one ought not "buy" a hypothesis until one has compared it with at least one other option.

Suppose one observes the following facts about one's next-door neighbor, an elderly widow: three daily newspapers have accumulated on her front steps; the window shades are pulled down; she has not been seen in three days; in the past, whenever she has gone away she has always informed her neighbors. What do these four facts add up to? One conclusion is that she has gone away and had to leave quickly without having time to notify anyone. But before buying that hypothesis at least one more should be constructed. Perhaps she is ill and in need of help. The second hypothesis then leads to some act, such as knocking on her door, calling her on the phone, or calling her relatives in the city to inquire about her. If one settles for the first hypothesis, one of course would do nothing. Obviously, then, one's choices can have very important implications.

Suppose a professor observes the following while proctoring a final examination: Student X has some notes on the floor near her feet, the student frequently looks in that direction, the student appears to be nervous whenever the professor comes close, and the student later is found to have gotten a grade on the test far higher than her previous grades. Should the professor conclude that Student X cheated on the final exam? If so, that would cause the professor to take certain steps, quite different from those taken if the professor concluded that the student did not cheat. Before the professor acted on that first hypothesis, it would be wise for him to hypothesize that the above facts do not necessarily point to cheating. For example, the notes may have been for another class, it is natural to look down at the floor while thinking, Student X is normally very nervous, and Student X may have worked very conscientiously in the last few weeks, which would account for the high grade. At any rate, the professor ought to construct the second hypothesis and consider it carefully before buying the first hypothesis.

Avoid Unnecessary Complexity

Avoiding the fallacy of unnecessary complexity is an unnecessarily complex way of saying that one's hypothesis should account for the given facts more simply than any other alternative hypothesis. In other words, usually the simpler the hypothesis, the better it is likely to be, for it does not interject so many variables.

In the case of the missing neighbor, suppose one hypothesized that she had had a heart attack and was in serious condition in one of the metropolitan hospitals, and that she would want you to mow her lawn, cancel her newspapers, and water her flowers. This five-point conclusion is rather complex, and each point needs to be confirmed before one makes any decision or proceeds to take any action.

Keep Wording Consistent

Arguers should not shift the wording on their way to the conclusion. Suppose Student Y consistently turns in assignments late. What kind of hypothesis can be constructed? "Student Y is a poor student"? But the work when turned in is of A quality; she is an excellent student. "Student Y is lazy"? Quite the contrary, for it is discovered that the reason for each tardiness was because she was taking a very heavy class load besides working at a part-time job. She certainly was not lazy. About all one can accurately say is that "Student Y is consistently tardy in turning in assignments." The temptation to assert something in a conclusion which is closely related to, but not exactly the same as, the quality brought out in the data is a temptation trustworthy arguers have to avoid. Being tardy with assignments does not equal supidity or laziness. One should not go beyond the data and wander uninvited into nearby pastures. Why do people wander? Sometimes it is because of carelessness, or laziness, or because of a preconceived notion which they want confirmed. That is, one had already concluded that Student Y was a lazy person, so one easily wandered from the category of "tardy" to "lazy."

Control bias

One ought not let one's bias dictate to one. Letting one's preconceived ideas push one to formulating conclusions which are not substantiated by the data is something people have to guard against constantly. One's bias often causes one to observe only what one wants to observe (selective perception), report only what one wants to report (selective reportage), remember what one wants to remember (selective retention). People should let the data push them toward their claims. It is easy and psychologically comfortable to follow one's preconceived biases, but that hardly does justice to the subject matter, to the people involved, or to the cause of truth.

REASONING BY COMPARING

Process of Comparing

Arguing from analogy is a common, important, and effective reasoning process. It involves a comparison of two bits of data. Argument from analogy holds that since two items are assumed to be similar in a number of aspects, they are probably similar in the additional aspect under consideration. For example, one might claim that since artificial turf has worked well in Stadium X, it should also work well in Stadium Y. One would be comparing the known experience of artificial turf in Stadium X with the unknown result in Stadium Y, making a conclusion about Y based on comparing it with X. This would be called a literal analogy, where the two elements being compared (artificial turf in stadiums) are similar entities. Another example would be to assert that Restaurant B probably has good food, for it is similar to Restaurant A, which has good food; the similarities might be such things as both are new, attractive buildings, the same size, both are expensive, and both have key locations at major freeway intersections. One would again be comparing two like things—two restaurants.

Arguing from historical analogy is a common use of the literal analogy. For instance, the 1938 Munich appeasement of Hitler, which stimulated his aggressive appetite, by giving in to his demands, rather than satiating it, was used to justify the United States' entry into Korea and Vietnam; and the strong stand against the Soviet Union's invasion of Afghanistan. Whether the comparisons were proper or improper is perhaps debatable, but the process involved was reasoning from comparison, from analogy. This enables one to profit from experience, but of course sometimes one might be misled by previous experiences, for one might apply them to new situations which are not comparable.

Suppose one claims that the operation of student government at one's college is like a smooth-running automobile engine. One then would be comparing two unlike things—student government and auto engines. This is called a figurative analogy. Such comparisons vivify, clarify, and illustrate, and thus can strengthen one's argumentative position.

Improving Argument from Comparison

Are the two things being compared really similar in the essential aspects? Do the comparative items really apply in drawing the conclusion? For example, suppose one claims that since College A abandoned inter-collegiate athletics with good results, College B would also reap good results if it, too, abandoned intercollegiate athletics. The arguer would probably want to show that the two colleges closely resembled each other in such relevant factors as size, type of students, type of curricular offerings, the current place of athletics in the overall mission of the college, and the importance of intercollegiate athletic contests in the larger surrounding community. If the two colleges do indeed resemble each other in these and other significant respects, then one's argument from comparison would be strengthened. Having the same number of ivy-covered buildings would not be a significant item in the comparison.

Suppose one claims that since Community X has utilized successfully unarmed traffic controllers instead of armed police, Community Y should adopt the same practice. One would probably demonstrate how the two communities were similar in such factors as size, type of people, traffic patterns, and rate of crime. The fact that the two communities have the same number of letters in their names would hardly be a relevant similarity.

In figurative analogies it becomes especially important to choose things which have similarities that are clear and apparent to one's audience. For example, is it immediately clear that student government and automobile engines are known entities and hence comparable as far as one's audience is concerned? This means knowing not only one's subject but also one's audience, for if the audience were not familiar with student government or automobiles, the comparison might escape them, or not make a very strong impression.

Are there enough items being compared? As one can see from the above examples, the comparison becomes stronger as the relevant items increase in number. This cumulative effect is important to keep in mind. If one contends that one's state legislature should have its proceedings televised because nine states have done it with success, rather than just two states, one strengthens one's case. If one can explicitly show that two restaurants are comparable in seven important respects, rather than only two, then one's argument becomes strengthened.

Are the differences few in number and insignificant in the compari-son? It is important not to overlook, ignore, or hide whatever differences may exist, for two colleges, two cities, or two restaurants are hardly ever completely similar, and it is often wise to acknowledge this as one makes one's claims. It would be refreshing to the audience to have this admitted openly. But one would have to hasten to suggest that what differences do exist are few in number and are not very important, so that one would end up showing that the similarities unquestionably do outweigh the dissimilarities. This is the goal to keep in mind when one engages in, or encounters, argument from comparison. The danger of overlooking or improperly deemphasizing important differences in one's desire to compare the two items is something to watch out for. One must be prepared to account for, and to refute, the claims of one's opposition that certain items are not comparable.

Can the argument from comparison be corroborated and strengthened by some other type of reasoning? For example, argument from authority is a helpful way to reinforce it. One might argue for elimination of intercollegiate athletics at College B not only on the basis of its comparison with College A but also because a famous local coach favors the claim. One may also argue from example, indicating that tennis courts, instead of being monopolized by the few members of the tennis team, could be used by a larger number of the student body if intercollegiate tennis were eliminated.

REASONING BY CONNECTING

Reasoning by connection includes two categories: arguing from *cause* and arguing from *sign*. The first is concerned with explaining, with answering the question of why something occurred. Argument from sign is concerned merely with describing or indicating; it deals with demonstrating association (correlation) between two phenomena, not causal linkage.

Cause-and-Effect Reasoning

Human beings operate on the assumption that everything has a cause, whether that cause be some person, some natural phenomenon (lightning), or some economic trend (inflation). Nothing happens without cause. Our human curiosity pushes us to ask why something happened, or to predict what will result from certain situations.

To claim that a causal relationship exists between two pieces of data is an important area of reasoning. Suppose a student contends that a splitting headache caused her to do poorly on an examination. A cause-and-effect linkage between those two facts—a headache and poor performance on a test—is asserted.

In an earlier chapter on problem analysis, locating the cause (the villain) of a social problem was discussed, so rereading that would now be helpful. Here the focus is mainly on suggesting some guidelines for improving one's cause-and-effect reasoning.

Improving Cause-and-Effect Reasoning

A common pitfall is to assume that since B follows A, the second event is caused by the first. This is known as the fallacy of *post hoc ergo propter hoc*: "after this, therefore because of this." If a student wore a certain shirt on a given day and later that day did well in his mathematics examination, he might feel that the first caused the second. Good luck charms are thus created, and so are superstitions, such as not walking under ladders. Three days after taking some patent medicine one's ailment disappears. Did the first event cause the second? If new neighbors move into one's area, and things begin to disappear from one's yard, one might be quick to accuse the new neighbors, and perhaps quite unjustly. This easy tendency to link two adjacent events into a cause-and-effect connection is at the heart of many faulty analyses of personal and social problems. People need to be especially careful not to link two events together causally just because they follow each other chronologically. In short, one ought to ask oneself whether chronological coincidence has been mistaken for causal regularity.

Is the alleged cause strong enough to have produced the result? Suppose early in a football game the quarterback fumbles the ball and the opposing team recovers it, and eventually goes on to win the game. Was that fumble so significant, so powerful a factor, that it can be cited as the cause of the loss of the game? Suppose a young man didn't smile at his fiancee one morning, and in the evening she returned her engagement ring to him. No doubt other more powerful factors caused her to do so! But one can hear him telling his friends, "Can you believe it?! She gave me back the ring because I didn't smile at her. Guess I'm lucky to be rid of her!"

Are we too quick to claim that a single cause is operating when in reality many factors are playing a causal role? In personal and social situations, usually multiple causes are operating, and one needs to broaden one's perspective so as not to focus too soon on just one cause. Increased crime usually has many causes, as do unemployment and unhappiness. Efficient government is brought about by many things, not just one factor. One's ability to do well in one's studies is the result of many things, such as innate intelligence, supportive parents, sufficient money, good roommate, good teachers, and good study habits.

A good testing exercise is to eliminate the alleged cause and see what happens. Suppose the drain in the corner of the street is clogged with debris, leading one to contend that that is the reason water accumulates in the street. One removes the alleged cause (the debris), and the water standing in the street is indeed altered, it now proceeds to go down the drain. Suppose a student claims that she is doing poorly in her studies because of her obnoxious roommate. She arranges to move to another room, but her work does not improve. The troublesome roommate really wasn't the cause after all, and one needs to probe for other factors which are causing one's poor performance.

Sometimes the alleged cause cannot be easily removed; instead one removes the cause mentally. One imagines what the situation would be with the alleged cause eliminated. Suppose a slightly drunk auto driver became involved in an accident. He claimed his two-year-old son distracted him, causing the mishap; his being drunk did not cause it. Was the alcohol or the son the real cause? If one imagines the scene with no son in the car, would the tipsy driver have had the accident? On the other hand, if the man had been completely sober, would the accident have occurred? These hypothetical situations sometimes need to be constructed in order to ascertain which factor is the prime cause in some social problem.

Is a person focusing only on the highly visible, recent, precipitating cause, and overlooking the not so visible long-range causes which may be in the background? In an above example, an obnoxious roommate was blamed as the cause for a student's doing poorly in her coursework, and it might very well have been *a* cause. But perhaps far more important causes were in the background, such as, the student was absent on two days when important test material was discussed, her heavy part-time job schedule has reduced her study time, and she admittedly read the text material only once. These more remote factors in the background, plus other intangible things, such as, she never has really liked the particular subject matter, and she does not see the relevance of the course for her future employment, may also be factors causing her to do poorly. Suddenly the obnoxious roommate is put in place, and the student realizes that long-range causes need to be ferreted out to account for her poor academic showing. A fight on the soccer field may be caused by one player allegedly tripping another, but in back of that precipitating cause may be a long-standing feud between those two players, long-standing animosity between the teams, or heightened edginess because the game was for the championship.

The above examples have illustrated that people deal with both cause-to-effect and effect-to-cause in their causal reasoning. Causal reasoning is involved with chronology, and we may move forward through time (wearing a good luck charm will bring good results on tests) or backward through time (seeking to know what in the past had caused the water to accumulate in the street). Whether one moves forward or backward along the time continuum, one can be on more solid footing by attending to the five suggestions just surveyed.

Arguing from Sign

Argument from sign is another type of reasoning involving the process of connection. Leaves turning color indicate that fall is coming. Telephone companies know from experience that when the number of telephone calls increase on Easter Sunday, they will also increase on Mother's Day; the former phenomenon is a good indicator, a sign, of the second. College entrance tests are indicators—of varying reliability—of how well a student is likely to do in college.

Argument from sign describes a situation, it does not analyze the "why" behind it. For example, suppose Hector enters a classroom consistently a few minutes before Dora does, so that one soon predicts that when Hector enters, Dora will soon follow. Hector does not cause Dora to enter the classroom, for it is just a simple association of facts, that as they walk from their previous classes, Hector arrives at this classroom shortly before Dora. It is a consistent association of events, not a causal connection. It might be tested by arranging to have Hector stay away one day. Dora *should* come, regardless.

The medical profession relies heavily on reasoning from sign when making diagnoses.

> Certain observable characteristics—sudden changes in mood or behavior, a loss of appetite, the development of phobias—may not be connected with specific diseases directly and inevitably, but they may accompany them often enough to justify the physician in making certain additional tests when he observes enough of these symptoms.[3]

A common pitfall is that one confuses associative signs as being causes. The fact that things occur together consistently is no sure indication that

3. Toulmin, Rieke, Janik, *Introduction to Reasoning*, p. 151.

there is a causal connection. One often hears the claim that crime has increased during the past decade, and so has the number of violence-dominated television shows, so it is supposedly clear that television is to blame. But during the same decade it might also be a fact that the number of ice cream parlors has increased, as has the number of foreign automobiles, and the use of garlic. So?

As a recent article has interestingly demonstrated, proverbs are very instructive guides to reasoning from sign (as well as reasoning from cause, analogy, generalizing, and others). For instance, warnings against deceiving appearances are numerous: "All is not gold that glitters"; "You can't judge a book by its cover"; and "Not every man is a huntsman who can blow a horn."[4]

One can strengthen one's use of arguing from sign if one is careful to use reliable signs. If, for six weeks, Hector serves as an accurate indication of Dora's coming into the room, Hector's arrival has become a rather reliable sign. In addition, one should seek to corroborate one's claim with other types of reasoning and with other evidence which might be available.

SUMMARY

This chapter has surveyed the inductive process of reasoning, that is, arguing from generalization, comparison, and connection. Closely examining the metaphors of arithmetic, jumping, and pointing has helped to clarify the inductive process. Inductive reasoning involves tentativeness and risk. To improve one's ability to generalize more accurately and responsibly, the following guidelines should be helpful: avoid hasty generalizing, obtain enough instances, carefully select one's quantifiers, avoid exaggerating, secure typical instances, have the hypothesis cover all the relevant facts, think of at least one possible alternative hypothesis before coming to a conclusion, avoid the fallacy of unnecessary complexity, do not shift wording in the conclusion, and do not let bias govern one's conclusions.

Reasoning by comparison includes both literal and figurative analogies. To strengthen one's command of this type of reasoning, one ought to ask the following questions: Are the two things being compared really similar in the essential aspects? Are there enough items compared? Are the differences few in number and relatively insignificant? Can the

4. Paul D. Goodwin and Joseph W. Wenzel, "Proverbs and Practical Reasoning: A Study in Socio-Logic," *Quarterly Journal of Speech*, 65 (1979): 289–302.

argument from comparison be corroborated by other types of reasoning?

Reasoning by connection includes cause-and-effect linkage and argument from sign. To strengthen one's command of cause-and-effect reasoning, the following suggestions should be helpful: avoid the *post hoc* fallacy, determine if the alleged cause is strong enough to produce the result, look for multiple causes, eliminate the alleged cause and see what results, and look for long-range background causes as well as immediate precipitating causes. Reasoning from sign simply describes a situation, it does not analyze the "why" behind it, as causal reasoning does. One should search for reliable signs, and seek corroboration from other types of reasoning.

EXERCISES

1. Reflect on some personal episodes in recent days or weeks in which you have violated some of the guidelines in the generalizing process discussed in this chapter. Summarize your experiences in a 500-word essay, and share your information with the class in an informal discussion.

2. Examine a published speech in *Vital Speeches*, or elsewhere, and evaluate how well the speaker lived up to the guidelines in the generalizing process. Summarize your analysis in a 500-word essay or in a five-minute oral report.

3. Study advertisements in magazines, newspapers, billboards, or elsewhere, and note their use of quantifiers in their claims. Note the instances in which the absence of quantifiers clearly implied "all". Construct a 500-word essay on your findings. Bring some of the advertisements to class and share your observations and analysis in an informal discussion.

4. Analyze a published persuasive speech or a persuasive article in a magazine and evaluate how well the author made use of analogies. Summarize your findings in a 500-word essay. List the analogies in a concise manner as an appendix to your paper.

5. Together with three to five of your classmates, listen to an intercollegiate debate or some other public speech and analyze the role of inductive reasoning as you observed it. Summarize your comments in a 500-word paper, and in a class discussion compare your analysis with those of your classmates.

9

Deductive Reasoning

The Nature of Deduction
Categorical Syllogisms
Enthymemes
Hypothetical Syllogisms
Disjunctive Syllogisms
Summary
Exercises

Having a clear understanding and firm command of deductive reasoning is an additional valuable means for arguers to increase the likelihood of winning adherence from their audience. We all use deduction constantly in everyday argumentation whether we realize it or not. For example, our first impressions of people depend on generalizations we carry in our mind based on prior experience, which may be accurate or misleading. When we first meet a student from England, for example, perhaps we have a prepared image which says that all English people are haughty. We then fill out the reasoning, noting that Jerome is an Englishman, and therefore concluding that Jerome is haughty. We may soon discover, of course, that he does not fit that characterization, or may fit it, or may partially fit it; but whatever the truth of the situation, the point is that deduction was employed in formulating our initial judgment of that new acquaintance. Deduction is imbedded in public speeches, editorials, and essays.

It is beyond the scope of this textbook to become too deeply involved in the endless detailed rules of logic, but an overview such as this chapter will give should be helpful without being too complicated. The nature of deduction will be sketched, including its definition, its relationship to induction, its formulation in syllogisms, and the distinction between validity and truth. The three types of syllogisms—categorical, hypothetical, and disjunctive—will be analyzed, and their valid forms clarified.

THE NATURE OF DEDUCTION

Deduction Defined

Deduction is engaging in a process of reasoning whereby the flow of argument moves from the general to the particular, the reverse of induction. The term "deduction" is from the Latin *de* ("down") and *ducere* ("to lead"), thus communicating the notion of leading down from something. Deduction relates a general statement to a particular case, thus facilitating the emergence of a conclusion. Deduction is a rule-governed process, and if the rules are followed correctly, the conclusion necessarily follows, in contrast to induction, whereby moving to the conclusion always involves probability, a leap. We compared induction to arithmetic; likewise we could compare deduction to geometry. As it is necessary to apply correctly certain rules of geometry to progress correctly in some mathematical circumstances, so it is necessary to apply rules of logic to achieve valid deductive reasoning.

Deduction-Induction Interaction

Deduction and induction move back and forth in much of our reasoning experiences, complementing each other. They ought not to be thought of as antagonistic opposites but, instead, as supplementing each other. Neither is better than the other, and neither is more fundamental to reasoned behavior. The following sequence of events will illustrate how induction and deduction are complementary.

1. Last week Walter overheard someone on campus say that members of the XYZ Sorority had high grade-point averages.
2. On Monday of this week his friend Tai, a member of the XYZ Sorority, mentioned in conversation that all of the members of her sorority had high grade-point averages.
3. On Wednesday the campus newspaper carried a story about the XYZ Sorority in which it was mentioned that all of its members had high grade-point averages.
4. On Thursday Walter mentioned to a friend that all of the members of the XYZ Sorority had high grade-point averages.

Walter arrived at that conclusion through induction, and on Thursday was ready to state it publicly. That is, the bits of evidence (1, 2, and 3) added up to, pointed to, the conclusion (4) he uttered.

Now deduction enters the picture, for the conclusion arrived at inductively serves as the beginning premise for the deductive process of reasoning.

5. On Friday Walter discovers that Harriet, a girl in his physics class, is a member of the XYZ Sorority.
6. Friday evening he says to a friend, "I bet Harriet must have a high grade-point average."

He arrived at his conclusion through a mental process. No one had told him that Harriet had a high grade-point average, and he had not seen her transcript or any other evidence. He simply deduced it. Assuming Walter had a liking for girls with high grade-point averages, this new insight may lead him to strike up a close friendship. The excitement of thus arriving at some conclusion through this mental process should not be overlooked, for it is indeed exciting to be able to exclaim, "Hey, guess what I just figured out!"

The following diagrams will illustrate the processes in the above sequence. The inductive step indicated that the three bits of evidence "added up" to, or "pointed to" a conclusion:

The deductive step is characterized in the following syllogism:

4. All members of the XYZ Sorority have high grade-point averages.
5. Harriet is a member of the XYZ Sorority.
6. Therefore, Harriet has a high grade-point average.

Syllogism

Deductive reasoning is carried on in syllogisms. The roots of the term "syllogism" give helpful insight into what is involved. It springs from the Greek *syllogismos*—which is a combination of *syn*, meaning "together," and *logismos*, meaning "logical discourse." Terms like "synagogue," a place where people congregate for religious purposes, and "synthesis," an intellectual bringing together of ideas and facts, depict the notion of bringing together something. A syllogism is a bringing together of two statements to arrive at a conclusion. Of the two statements, one is a generalization and the second is a specific factual statement related to the general statement.

GENERALIZATION: All Americans believe in freedom of speech.
SPECIFIC FACTUAL STATEMENT: Martin is an American.

The conclusion brings those two statements together. No new substance is brought into the conclusion which was not in the two premises, but the substance in the two statements is rearranged, linked together, in such a way as to produce a new assertion, which, in this example, would be, "Therefore, Martin believes in freedom of speech."

To return to the earlier example, the substance in statements 4 and 5 is rearranged in the conclusion (6). No new substance appears, but the arrangement of, the relationship among, the items is what is new. A syllogism, then, is a bringing together of known material into a new assertion.

The generalization in a syllogism ("All Americans believe in freedom of speech") is the "major premise." The specific factual statement related to that major premise is the "minor premise" ("Martin is an American"). The resultant assertion ("Therefore, Martin believes in freedom of speech") which brings the two premises together is the "conclusion."

It might help to relate these labels to the Toulmin terminology learned earlier; that is, the conclusion is the claim, the minor premise is the evidence, and the major premise is the warrant. In the above example the claim-maker asserts that Harriet has a high grade-point average based on the factual evidence that she is known to be a member of a given sorority, and the linkage of the evidence to the claim, that which warrants that linkage, is the major premise that all members of that sorority have high grade-point averages.

With the stress in recent years having been placed on the Toulmin system of functional analysis of reasoning, the emphasis on the older formal analysis of syllogistic patterns has decreased, but scholars[1] are now suggesting a return to the syllogism to supplement the Toulmin system. The syllogism can give helpful insights into argument analysis. One can see more clearly the premises, some of which might be only implied, and one can better test the soundness of the conclusion. It

---

1. For instance, see Dale Hample, "The Toulmin Model and the Syllogism," *Journal of the American Forensic Association*, 24 (1977): 1–9.

enables one to examine reasoning structures with more precision and accuracy, and in debate it is very helpful in refuting an opponent's claims. It alerts one to the need for support in one's own argument, helps one see the need for revision of one's premises, and tests one's own reasoning process.

The nature of syllogisms will become clearer when we analyze the three main types: categorical syllogism, hypothetical syllogism, and disjunctive syllogism. Before we do so, however, it is important to understand the distinction between validity and truth.

Validity and Truth

In everyday communication people use these terms interchangeably as if they were synonymous: "That's a valid (true) statement if I ever heard one." We need to distinguish between them, however, for in the technical language of logic the two are distinctly different. Truth refers to content, substance, to the accuracy of the statement in light of the realities of life. It is concerned with individual statements, whereas validity is concerned with how statements are put together. Validity refers to procedure, to form, to the way statements are linked together.

> The following example will help to clarify the distinction:
> All students at Augsburg College are seven feet tall.
> Harvey is a student at Augsburg College.
> Therefore, Harvey is seven feet tall.

The conclusion is valid, for the argument proceeds correctly according to rules of logic (which will be clarified shortly), but we would say that based on our experience, observation, or common sense, the initial premise is not true to life. Thus, technically, a conclusion may be valid but untrue. Another example will help imbed that notion:

> All people with a fever have appendicitis.
> Lucile has a fever.
> Therefore, she has appendicitis.

Based on our experience with life, we would say that the major premise simply is not true, and hence the conclusion is untrue, even though it is valid.

The central point here is that a sound deductive argument rests upon having true premises and valid relationships in order to formulate a valid and true conclusion.

CATEGORICAL SYLLOGISMS

Definition

In a categorical syllogism, sometimes called the classical or traditional syllogism, a person is involved with categories, with classes. These are called "terms." To illustrate, a former example can be used:

MAJOR PREMISE: All members of the XYZ Sorority have high grade-point averages.
MINOR PREMISE: Harriet is a member of the XYZ Sorority.
CONCLUSION: Therefore, Harriet has a high grade-point average.
MAJOR TERM: those people who have high grade-point averages
MIDDLE TERM: members of the XYZ Sorority
MINOR TERM: Harriet

It will be noted that the middle term is the one that appears in both the major and minor premises; it links the two together. Thus, the middle term does not appear in the conclusion. The major term appears in the major premise and in the conclusion; the minor term appears in the minor premise and the conclusion. Thus, the major and minor terms, referred to as the "end" terms, come together in the conclusion through their relationship with the middle term.

There is a spatial characteristic associated with categorical syllogisms, that is, one thinks of putting things "into" other classes. One thinks of whether an item is inside of, or outside of, some other group. This concept of inclusion and exclusion is fundamental.

A   B

    All members of the XYZ Sorority have high grade-point averages.

      C
Harriet is a member of the XYZ Sorority.

Therefore, Harriet has a high grade-point average.

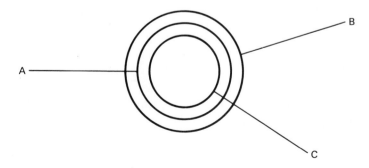

The circle diagram shows that term A (members of the XYZ Sorority) falls within term B, the group of people who have high grade-point averages. Term C (Harriet) is to be found within the members of the XYZ Sorority (A). The spatial image here might be compared to having one's sandwiches inside of a brown bag which is inside of one's briefcase.

Basic Conditions for Valid Categorical Syllogisms

1. There should be three and only three statements, each containing two terms.
2. A syllogism must have three and only three terms. Each term must be used twice and no more. If there were no middle term appearing in both premises to link them together, nothing could be logically inferred. It would mean that four terms were present, thus committing the four-term fallacy. For example:

     A   B
All members of the XYZ Sorority have high grade-point averages.
     C   D
Harriet is a member of the MNO Sorority.
Therefore? (Nothing can be concluded, for there is no linking middle term; there are four terms: A, B, C, D.)

Distribution

Fundamental to validity is the notion of "distribution." A term is distributed when all of the members of the given class are being considered; an undistributed term does not refer to an entire class. If it is said, "*All* members of the Twins baseball team are...," then that term would be distributed (universal, unqualified). If it is said, "*Some* members of the Twins baseball team are...," then that term is said to be undistributed (particular). When a quantifying adjective is omitted, "Members of the Twins baseball team are...," then "all" is implied and, frequently, much needless disagreement results. It is very important that the quantifier (words such as "all," "no," "some," "many," "every," "a few") be clearly understood.

The following concise summary[2] gives a good overview; U = universal, P = particular, A = affirmative (positive), and N = negative.

2. Monroe C. Beardsley, *Thinking Straight* (4th Ed.; Englewood Cliffs, N.J.: Prentice-Hall, 1975), p. 61. For a more extensive discussion of many points in this chapter see pp. 21–83.

UA STATEMENT: subject distributed, predicate undistributed
PA STATEMENT: subject undistributed, predicate undistributed
UN STATEMENT: subject distributed, predicate distributed
PN STATEMENT: subject undistributed, predicate distributed

From this, it will be noted that universal statements distribute their subject terms, and negative statements distribute their predicate terms. Each of the above truncated statements needs to be illustrated.

First, a universal affirmative (UA) statement has its subject distributed and its predicate undistributed. "All members of the XYZ Sorority have high grade-point averages" is an affirmative statement. The subject (all members of the XYZ Sorority) is distributed, for "all" is what is being asserted. The predicate (those people who have high grade-point averages) is undistributed, for that whole class is not being spoken of. For instance, other people who are not members of that sorority also have high grade-point averages.

Second, a particular affirmative (PA) statement has its subject undistributed and its predicate undistributed. "Some members of the XYZ Sorority have high grade-point averages" is an affirmative statement. The subject (some members of the XYZ Sorority) is undistributed, for "some," not all, is what is being asserted. The predicate (those people who have high grade-point averages) is undistributed, for the same reason as in the previous UA example.

Third, a universal negative (UN) statement has its subject distributed and its predicate distributed. "No members of the XYZ Sorority have high grade-point averages" is a negative statement. The subject (no members of the XYZ sorority) is distributed, for all of the members are being considered. The predicate is distributed, for all members of the class of people who have high grade-point averages are being considered, as the assertion contends that everyone is excluded from that class.

Fourth, a particular negative (PN) statement has its subject undistributed and its predicate distributed. "Some members of the XYZ Sorority do not have high grade-point averages" is a negative statement. The subject (some members of the XYZ Sorority) is undistributed, for we are speaking of only some, not all, of the members of the sorority. The predicate (those people who do not have high grade-point averages) is distributed, for everyone in that category is again being spoken of.

Fallacies in Distribution

First, the fallacy of the undistributed (underdistributed) middle term occurs when the middle term is not distributed at least once in one of the premises.

        A   B

All members of the XYZ Sorority have high grade-point averages.

        C

Pauline has a high grade-point average.

Pauline is a member of the XYZ Sorority.

Common sense tells us that something is wrong, and having a command of the concepts and terminology that we have now acquired permits us to say specifically what pitfall of logic is being demonstrated. The middle term (those people who have high grade-point averages [B]) is not distributed at least once. In the major premise the middle term is the predicate of a UA statement and thus is undistributed; the minor premise is a PA statement, so the middle term is likewise undistributed. A circle diagram will help to illustrate this fallacy. It is asserted that all of A falls into B:

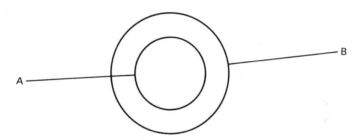

Then it is asserted that C falls within B, but since it could come anywhere within the B circle, it does not necessarily fall within the A circle, hence the conclusion is invalid.

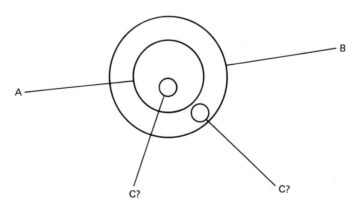

nother example would be the following:

      A   B
Communists oppose tipping.

     C
George opposes tipping.
Therefore, George is a Communist.

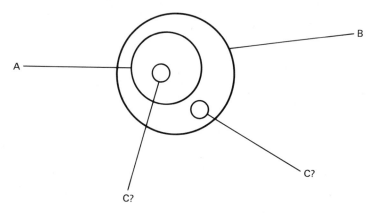

The fallacy of the undistributed middle term sets up, then, a faulty analogy; what is commonly called, in this instance, guilt by association. We falsely link together two entities simply because they happen to have one characteristic in common.

Second, the fallacy of the overdistributed middle term can be illustrated as follows:

      A   B
All members of the XYZ Sorority have high grade-point averages.

                               C
All members of the XYZ Sorority are attractive.
All attractive women have high grade-point averages.

Again, common sense tells us that something is wrong, but, more precisely, we can now point out that the middle term (all members of the XYZ Sorority) is overdistributed. It is distributed in both premises, for in both it is the subject of UA statements, and in such statements, as we have seen, the subjects are distributed. Another example may help to imbed this type of fallacy:

All baseball players chew tobacco.
All baseball players are in good condition.
All people in good condition chew tobacco.

These fallacies of the underdistributed middle and the over-distributed middle are sometimes presented as two subtypes of the fallacy of the maldistributed middle.

Third, the fallacy of unwarranted (illicit, unequal) distribution occurs when a term that was undistributed in a premise, is distributed in the conclusion. To put it another way, if a term is distributed in the conclusion, it must be distributed in the premise.

   A   B

All political campaign speeches are emotional speeches.

C
None of Carol's speeches are political campaign speeches.
Therefore, none of Carol's speeches are emotional speeches.

The end term "emotional speeches" is undistributed in the major premise, for it is the predicate of a UA statement; but in the conclusion that term is the predicate of a UN statement, and hence is distributed. It is distributed in the conclusion unwarrantedly.

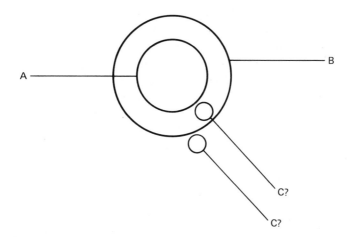

It is asserted that all political campaign speeches (A) are to be found in the category of emotional speeches (B). Then it is asserted that none of Carol's speeches (C) are to be found in the category of political campaign speeches (A). We do not know where to put them, but at least we know where not to put them, for they do not belong in the A circle. The conclusion thus is invalid, for Carol's speeches may fall in the non-A portion of circle B, or may fall outside of circle B, so her speeches may or may not be emotional speeches.

A number of additional corollaries also could be listed:

1. If both premises are particular, no conclusion can be drawn.
2. If one of the premises is particular, then the conclusion must be particular.
3. From two positive premises only a positive valid conclusion is possible.
4. From two negative premises no valid conclusion is possible; in other words, at last one of the premises must be positive.
5. If one premise is negative, the conclusion must be negative.

ENTHYMEMES

In everyday discourse, people seldom express themselves in fully formed syllogisms. Instead, truncated syllogisms, with a premise or conclusion unstated but implied, are the usual experience most of us have with syllogisms in our informal oral argumentation. Such a fragmentary, elliptical syllogism is called an "enthymeme." It is rooted in the Greek term, *enthymeesthai*, meaning "to think"; that is, *en* plus *thymos*, literally "in the mind." In other words, the omitted premise in the enthymeme is to be supplied in the mind of the recipient; thus there is a sort of co-creation taking place between sender and receiver. As Bitzer put it, the successful construction of an enthymeme "is accomplished through the joint efforts of speaker and audience, and this is its essential character....Enthymemes intimately unite speaker and audience and provide the strongest possible proofs."[3]

Consider the following example:

Naturally he doesn't know much about cars, he's a professor.

By filling out this assertion into its formal categorical syllogism structure, we can see its reasoning more clearly:

(All professors know very little about cars.) (implied, unstated)
He is a professor.
Therefore, he does not know much about cars.

Usually it is, like the above example, the major premise which is missing, but it can also be the minor premise:

All students at the university are hardworking.

3. Lloyd Bitzer, "Aristotle's Enthymeme Revisited," *Quarterly Journal of Speech*, 45 (1959): 408.

(Alice is a student at the university.) (unstated, implied)
So, Alice must be hardworking.

In such a case, it is assumed that the audience would supply the minor premise in their own minds, so there is no point spending the time and energy to state it. Similarly, in the previous example, it would be assumed that the audience would supply the missing major premise (all professors know very little about cars), and thus co-create the syllogism with the speaker.

The conclusion might also be the missing ingredient in an enthymeme:

Honor students aren't interested in going to hockey games.
Jim is an honor student.
(Jim is not interested in going to the hockey game). (unstated, implied)

Filling in the implied statement is indeed helpful in understanding, analyzing, and evaluating the assertions of an arguer, who of course is obligated to defend the statement even if it is unstated. If arguers are in doubt whether the audience will easily supply the omitted statement, they should state it explicitly. Enthymemes aid brevity and conciseness, and, by moving the argument along, reduce potential boredom.

There is a second definition of an enthymeme, which goes back to Aristotle, and which may or may not omit one of the statements. Reflecting informal everyday argumentation, it focuses on the notion of probability.

All sports which teach teamwork should be in the curriculum.
Baseball *may* teach teamwork.
Therefore, baseball should be in the curriculum.

In this case all statements are uttered. The minor premise asserts the probability, not the certainty, that baseball teaches teamwork.

HYPOTHETICAL SYLLOGISMS

Definition

Many assertions are formed with conditions attached, that is, with "if" clauses. "I'll come for you at 7:00 tonight, if I can get the car to start." Cast into a formal syllogistic argument it would be:

> If I can get the car to start, then I will come for you at 7:00 tonight.
> I can get the car to start.
> Therefore, I will come for you at 7:00 tonight.

Since the major premise sets up a hypothetical or conditional situation, the resultant syllogistic form is labeled as a hypothetical or conditional syllogism. The "if" conditional dependent clause is called the "antecedent" and the "then" independent clause is called the "consequent."

ANTECEDENT: "If I can get the car to start...
CONSEQUENT: ...then I will come for you at 7:00 tonight."

The consequent is that which will result if the antecedent is fulfilled. There is an inherent cause-and-effect structure involved in the sequence. Other terms instead of "if" which might be used in colloquial situations would be: "assuming," "suppose," "on condition that," "or in the event that."

Validity in Hypothetical Syllogisms

A valid form of the hypothetical syllogism is one in which the minor premise affirms the antecedent.

> If I can get the car to start, then I will come for you at 7:00 tonight.
> I can get the car to start. (antecedent is affirmed)
> Therefore, I will come for you at 7:00 tonight. (consequent is affirmed)

Stating the same rule negatively, an invalid form is created when the antecedent is denied; this is the fallacy of denying the antecedent.

> I cannot get the car to start. (antecedent is denied)
> Therefore, I will not come for you at 7:00 tonight. (consequent denied)

The conclusion is invalid, for it may not necessarily be the case, as perhaps the person was able to borrow a friend's car or could come on the bus. If the original assertion was, "If, *and only if*, I can get my car to start,..." then the situation would be quite different.

> A second valid form is one in which the minor premise denies the consequent.
> I will not come for you at 7:00 tonight. (consequent is denied)
> Therefore, I cannot get my car to start. (antecedent is denied)

An invalid form thus is created when the minor premise affirms the consequent, which is known as the fallacy of affirming the consequent.

DISJUNCTIVE SYLLOGISMS

A disjunctive syllogism is characterized by the major premise presenting two alternatives in an "either/or" relationship.

> Either I will study in the library this afternoon or I will go to my room to take a nap.

The syllogism is completed correctly when the minor premise goes on to deny one alternative, and the conclusion affirms the other.

> I will not study in the library this afternoon.
> Therefore, I will go to my room to take a nap.

A first test for validity in a disjunctive syllogism is that the major premise must include all of the possible options; that is, there must indeed be only two available options.

> Either love America or leave it.

This illustrates the setting up of only two choices when there might indeed be others. For example, one might not like everything about America, but one might stay and try to reform it. One ought not to have to choose between accepting everything as it is or leaving the country.

Second, the two alternatives must be mutually exclusive; that is, they both cannot be present, they should not overlap. To accept the one should force the rejection of the other. In the earlier example, one might study in the library for two hours and then go to one's room for a nap for two hours, so that both alternatives might be followed; one does not force the rejection of the other. "She went to the university either to catch a husband or to get an education." Obviously they are not mutually exclusive, for both objectives might well be present. But if one says, "Either the fire was set by an arsonist or it was accidental," one has set up two mutually exclusive options. That is, the fire was either planned or unplanned. The following are also mutually exclusive:

> Either the goldfish are dead or they are alive.
> Either the student is present or she is absent.

SUMMARY

Deductive reasoning, moving from the general to the particular, is a common and important mode of reasoning, constantly complementing inductive reasoning. It is important to note the distinction between truth and validity: truth has to do with the substance of a single statement; validity is concerned with how statements are put together, linked correctly according to set rules of logic. A basic contention is that arguers are more likely to win adherence if they employ true statements and formulate valid conclusions. Categorical, hypothetical, and disjunctive syllogisms have their distinctive formats, and their special rules for validity. The enthymeme is a truncated syllogism, and is the form encountered most in oral argumentation.

EXERCISES

1. Fill out the following enthymemes into complete syllogistic form:
   a. Certainly she's beautiful, she's a receptionist.
   b. You can be sure he'll be a wealthy man some day. He's going to the university, isn't he?
   c. Of course he's no brain, he's just a country boy!
   d. I suppose you like all this snow. You're from Minnesota, aren't you?

2. Examine newspaper editorials, letters to the editor, an article in an opinion magazine, or campaign literature and analyze its deductive reasoning. Construct the syllogisms that you see imbedded in the argumentation. Evaluate how sound you think they are. Apply specific tests discussed in this chapter.

3. Select three textbooks in argumentation and compare and contrast how they deal with the material discussed in this chapter. Summarize your findings in a 500-word essay.

4. Listen to a speech on campus or in the community, or have an advocate speak to the class, and analyze the deductive reasoning. Reconstruct the major syllogisms that you perceive, and evaluate the strength of each. Share your evaluations orally with the rest of the class.

5. Observe and analyze the deductive reasoning you encounter in everyday conversations during a given day, or portion thereof. You may be a participant or an observer. After recording the syllogisms, evaluate each.

10 Pseudo-Reasoning

In the two chapters on deduction and induction, we discussed the formal fallacies and pitfalls which may occur if those modes of reasoning are not used correctly or wisely. In a later chapter we will discuss weaknesses in arguing which stem from language usage. Here we are concerned with unsound reasoning which is furthered by various procedures being used unintentionally by arguers in everyday informal situations.[1]

Coming from the Latin root, *fallere*, meaning "to deceive," the term fallacy often has that concept of deception inherent in its definition. Deception of course involves the intentional, deliberate act of misleading people. As such, it is a moral problem, and ethics were discussed in an

1. For some books which focus on informal fallacies, see S. Morris Engel, *Analyzing Informal Fallacies* (Englewood Cliffs, N.J.: Prentice-Hall, 1980); Howard Kahane, *Logic and Contemporary Rhetoric: The Use of Reason in Everyday Life*, 2nd ed. (Belmont, Calif.: Wadsworth, 1976); Ralph H. Johnson and J. Anthony Blair, *Logical Self-Defense* (Toronto: McGraw-Hill Ryerson, 1977). The last book's examples from a Canadian context supplement well Kahane's examples, which are set in the United States.

earlier chapter. But seldom do arguers consciously say to themselves, "Now I'm going to mislead my audience by inappropriately shifting the burden of proof." More often than not, arguers use this or some other misleading process more out of ignorance than malice. Thus, it is an intellectual failure and needs an intellectual corrective.

Readers are probably already reacting, however, thinking, "But fallacious reasoning is often a combination of intentional deception and unintentional unsoundness." This is quite right. We cannot neatly divide the moral and intellectual into two mutually exclusive pigeonholes. But it may be helpful to focus more on the unintentional dimension, for that probably is where unsound reasoning springs from in much of our general argumentation. We often unknowingly deceive ourselves with such "pseudo-reasoning," a term which best reflects the focus of this chapter. Coming from a Greek root, the term "pseudo" means something false, counterfeit, not genuine. This more general term is helpful in broadening our view beyond the specific technical term "fallacy," that is, a violation of precise logical rules.

We need to avoid using these pseudo-arguments ourselves, and to neutralize them when used by other arguers. Pseudo-arguments give the impression of being sound without being so grounded. They distort, divert, confuse, and manipulate. The goal is to lessen our self-deception and the deception of others; or to put it positively, the goal is to achieve a greater measure of soundness in our argumentation efforts, and a greater proficiency in our evaluation of the reasoning of others. Pseudo-arguments unfortunately can be highly persuasive, so our objective in this chapter is to strip them of their ill-deserved power.

How best to group the many pseudo-arguments is indeed a problem, but the following categories should be helpful: (1) substitution of emotional appeals for soundness of reasoning; (2) "stroking" the audience as a substitute for reasoning; (3) substitution of compelling mannerisms for soundness of reasoning; (4) diversionary maneuvers as substitutes for soundness of reasoning; and (5) miscellaneous procedures as substitutes for soundness of reasoning.

SUBSTITUTION OF EMOTIONAL APPEALS FOR SOUNDNESS OF REASONING

The following are appeals which frequently take the place of soundness of reasoning in the claim-making of all too many arguers: inappropriate appeal to pity; inappropriate appeal to fear; inappropriate appeal to the majority; inappropriate appeal to authority; and inappropriate appeal to tradition.

Inappropriate Appeal to Pity

To endeavor to modify ideas and actions out of a sense of concern and pity is of course commendable, and we probably need more of it. But it becomes unwise and even dangerous if pity is the sole basis of our thinking and action, if it diverts us from reasoning out carefully all aspects of the situation. Defense attorneys may eloquently appeal for pity in behalf of their clients, but the jury cannot let a sense of pity for an accused person cloud and distort its task of looking at the facts involved. Suppose Samphi successfully convinces his family to take in three stray cats because he feels sorry for the homeless creatures; he appeals to their sense of pity, but probably does not give careful consideration to his ability to adequately care for them, and to how his action will affect his family and neighbors. Suppose a city official dwells only on pity when arguing against putting a freeway through the city, because such a project would dislocate many aged people who had spent all their lives in their houses. Pity can be a very faulty and even unfair criterion for rational decision-making. If we feel sorry for the accused person, the homeless cats or the dislocated people, to the point that we fail to let reason operate, we create more problems than we solve, and do an injustice greater than we imagine. Of course, it is obviously a matter of degree, for pity is often relevant, but excessive pity can be an inappropriate distortion and diversion in some situations.

Inappropriate Appeal to Fear

At the outset it would be well to admit that at times a person legitimately needs to appeal to fear. When an enemy attack is imminent, a serious epidemic of illness is known, or a fire occurs, obviously people will be making claims which rest heavily on the appeal of fear. Even then, of course, the appeal would have to be tempered so as not to paralyze the audience into inaction. But for all the instances calling for legitimate appeal to some degree of fear, there are far more instances in which this appeal is grossly magnified and distracts our attention from the rational consideration of the situation. Deodorant advertisers warn us of devastating social ostracism, Pentagon officials warn us of complete annihilation, and political leaders warn us of total collapse of the economy. Our fear, rather than our rational consideration of the situation, begins to dictate our response, often with unfortunate results. Many studies in speech-communication, political science, sociology, psychology, and other areas have analyzed in experimental and natural settings the effect of the fear appeal.[2] While results of such studies are variable, it can be asserted that when advocates appeal inappropriately to fear, and exclude or offer minimal presentation of facts, individuals and society suffer.

Inappropriate Appeal to the Majority

Fear of being isolated is experienced at some time or another by most people. Hence, arguers often take advantage of this by warning us to agree with their claim or suffer the consequence of being alone, of not being "with the crowd." One's roommates may urge one to come with them to the dance, because "everybody in the dorm is going." Advertisers urge us to buy their product, for "three out of four people use it." A classmate may tell one to take Astronomy 1234 next term, for many acquaintances are doing it. Immediately we need to admit that majority opinion and action is important, and in many instances is a wise and safe guide. But to believe or to do something merely because the majority believe or do it is a weak basis for a claim. Even if most of the dorm residents are going to the dance, one may have good reasons for not going. Certain products may not suit one's tastes or pocketbook; and one ought not to register for a course only because others are doing so. This inappropriate appeal to the majority is referred to as the "bandwagon" device. The metaphor is an apt one, for it suggests that we ought to climb aboard a wagon on which many others are riding.

But we need to remind ourselves that the majority is not by definition "right." We in a democracy are accustomed to asserting, quite correctly, that the majority "rules," and we allow majority vote to decide election contests and most other issues, but we ought not to confuse that with the notion that the majority is always right. Legislatures, for example, may change their minds next year and retract one of last year's decisions, so that the majority in the second year says that the majority in the prior year was wrong. If we let the majority decide for us, and we lived in a community that was ninety-five percent Buddhist, or Methodist, or Mormon, or Moslem, we presumably would allow that majority to

2. For a concise summary of some studies, see Brembeck and Howell, *Persuasion: A Means of Social Influence*, pp. 113–17.

determine our religious views, which most thoughtful persons probably would not want to do. Or if our circle of acquaintances believes in premarital sex, heavy drinking, and is "into" drugs, we ought not to be pressured into participating in these activities by the power of numbers, by the pressure of conformity. We may want to let the bandwagon roll by without us.

Inappropriate Appeal to Authority

In addition to appealing inappropriately to the majority, occasionally arguers will inappropriately appeal to authority. In an earlier chapter argument from authority was discussed and identified as an important mode of reasoning. Arguers who use it well and appropriately can strengthen their claims considerably. But if the appeal to authority is handled inappropriately, it can serve to stop further thought. Suppose a wife claims that the family car is not worth repairing and should be traded in for a new one, but her husband asserts that he does not want to purchase a new car because their friend Ken, an excellent mechanic, tells him what a good car it is. The wife feels that she cannot dispute Ken's expertise and so the discussion stops, whereas it might have been wise to keep the issue open and to continue to discuss it. Suppose Vin and Fran are discussing religion, and Fran stops the process by saying that Rev. Hanson, their minister, holds the same view she does. Assuming that Vin accepts the minister as a reputable authority, the discussion probably will stop.

Inappropriate transfer of "authority" from one field to another is also something to be alert to here. A person who excels in the theater may not necessarily be an authority on foreign policy; a respected medical doctor may not necessarily be an authority on inflation; a superstar football player is not necessarily an authority on nutrition.

Inappropriate Appeal to Tradition

"*Why* do I have to be in at midnight?" the teenage daughter angrily shouts at her parents. They stiffly respond: "Because that's what we demanded of your older sisters and brothers. That's a family rule!" To expect an audience to accept a claim *merely* because "that's the way it has always been done" is an inappropriate tactic, often designed to terminate the communication. The daughter above was expected to cease the discussion, for she had been given the ultimate answer. The family was not about to change its tradition to fit her desires; altering time-honored customs would be unthinkable. But it is easy to see that perhaps the discussion should have continued, that factors may be present which should call for a modification of that family tradition. Obviously, appeal to tradition, to custom, is a legitimate appeal in many contexts, but to cite it as the *only* ground on which to make a decision, without consideration of other aspects, and with the intent to terminate further thought and discussion, is an inappropriate use of appeal to tradition. The political figure who asserts that it is "common practice" for public officials to put their friends and relatives into good jobs, and the school administrator who asserts that a huge percentage of the budget should go into athletic uniforms, "because that's been the tradition of the school," are inappropriately attempting to terminate thought and discussion. We have strong emotional ties to "tradition," and the crime of "going against tradition" is one that few people are ready or willing to commit. The arguer who appeals to it must do so with care and with perspective and responsibility.

"STROKING" THE AUDIENCE AS A SUBSTITUTE FOR REASONING

Making people "feel good" is certainly a legitimate action. But when arguers do it as a substitution for reasoning, then it needs to be exposed for what it is. The term "stroking" is a common one in interpersonal communication, and such "a light, caressing movement" is obviously helpful to harmonious interrelationships. Needless to say, it is meant as a metaphor, not as actual physical stroking. There are at least four ways in which such "stroking" might be inappropriately used as a substitute for reasoning: (1) appeal to flattery, (2) appeal to snobbery, (3) appeal to plain folks, and (4) appeal to humor.

Inappropriate Appeal to Flattery

"It's a pleasure to be with such a fine audience today. You are the nicest people I've met on this tour." The speaker is intending probably not only to make the audience "feel good" but also to get them to be less critical of anything that is subsequently said. In short, flattery of the audience often serves as a cover-up for an arguer. The audience is lulled into a mood favorable to the speaker, and the claims which are made are not questioned so rigorously as they might otherwise be. The universal human desire to have one's ego stroked makes the appeal to flattery a procedure to be used with care and responsibility.

Inappropriate Snob Appeal

The desire to be "outstanding," to be part of an elite, to be distinguished from the general populace is a strong desire on the part of many people. Arguers sometimes suggest that we can gain such distinction in a simple manner which requires little thought or effort, by, for example, merely purchasing a certain product. "Men of distinction" ads are familiar. We are urged to purchase a certain automobile, beverage, or house, or to join a certain sorority/fraternity, or to attend a certain school, because it will mark us as being exclusive, distinctive. Again, admittedly, such stroking, up to a point, is not necessarily bad, but when it replaces reasoning or is used to an abnormally strong degree, then it is cause for concern.

Inappropriate Appeal to "Plain Folks"

At the other end of the continuum from snob appeal is the attraction most of us have, especially in democracies, to identify with the "common man." People running for political office of course rely heavily on this, for they try to reach as many voters as possible, and, by definition, there are more "common" people than "distinctive" ones. Many times arguers will inappropriately identify themselves with "plain folks," pretending to be part of that vast part of humanity. "I'm just a plain farmer like the rest of you," sounds a little hollow when uttered by an absentee landlord who owns a thousand-acre farm. Obviously, one can use the "plain folks" appeal legitimately, but when such an appeal is artificial and when it distracts from reasoning, then it is suspect as a motivator for accepting some claim put forth by an arguer.

Inappropriate Appeal to Humor

When humor is used appropriately to strengthen a sound presentation, then it obviously can be very helpful. But when it is substituted for sound reasoning, as it so often is, then it becomes a serious flaw. We all enjoy being stimulated to laughter—witness the size of the entertainment industry in the United States, and the large amount of humor in commercials. This does leave us vulnerable to accept all too readily the message of the arguer, however.

Humor may hide some imbedded persuasive message, and we agree with arguers or at least develop goodwill toward them without realizing it. People who make an audience laugh leave the impression that they are on the audience's side in a controversial situation. "He who laughs with us, is for us" can be a very powerful and misleading notion. Humor can divert our attention from the issues.

When we are the arguer, we ought not be misled into thinking that when our audience laughs at something we say, that they necessarily agree with our claims. Laughter does not necessarily mean assent. The sweet siren song of hearing an audience laugh lulls many speakers into the false notion that they have won over the audience. The audience may be laughing at the humor, but withholding assent; in fact, sometimes they may be laughing *at* us, not *with* us. Often, both speaker and auditor "wake up" to discover that the temporary ecstacy is soon dissipated, and that later a backlash of animosity may set in. We ought to base our claims on solid substance, not on humor.

SUBSTITUTION OF COMPELLING MANNERISMS FOR SOUNDNESS OF REASONING

All too frequently arguers seem to assume that the display of some compelling mannerism will suffice instead of reason and evidence in trying to sell some claim to an audience. All too frequently they are successful. We need to sensitize ourselves to this problem by understanding more fully the power of such compelling mannerisms as bombast, anger, assurance, sincerity, and conciliatoriness. Again, it is obvious that these are "good" in certain contexts, but they are potentially dangerous to sound reasoning when they are substituted for, or divert attention away from, sound reasoning and needed evidence.

Bombast

A loud voice, vigorous gestures, belligerent manner, air of certainty, forcefulness, and a rapid rate of speech are some verbal and nonverbal characteristics of a bombastic manner. Some parents all too often raise their voices to their children and seem to assume that their assertions are more valid simply because they have increased the volume of the utterance. We are familiar with arguers who try to overwhelm their opponents with this mode of behavior rather than by thoughtful reasoning. Such arguers usually assume that because their audience remains silent and is somewhat intimidated, they (the arguers) have won the day. But silence in the presence of bombast does not mean assent, and the arguer ought not to be deluded into thinking it does. "Did I tell him a thing or two!" "They didn't say a word!" "They were quiet as church mice!" These triumphant reports reveal such delusions. In most cases the audience was probably just waiting out the storm, and then went on its own way with no change in its original position, except perhaps to hold to it more tenaciously. Childhood literature should have taught us that a gentle sun rather than a boistrous wind is more successful in convincing people to take off their coats. The auditors were probably afraid, bored, or not willing to engage in an unpleasant exchange, and so remained silent at the moment, in the arguer's pressence, which gave the arguer the erroneous impression that the audience agreed with her. An animated, excited, vivacious manner can be very persuasive. The enthusiastic salesperson, presumably convinced of the quality of the product (and dreaming of the commission to be made if successful), energetically races along, assuming that enthusiasm is a sign of a sound case for the product. Evangelistic fervor and bombast are not to be confused with sound reasoning. When listening to these bubbling, self-confident enthusiasts, we need to erect dams to contain the overflowing enthusiasm until we have had time to examine calmly the reasoning and evidence presented or omitted.

Anger

Related to bombast is anger, although the former does not necessarily include the latter. Too many arguers seem to feel that simply showing anger will convince the opponent. When anger is thus used as a substitute for reasoning, it is to be condemned. On the other hand most of us applaud "righteous indignation," whereby anger has been gener-ated by unjust actions, and hence rests on facts. People who are denied housing or employment day after day because of their color soon develop appropriate indignation. But all too often the anger is the result of personality shortcomings, an inability to control one's emotions, an attempt to cover-up for lack of data, or a desire to force someone to do something. Needless to say, anger often stops thought and discussion, and produces instead silence, animosity, or superficial and grudging acquiescence.

Assurance

Related to bombast and anger, but also quite distinct, is assurance. After all, this exuding of great self-confidence, "putting on a bold front," can also be a quiet, unemotional mannerism. The audience becomes so impressed with how sure the advocates are of their position, that it is readily assumed that the advocates must be right. "You were so *sure* that was the right road to take that I never questioned it, " laments the wife to her husband as they try to discover where they are. A general who is *sure* his strategy will defeat the enemy may convince his fellow officers not by his logic but by his confidence. "No one could be wrong who is so confident!" This total assurance flows from many debating chambers, pulpits, commercial advertisements, and everyday conversations. Part of its appeal is of course the high degree of trust we have in people, but it is also plain laziness, for we like to assume the speaker is right, as that relieves us of the work of thinking through the issues. If such assurance on the part of the arguer takes the place of sound reasoning and evidence, then it is pseudo-reasoning, and is dangerous indeed. If it supplements sound reasoning and evidence, then it is a worthy and welcome ally.

Sincerity

Too many arguers assume that their sincerity in espousing beliefs is the same as sound reasoning. "How can I possibly be wrong? I'm so sincere!" This attitude can indeed create much mischief, for it can mislead both the arguer and the audience. While, obviously, sincerity is to be advocated and commended, it ought not to be a substitute for solid intellectual substance. Many cruel things have been done under the cloak of sincerity. Hitler and various notorious cult leaders have all apparently been "sincere" in their twisted teachings.

Conciliatoriness

The other end of the continuum from bombast is a meek, mild, conciliatory demeanor, which, if not genuine, can often simply be a diversionary tactic and inappropriate for a responsible arguer. It attempts to convince the listeners that they should agree with the speakers because the latter are so nice and conciliatory. Even if that spirit were genuine, we ought to test and accept or reject ideas on their own merits. We ought not to let even a genuine conciliatory nature of the person putting forth the claims to sway us in our decision-making.

DIVERSIONARY MANEUVERS AS SUBSTITUTIONS FOR SOUNDNESS OF REASONING

A number of diversionary maneuvers sometimes are employed knowingly or unknowingly as substitutions for soundness of reasoning, and when they are, we ought to view them with concern. Among such maneuvers would be shifting burden of proof, shifting ground, shifting to a countercharge, shifting focus from the issue to the person, and shifting between the parts and the whole.

Shifting the Burden of Proof

"The Yankees are the best team in baseball. Prove to me that they aren't!" Here the person making the claim that the Yankees are the best team has shifted the burden of proof to those who would oppose that claim. In the excitement of a discussion this tactic often goes unnoticed, as the person challenged to prove the negative is pushed into defending why the Yankees are not the best team. It is the procedure whereby accused people are handed the burden to prove their innocence, whereas the burden of proof rests on the accusers. Innocent until proven guilty is a fundamental premise. "Space ships from outer space must exist, for no one has proved that they don't exist" is another example of this shifting of the burden of proof. Responsible arguers will avoid this tactic and take on the task of proving their contention rather than shifting it to the opposition. We should become immediately suspicious when an arguer tries to put onto us his job of proving his claim.

Shifting Ground Inappropriately

Suppose Helen asserts that the Beauty Queen Hairdresser Shop has expert beauticians on its staff. Maria retorts that she has had very bad experiences with them, and so have two of her friends. Helen responds, "But you have to admit that their prices are very reasonable," a fact with which she knows Maria will have to agree. Helen has thus shifted ground to a more easily defensible contention in order to keep the upper hand. This is often done very subtly or swiftly so that the shift is not noticed by the second party. Indeed, the contention might be made that in such an example as the above, there was no basic shift, for expertise and price are merely subclaims to the major unstated claim by Helen that the Beauty Queen Hairdresser Shop is a good place to patronize, and if Maria would not go there because of the lack of expertise of the employees, then she should go there because of the reasonable cost. But whether the shift is in the subclaims or in the major claim, it still is a tactic of diverting focus from the original contention to another, more easily defended assertion. Of course, it should be acknowledged that indeed sometimes it might be wise and appropriate to shift ground if one sees one is on a weak platform and perceives a stronger one to move to, but it should be done openly and not with intent to divert attention or in the spirit of one-upmanship.

Inappropriate Shifting to a Countercharge

Suppose Candidate A is charged by Candidate B with being insensitive to equal rights for women, and Candidate A responds: "Your record on equal rights for blacks is certainly far from being satisfactory." This diverts attention from the original charge to a countercharge. It might very well be appropriate, of course, to bring into the discussion at some point the poor record of Candidate B on race relations, but to do so without speaking to the original charge of being insensitive to women's rights is an unfair diversionary technique. Candidate B is almost forced to respond to the charge, and Candidate A may in the heat of discussion manage to avoid commenting at all on the charge of his being insensitive to women's rights. Does the following sound familiar? Student X: "So you got a D in math last quarter, eh? What's the matter, can't you understand that simple stuff?" (Translated: "You are certainly dumb!") Student Y: "How about that D you got in Philosophy?" (Translated: "*You* certainly are dumb!") A perceptive listener of course no doubt will note the shift, but all too often sidestepping an original charge by making an immediate countercharge succeeds in diverting attention to something else. If one is in the audience, one should be alert to its use; if one is the arguer, one should avoid the temptation to utilize it.

Inappropriately Shifting Focus from the Issue to the Person

Suppose Rachel asserts that she is not going to vote for Candidate X because he talks too fast and is bald, or she does not intend to buy a particular vacuum cleaner because the salesperson is not neatly groomed. Instead of focusing on the political issues or the qualities of the vacuum cleaner, we all too often make our decisions on some personal characteristics of the persons making the claims. This diversionary tactic is often identified by the Latin expression, *ad hominem*, literally, "to the man." "How can you trust him in a government post? He's been divorced twice." "Everybody knows he's a scoundrel, therefore his proposal to subsidize intramural sports is obviously no good." This kind of argument no doubt sounds familiar. Often the *ad hominem* is utilized when an arguer cannot handle the ideas involved, and so turns on the person. It is sometimes referred to as "poisoning the well," that is, one claims that any idea coming from a particular source is unhealthy because of the source. We discredit an idea by simply asserting that since the proposal comes from "do-gooders," "radicals," "reactionaries," or "socialists," it must not be any good. Of couse, often it is indeed appropriate and necessary to focus on the personal characteristics and qualifications of the arguer, as we will note in a later chapter when we discuss the imporantce of ethos. But when we focus inapproriately on the speaker, and when the issues as a result are inappropriately deemphasized or even skirted, then shifting attention "to the man" becomes a device of pseudo-reasoning.

It is indeed legitimate and important to note and publicize any lack of consistency in a person's claims over a period of time. But to magnify an inconsistency which is relatively insignificant or irrelevant in an endeavor to attack the person's credibility is a type of *ad hominem* argument. It serves to divert attention from the issue to the person. We need to realize that inconsistency in certain contexts may be a sign of mature modification of views. For example, if Don says in December that a certain ski area is a poor one, but after using it a number of times he ends up saying next December that that ski area is a good one, he could be praised for being willing to change his opinion after further experience with the facts. Likewise, a public official who three years ago favored high military spending now may favor trimming the military budget, because of a change in the times and his experience and study over those three years. Thus, it should not be considered a crime to change one's mind. But random, flightly, opportunistic changing of one's mind is indeed open to criticism. We need to remember, however, that just hurling the accusation of "inconsistency" at someone as the sole ground for rejecting their claims is not necessarily coming to grips with the issue being discussed.

Inappropriately Shifting between the Parts and the Whole

When we inappropriately extend our claim by asserting that what is true of the parts of something is also true of the whole thing to which the parts belong, we are committing what is called the "fallacy of composition." It asserts, for example, that since each individual item in a watch is an excellent item, therefore the watch is an excellent watch. Putting the parts together to make a smooth-running watch goes beyond the simple excellence of each part in isolation. This fallacy asserts that what is good for the state of Texas is good for the nation, or that what is good for Ford Motor Company is good for the nation. It asserts that since a certain family has five wonderful children, the family relationships are wonderful. Yet we know that five wonderful individuals may create disharmony.

The reverse of the fallacy of composition is the "fallacy of division," that is, when it is asserted that what is good or true for the whole is good or true for each individual part. For example, it may be considered good for the nation's economy to eliminate subsidies to wheat farmers, but that may be disastrous to the wheat farmers. It may be considered true that Americans are talkative people, but there sits silent Mary in the corner.

MISCELLANEOUS PROCEDURES AS SUBSTITUTES FOR SOUNDNESS OF REASONING

A variety of other procedures may serve at times as substitutes for reasoning, and hence in those contexts would be thought of as pseudo-reasons. These would include: repetition, reducing claims to an absurdity, limiting the audience to only two choices, "two wrongs make a right," reliance on lack of contrary evidence, underlying assumptions go unexamined, and focusing on a trivial point.

Repetition

Often we seem to think we are adding to our argument by merely repeating our contentions. The repetition is treated as if it were proof of the original claim, and we delude ourselves and any unsuspecting auditor when we assume that mere repetition means increasing the truth of something. In an argumentative context, we often ignore the opposition's claim, and merely repeat our own. The advertising industry relies heavily on repetition. In some instances, repetition can be related to the "big lie," a technique utilized so blatantly by Hitler and by others; that is, simply repeating a lie often enough will eventually imbed it in the minds of the auditors to the degree that they will begin to believe it is true. Actually, repetition probably suggests that we have run out of arguments and are simply trying to inflate the thin arsenal at our disposal, trying to make it seem larger than it really is. When repetition begins to set in, it should be a warning signal to us, whether we are the speakers or listeners, that the full extent of the case probably has run out. It is thus actually helpful in indicating boundary lines to the argument. We know we have reached the end when we hear arguments repeated. Obviously, appropriate repetition does add argumentative strength, and imbeds our claim more firmly into the consciousness of our auditors, but here we are concerned with the inappropriate reliance on repetition as a substitute for reason.

Reducing a Claim to Absurdity

Usually referred to by the Latin phrase, *reductio ad absurdum*, this procedure extends a comparison to such an outlandish extreme so as to make it ridiculous. "Trying to wake up Joe in the morning is like trying to wake up a hibernating bear." The claim, "Joe is difficult to wake up," is thus exaggerated and put in a humorous light. "Wanting to go to Florida during spring break is like wanting to go to the moon, as far as my finances are concerned." Again, the comparison is so dissimilar as to create exaggeration and humor. This process of pushing claims to an absurdity of unreasonable extension, shunts aside reasoning, and hence we again are involved in pseudo-reasoning.

Inappropriately Limiting the Audience to Only Two Choices

In many communicative situations the audience is inappropriately presented with only two choices: "Vote for Candidate A or Candidate B"; "Either we go to Movie M or Movie N." This type of oversimplified "either/or" proposition often inappropriately narrows our options to only two; in reality, there might be more possibilities. One might vote for Candidate C or D, though they are not candidates of major parties, or one may abstain from voting altogether. One might go to Movie O or P, or go bowling instead. Certain common metaphors entrench this "two-choice" limitation in our thinking; for example, "sink or swim" overlooks the possibility of "treading water." (Of course, some situations *may* have only two possible options.)

Some two-choice situations are constructed so that one choice is obviously the "good" one and the other is obviously to be rejected. "Either you go to college or you will be ignorant the rest of your life." The pressure is directed toward selecting the first option. But we realize that knowledge can be gained many places other than college, so other options do indeed exist. Too many textbooks still refer to this type of two-option situation as "black-and-white" thinking, but we have purposely avoided it, as this subtly perpetuates the color prejudice which suggests that "black" things are bad, and "white" things are good.

When both options are bad, we have a *dilemma*, and when the posing of two undesirable options is inappropriate, we then have a *false dilemma*. "Either you marry me or I'll jump off the bridge!" The second party presumably would want neither of those things to occur. Political figures, unfortunately, are often adept at creating false dilemmas: "The opposition is either ignorant of the facts or is covering them up! Which do you prefer?"?!!

"Two Wrongs Make a Right"

The ancient concept of "an eye for an eye and a tooth for a tooth" is not dead. It persists in many argumentative situations today, for we justify some statement or action on the ground that since the opposition did something wrong, it is thus permissible for us to do so, too. For example, if a customer knows that the salesman is lying about something, the customer might lie in return with no disturbance of conscience. "If he can lie, so can I!" We justify our action with the familiar idiom, to give someone "a taste of her own medicine." It should be obvious that this does not further rational decision-making.

Inappropriate Reliance on Lack of Contrary Evidence

The defense attorney may assert that there is no direct evidence that her client was at the scene of the bank robbery, therefore her client is innocent. A search committee for a new university president may assert that since they have discovered no claims against Candidate A's ability, therefore he must be capable. These are situations in which arguers claim that their contentions are sound and accurate, since there is no evidence to the contrary. While it is easy to agree that the absence of contrary evidence strengthens one's claims, it in no way completely proves them, for it may simply mean that the investigation has not gone far enough to turn up negative information, or that people are reticent about coming forward with negative information. Thus, we need to be careful not to claim too much from the absence of contrary evidence.

Underlying Assumptions Go Unexamined

The Latin phrase, *nonsequitur*, meaning, "it does not follow," identifies a common problem in argumentation. That is, does it follow that increasing faculty salaries will make them better teachers? Does it follow that buying new band uniforms will improve the school's music program? Such basic assumptions often go unexamined, and arguers go merrily on their way, hoping that no one will stop to question the assumptions.

When language is used in the assertion which assumes to be true the very thing that the arguer is supposedly setting out to establish, it is a form of "begging the question." For example: "Don't vote for that unfair, antistudent tuition increase." The term "unfair" and "antistudent" are included in the claim, and they are the very terms which need to be clarified and supported. Again the arguer assumes to be true the very thing she is supposed to demonstrate is true.

Inappropriate Focusing on a Trivial Point

Suppose in a debate one participant seizes on a minor mistake made by the opponent (for example, a speaker said "two hundred" when he meant to say "two million"), and blows it up as an indication that the opponent is unsure of the facts. This would be an endeavor to weaken the opposition and strengthen oneself by dwelling inappropriately on a trivial aspect. One ought to avoid the trap of believing one has refuted an opponent's case when one has refuted only a very minor point in that case. Often, arguers who dwell inappropriately on a minor point are doing so out of insecurity; that is, they are clutching for any point which they can boldly emphasize. Related to this is the setting up of a "straw man," something which they can easily knock down.

SUMMARY

In this chapter we have surveyed a number of examples of pseudo-reasoning with which students of argumentation need to be familiar in order to avoid using them and in order to expose their use by other arguers. First, a number of emotional appeals are often substituted for soundness of reasoning, such as the appeal to pity, fear, the majority, authority, and tradition. Secondly, "stroking" the audience is frequently employed as a substitute for sound reasoning, such as the inappropriate appeal to flattery, to snobbery, to "plain folks," and to humor. Third, compelling mannerisms are often substituted for soundness of reasoning, such as bombast, anger, assurance, sincerity, and conciliatoriness. Fourth, inappropriate shiftings occur as substitutes for soundness of reasoning, such as shifting the burden of proof, shifting ground, shifting to a countercharge, shifting the focus from the issue to the person, and shifting between the parts and the whole. Finally, additional miscellaneous procedures are engaged in as substitutes for soundness of reasoning, such as repetition, *reductio ad absurdum*, inappropriately limiting the audience to only two choices, assuming that "two wrongs make a right," inappropriately relying on lack of contrary evidence, permitting underlying assumptions to go unexamined, and focusing unduly on a trivial point.

EXERCISES

1. Discuss whether it is wise or even ethical to urge students to be cautious, to wait until all the facts are in, before asserting their claims. Does this permit the persons with an abundance of assurance (but perhaps not much solidity of reasoning or evidence) to take the lead in decision-making situations, and perhaps make it difficult if not impossible for the cautious person to influence the decision? That is, do we studiously ponder something, while the bold person with lots of assurance is determining policy for all of us?

2. Listen to a speech on campus or in the community and note what seem to be inappropriate appeals to pity, fear, tradition, and the majority. Summarize your findings in a 500-word essay and share them in class discussion.

3. Look at advertisements, wherever you might find them, and note their use of repetition and their appeal to humor, snob appeal, and flattery. Summarize your findings in a five-minute speech, using some advertisements as visual aids if appropriate.

4. Listen to some religious or political speech and note the presence of bombast, assurance, anger, sincerity, and conciliatoriness as substitutions for soundness of reasoning. Summarize your findings in a 500-word essay and share them in class discussion.

5. Ferret out an underlying assumption in each of the following, an assumption that probably would be overlooked in responding to the question:
   a. Who should sit at the head table?
   b. How should I spend the money I got for my birthday?
   c. How can I improve my golf game?
   d. What kind of meat should we have for supper?

11 Receiver Analysis

IMPORTANCE OF RECEIVER ANALYSIS AND ADAPTATION

Clarification of Terms

The very nature of the communication process demands that there be at least one recipient of a message, a reader or listener, who decodes the message of the writer or speaker. We use the term auditor when the recipient is only one person, and the term audience when there is more than one. These terms come from the Latin *audire*, meaning "to hear," and technically are limited to oral communication. Even though the term audience generally has been expanded to include written as well as oral communication, it is more appropriate to use the term "receiver," as this encompasses oral and written communication with greater accuracy and ease.

Common Practice of Analyzing and Adapting to Receivers

In our everyday conversation we analyze and adapt to our receivers much more than we probably realize. Suppose a fellow played golf with three of his buddies on Saturday, and on Sunday he discusses his experiences with various individuals. Think how differently he phrases his message to his girlfriend (who would have preferred to have gone to the beach with him rather than have him go golfing with his friends), to another golfing friend, to a friend from a foreign country who does not understand golf, and to his parents (who had wanted him to help with some work around the house). In a public speech or in a written piece of work, communicators also take their receivers into account, often without realizing it.

Need for Careful Analysis and Adaptation

In argumentation, where the communicator is seeking adherence from the receivers, it is crucial to secure an accurate picture of those receivers. As Perelman and Olbrechts-Tyteca have put it:

> In real argumentation, care must be taken to form a concept of the anticipated audience as close as possible to reality. An inadequate picture of the audience, resulting from either ignorance or an unforeseen set of circumstances, can have very unfortunate results.[1]

Aristotle's *Rhetoric* has stood for centuries as a touchstone for insightful audience analysis, and throughout history people sensitive to effective communication have admonished that verbal and nonverbal adaptations to one's varying audiences are of fundamental importance. The last three decades have witnessed an increased focus in periodical literature and in textbooks on the receivers.[2]

---

1. Ch. Perelman and L. Olbrechts-Tyteca, *The New Rhetoric: A Treatise on Argumentation*, trans. John Wilkinson and Purcell Weaver (Notre Dame, Ind.: U. of Notre Dame Press, 1969), p. 20.
2. Books focusing on the audience include: Theodore Clevenger, Jr., *Audience Analysis* (Indianapolis: Bobbs-Merrill, 1966); Paul D. Holtzman, *The Psychology of Speakers' Audiences* (Glenview, Ill.: Scott, Foresman, 1970); Carl H. Weaver, *Human Listening: Processes and Behavior* (Indianapolis: Bobbs-Merrill, 1972); Martin P. Andersen, Wesley Lewis, and James Murray, *The Speaker and His Audience* (New York: Harper & Row, 1964). Textbooks in argumentation and persuasion with an audience-centered approach include: Richard E. Crable, *Argumentation as Communication: Reasoning with Receivers* (Columbus, Ohio: Charles E. Merrill, 1976); Richard D. Rieke & Malcolm O. Sillars, *Argumentation and the Decision Making Process* (New York: John Wiley & Sons, 1975); Charles U. Larson, *Persuasion: Reception and Responsibility* (2nd ed.; Belmont, Calif.: Wadsworth, 1979).

Arguers must endeavor to gather as many facts as possible about the receivers and must endeavor to see things from their perspective. As Weaver put it, the goal is to "try to hear your message as he [the receiver] does,"[3] to empathize as fully as possible with the receiver. After all, receivers are the ones making the decision about an arguer's effectiveness, and as Crable wrote: "...regardless of the kind of claim you intend to advance, your receiver(s) will respond to it as the kind of claim they judge it to be."[4] Members of an audience, even a captive audience, do not have to listen if they do not want to, so arguers have to mold their comments accordingly to meet the interests and aspirations of the receivers, to secure a high degree of attention, understanding, and favorable response. Arguers with sensitivity will choose their topics wisely, select supporting material and illustrations with care, phrase their remarks appropriately, arrange their arguments effectively, use accepted authorities, and tap appropriate appeals. Obviously one cannot find out everything about a group of receivers, but the important thing is to have a questioning mind, even though all the answers may not be forthcoming. Arguers will want to know as much as possible about the nature of the receivers, their probable knowledge of, and attitude toward, the subject, and their probable attitude toward the arguer. These will be discussed later in this capter.

Homogeneity Illusion

We often erroneously think of a group of receivers as being *an* audience, a singular entity, with virtually similar characteristics. Obviously, considerable homogeneity does exist, for example, in college and university speech and communication classes, for one's classmates are of the same approximate age, possess similar intellectual capabilities, have common interests and goals, and have somewhat similar backgrounds. But we ought not to be misled by such assumed homogeneity, for we soon discover that an astonishing variety exists: in work opportunities, in family backgrounds, in travel experiences, and in attitudes toward social, political, religious, and cultural issues. This applies to other groups of receivers also that arguers may encounter. We ought not be misled into thinking that all members of the audience are alike simply because they belong to the same group. They are a collection of individuals. The notion of a single entity is a generalized abstraction which, while often helpful to create in one's mind, also can be misleading.

3. Weaver, *Human Listening*, p. 107.
4. Crable, *Argumentation as Communication*, p. 133.

Target Audience

Not infrequently, arguers will want to aim their remarks at one specific segment of a group of receivers. Advertisers, for example, prepare their campaigns with a particular audience in mind, that is, those most likely to purchase that product. A speaker in a large convention hall may be more concerned with winning favorable responses from the nationwide television audience. The President in an address to the nation may often phrase his statements with foreign audiences in mind, both foes and friends. A speaker at a high school commencement may virtually ignore the parents, friends, and school officials in the audience and instead speak only to the graduating seniors. Noting that women outnumber the men in an audience ten to one, an advocate might adapt remarks to appeal to that majority. A brother arguing with a sister might couch his statements in such a way as to please the parents who are within listening range. Obviously, if arguers are to pinpoint segments of an audience, they need to analyze the audience factor very carefully.

Universal Audience

While arguers focus on the known, specific receivers, if possible, arguers also often have to operate without knowing much about the receivers. A person speaking on radio or television, and many if not most writers, simply does not know who her receivers will be. Guesses have to be made. An arguer assumes a competent, informed audience, people who have normal reasoning and judging capabilities. Students training to become historians are told that a qualified historian

> ...must write always as if addressing the whole educated community. His yardstick is: can another trained mind, not expert in my subject, understand what I am saying?[5]

This would also apply to an arguer. But the very concept of a universal audience is of course an abstraction; one has to imagine it.[6] Such imaginative speculation can of course be misleading, but it still is in most situations all an advocate can operate on, and can be indeed functional and accurate.

5. Jacques Barzun and Henry F. Graff, *The Modern Researcher* (3rd ed.; New York: Harcourt, Brace, Jovanovich, 1977), p. 27.
6. Perelman and Olbrechts-Tyteca, *The New Rhetoric*. p. 31. See also John W. Ray, "Perelman's Universal Audience," *Quarterly Journal of Speech*, 64 (1978): 361–75.

Perspective

Before we go further, it would be wise to inject a word of caution and secure proper perspective on receiver analysis. All of this emphasis on the importance of the receiver might well give some students the erroneous impression that the content of a presentation should be a "slave" to the audience. It might seem to condone or even advocate hypocrisy, suggesting a person ought to say one thing to one group but something else to another, such as advocating abortion if one audience is in favor of it, and opposing it if another opposes it. Such an impression would be disastrous. What we are trying to say is that an accurate analysis of the receivers is highly important to effective argumentation, that it is one of many elements to keep in mind. It certainly does not suggest lessening one's commitment to truth, as perceived by the arguer.

SOURCES FOR INFORMATION ABOUT THE RECEIVERS

Prior to the Communication Event

To explore the different avenues one could utilize to secure information on the receivers, let us focus on a particular episode, and the readers can make the obviously needed adaptations to other kinds of communication situations. Suppose Joe has been invited to speak to the local League of Women Voters about the virtues of a particular political candidate. One thing he can do is talk with one or more members of the group over the telephone or at a prearranged get-together, such as over lunch. He may have friends and acquaintances who are, or used to be, members with whom he could talk. He would probably get some information from the program chairperson who arranged for him to give the speech, and he could get in touch with some of the other officers of the group. He might have followed in the mass media in past months and years the activities and statements of the League of Women Voters so that he knows quite a bit about their organization and its purposes and functions. He might have read their newsletters, their constitution, or any other document published by them. He might get a membership list. He might prepare a formal questionnaire which could be filled out by the membership and returned to him sometime prior to his speech.[7]

7. In addition to the questionnaire, Clevenger (*Audience Analysis*, pp. 66–75) discusses six other formal procedures that one might employ in seeking to gather data on the audience.

Of course, he would recognize that he was assuming that responses there and elsewhere were truthful. He might have had experience with a similar group in another city, and reasoning by analogy would suggest to him that this group is probably similar.

During the Communication Event

Immediately before the program begins, Joe might informally converse with some of the officers or other members of the group, finding out something about the membership and their ideas. During the actual speech, he might ask for a show of hands on how they feel about certain candidates or issues. He might carefully observe nonverbal cues during the speech, such as smiles, laughter, head nodding or head shaking, drowsiness, puzzled looks, or applause, indicating the audience's degree of agreement, enjoyment, interest, and comprehension. It would be very important, of course, to interpret accurately the cues demonstrated. Also, it would be important not to narrow one's observation to only those anticipated effects. For example, a comedian, or an arguer, intent on being funny, may look only for smiles and laughter, thus overlooking other cues. Joe should keep in mind the state of readiness of the audience; that is, they may laugh very quickly at a comedian because they expect her to be humorous, but since they do not expect Joe to be humorous, they may be slow to respond—they were not ready to do so.

Collecting audience response during and immediately following a presentation can be extremely helpful for future speeches. Those advocates who are playing for high stakes, such as national advertisers or political campaigners, are very careful to thoroughly record audience reactions in order to improve and refine the message in the future.

CHARACTERISTICS OF THE RECEIVERS

What information is most necessary for an arguer to secure about any particular audience of course depends on each situation, but there are a number of fundamental components which the arguer would be wise to learn as much about as possible. Admittedly, one may end up with only a small amount of data, but every little bit helps, and a small amount of information on a crucial aspect or two may make a great deal of difference in the arguer's effectiveness. The arguer is concerned, then, with demographics, a term coming from the Greek *demos* and *graphos*, meaning "people" and "to write," respectively. In other words, one is writing a summary of a group of people, creating a word picture of their characteristics. Fields of study such as communication, sociology, and political science are deeply interested in demographics, identifying items which are to some degree measurable and quantifiable. Some characteristics the receivers possess through no choice of their own, and some characteristics are theirs through at least some degree of free will. We will first survey the former, then those in which choice is operating.

Nationality and Race

How many readers voted at birth what nationality or race they wanted to be? The secret ballot was hardly operating. An arguer should carefully determine if possible what nationalities and races are likely to be represented in the group of receivers. Fortunately, people today are increasingly sensitive about showing fairness and justice to all, and any advocate who violates this is deservedly going to be less effective. In conversations, or in public oral or written utterances, no advocate has the right to offend any group because of race or national origin. Jokes, illustrations, or terminology likely to be offensive to any given group should certainly be avoided.

On the positive side, an arguer can use knowledge of the nationality and racial composition of her receivers to build a more appealing case. For example, recounting a familiar Spanish folktale before a predominantly Spanish-speaking audience, being knowledgeable on the special problems of Vietnamese immigrants when large numbers are present in the audience, or quoting a respected authority, like Martin Luther King, Jr., to predominantly black audiences, would add to favorable reactions.

Age

What is the age range and dominant age group among the receivers? Inexperienced and idealistic youth has insights and interests which tend to differ from those of experienced and realistic older people. While youth revels in activity, old age finds pleasure in quiet pursuits. Young people are quick to suggest changes in the status quo, while successful adults insist that conditions and procedures ought to remain as they are. Not infrequently, however, the attitudes of young people, lacking a certain intellectual maturity, may be rigid and reactionary; similarly, not infrequently increased age brings a mellowing mind and flowering of the liberal spirit. But, generally, the elderly want to hold, to conserve, what they have acquired through conformity to numerous demands and restrictions of society on them through the decades; youth has not yet acquired much to conserve. Age glories in what was; youth glories in what will be. Long ago Aristotle insightfully summarized the different outlooks of youth and older people; consider his comments on their differing attitudes on money:

> ...[youth] love [money] very little, not having yet learnt what it means to be without it....[Old people] are not generous, because money is one of the things they must have, and at the same time their experience has taught them how hard it is to get and how easy to lose.[8]

While arguers are adapting to these general mind sets of the different ages, arguers also ought to be sensitive to the various pretensions of age. That is, youth often pretends sophistication, middle age pretends youth and realism, and old age pretends Olympian virtues.

But whatever the situation, sensitive arguers need to analyze as accurately as possible the age component. Sometimes a slight miscalculation can make a big difference. Take, for example, the time a political official addressed a group of college students under the mistaken impression that they were high school students. What could be more disastrous than to talk to college and university freshmen as if they were mere high school seniors?

Sex

With more women entering the professions, the business world, and the labor force, their experiences and interests are not so different from men's as would have been true a generation ago when women were more housebound. But despite the fact that men and women have increasingly more in common, enough differences still exist so that an advocate needs to be sensitive to those variations. Some studies suggest that women, for instance, are more easily persuaded than men, but the studies are inconclusive and may result from the fact that the topics used in the studies were of less importance to women.[9]

8. Aristotle, *Rhetoric*, 1389a, 1389b. Students may enjoy reading Aristotle's comments about youth, middle age, and old age, and will be surprised how modern and contemporary they sound (1389a–90b).

9. Kenneth E. Andersen, *Persuasion: Theory and Practice* (2d ed.; Boston: Allyn and Bacon, 1978), pp. 96–97.

Size of Audience

To speak before a group of ten or a gathering of five hundred often necessitates some variation in handling of material. It surely helps arguers to prepare themselves psychologically if they can determine ahead of time the approximate number in the group of receivers.

Habitat

None of us chose the location of our birth. And while it is becoming increasingly easy for people to move either temporarily or permanently, there still are many who live out their lives in one geographical area and have a fierce loyalty to it. Farming illustrations would be comprehended and appreciated more by people in rural rather than urban settings. From what states or foreign countries have the receivers come? College and university students today are certainly widely traveled. Many have been on family vacations in other states, some have gone to the beaches or the ski resorts during school vacations, some have been abroad in military service, and many have had summer employment or temporary jobs in other cities and states. Arguers would be wise to determine the variations of habitat experiences, and weave them into the message appropriately.

Marital Status

Arguers would do well to be attuned to the number of single, married, divorced, or widowed people among their receivers. Illustrations drawn from family tensions or children's antics have a depth of meaning to married people, but are less appreciated by those who are single. Advocacy of drug control, for example, probably would be more favorably listened to by parents who are rearing children.

Educational Level

Children raised in the United States and certain other countries secure a high school level education through no choice of their own. They are forced by law to get that much education. Many countries do not have the resources or will to guarantee an education much beyond primary level, if even that much, and then, often, only for boys. But beyond high school the educational level one attains is largely a matter of choice, though it may not be without great financial and other burdens. Formal education and intellectual capability are of course not synonymous, but knowing the educational background of their receivers will help arguers determine the choice of subject, and the manner and depth of treatment of material. A doctor who has to explain the nature, cause, and cure of a particular disease to an illiterate patient has a task quite different from that were her patient a college graduate. Jokes and supporting materials drawn from a college setting may be very interesting to the college student in the audience, but someone who finished only high school may feel left out and slighted.

Socioeconomic Level

Subjects such as Social Security, rent and price controls, government health insurance, and unemployment compensation would stimulate considerably varying reactions depending in part on where the member of the audience was on the socioeconomic scale. An arguer would probably create little interest and considerable animosity by using an illustration based on playing the stock market when addressing a low-income audience which has never had the surplus money available to invest in stocks. Knowing the average income of the receivers would be an instructive bit of data for the advocate.

Occupations

Closely related to socioeconomic levels would be determining the types of occupations engaged in by the receivers. Arguers could then cite examples or create hypothetical illustrations from the appropriate occupations. An illustration based on the carpenter's trade might not be understood or hold much interest for a banker, and vice versa. It the receivers are students, who perhaps have not held many permanent occupations as yet, it would be wise to determine their part-time work experiences and perhaps the occupations pursued by their parents. Occupations may also carry with them union or other types of affiliations which are very important. Membership in a labor union, the chamber of commerce, or the American Medical Association could be a significant indicator of the receiver's ideas. A non-AMA doctor, for instance, or a nonunion teacher may have political and social views quite different from their union-member colleagues.

Political Preferences

It often would be very helpful for arguers to have some idea of the political leanings, if not the outright political party affiliations, of the receivers. Knowing the political atmosphere of a group will enable arguers to adapt accordingly, to choose acceptable authorities, to develop certain arguments more than others, and to phrase statements appropriately.

Religion

Many people of course do not choose their religion; they have been born into it. But their views are often strong, whether they have been arrived at through birth or choice, and arguers would be aided if they knew what religious beliefs and affiliations are represented in the group of receivers. Surely the effectiveness of arguers will sharply decline if the religious viewpoints of the receivers are carelessly or unkindly imposed upon. Many social and political issues, such as birth control, are intimately intertwined with religious premises, and this should be taken into account by sensitive arguers. Reference to certain religious leaders would have great weight with some receivers and very little with others.

Interest Groups

If arguers knew that many of the receivers belonged to such organizations as the Shriners, Rotarians, Parent-Teacher Association, YWCA, or League of Women Voters, then appropriate arguments and illustrations could be developed. Obviously arguers cannot comment on every organization represented among their receivers even if such information were known, but by referring to one or a few interest groups the arguer gives the whole audience the feeling that their interests are being noted and appreciated. There is a sort of vicarious sharing among the receivers. With an audience of college and university students it would be important to know to what campus organizations and interest groups they belonged.

Recreational Interests

We know that nothing brightens up a listener's eyes so much as bringing into the conversation (in a favorable way, of course) his favorite hobby, say, operating a ham radio, or his favorite sport, perhaps golf. Perhaps no richer source of illustrative materials or metaphors can be found than in the area of recreation, for these pastimes are shared by so many and bring such pleasant connotations. Politicians, for example, will claim that if elected, they will deliver a knockout blow to racketeers, or will be effective team players in the legislature. With a large heterogeneous group of receivers it would be wiser to employ sports with a broad appeal, such as baseball or football. Reference to cricket would have little or no positive impact on an American audience, although it would create a real sense of identification with students from England. Arguers have to be careful to use recreational interests of their receivers, and not their own; an avid handball player makes little headway by bringing in references to the game if the receivers are unfamiliar with, or uninterested in, that particular sport. Arguers who do not draw on the rich source of recreational interests to make their case more clear, interesting, and compelling, are missing a fine opportunity.

PHYSIOLOGICAL AND EMOTIONAL NEEDS

Common biological, social, and emotional needs in all human beings emphasize the oneness of, the similarities present in, all members of a given audience. Psychologist Abraham Maslow has crystallized and categorized these into a pyramid configuration which has been widely used in communication textbooks for many years.

At the base of the pyramid are basic universal physiological needs. Nature has decreed that all normal human beings possess the same basic biological demands for food, water, oxygen, sex, elimination, and sleep. These needs have to be satisfied in order for life to function. Of course, humans can control some of them to some degree, such as fasting or electing to remain celibate, but this is atypical. The biological brotherhood of human beings enables arguers to predict with some accuracy how the receivers will react. These basic physiological needs have to be satisfied first, then other levels of the pyramid are able to exert influence.

The next level is called security needs, that is, the desire for economic security, for job stability, protection from bodily harm, or security from invasion by other nations. One has the desire, in other words, to live in safety.

The third level going up the pyramid is belonging needs. Humans have the desire to be a part of some group larger than themselves, such as a family, a fraternity/sorority, a religious group, some sports team, some political group, some institution, or some movement. In a sense, it is the security of conforming to, being a part of, some unit in society.

The fourth level is love and esteem needs. We desire not only to be a member of a sorority/fraternity but we also desire to be a respected member of it, to be recognized and acclaimed. We thus obey all the rules, willingly do our share of the work, and perhaps aspire to a leadership role.

Finally, at the top of the pyramid is self-actualization, that is, the peak experiences of self-fulfillment and happiness. We sense the thrill of adventure, of creating something, of excelling in an endeavor, of being a part of some higher cause, of living up to the potential we feel is in us.[10]

The basic premise undergirding Maslow's pyramid is the notion of prepotency, that is, the lower levels have to be satisfied before higher levels have much potency. The appeals of the secret ballot in the democratic process, or the appeals of some perfume advertisement, will have little infleunce on people in some underdeveloped country faced with continual starvation. It is difficult to be convinced to join some evening bowling league when one is frightened to be in that neighborhood at night.

Seldom does any one of these five levels operate in isolation, for usually a number are jointly called into play in varying strengths in any given situation. A group of receivers, for example, may be assured of bodily comfort and social prestige if they purchase a particular automobile or a particular coat. Volunteers may feel a sense of belonging and self-actualization by joining the Peace Corps or the Marine Corps. If arguers can successfully appeal to multiple levels present in each of the receivers, the arguers will increase the likelihood of securing attention and adherence.

VALUE CLUSTERS

Like physiological and emotional needs, values are at a low level of awareness in all of us. That is, they operate powerfully in the subconscious, but we take them for granted and seldom verbalize them. Arguers need to be alert to the values which pervade any given society and which are imbedded to varying degrees in any group of receivers from that society. Small subcultural groups have distinctive values. For

10. For an extensive discussion of the role of drives, motives, emotions, and societal pressures, see Brembeck and Howell, *Persuasion*, pp. 80–173.

example, Family C will have decidedly different values from Family B, often much to the surprise of school children when they visit each other's homes. A gang of juvenile car thieves will have values quite different from other youngsters their own age. Inner-city slum-dwellers and suburbanites have different value preferences. Any interest group, be it a high school athletic team, a college debate squad, or a group of volunteers in a hospital, all have distinctive value clusters.

It is common to think in terms of a nation's value system. Much, for instance, has been written on the American value clusters, which would include the following emphases.

First, a strong moral, Puritan conscience has been ingrained into the American fiber ever since the early settlers arrived. It is a sense of living in accordance with some strict, stern, moral law of the universe, of following God's will, of seeing life in terms of sharp distinctions between good and evil, with little in between. One's life is not to be passed in idleness, and one is to be held accountable to God at the end.

Second, America has emphasized that hard work is a virtue and that it will lead ultimately to success. People operate on the optimistic assurance that a bountiful harvest, in both the tangible and intangible, will be theirs eventually if one works hard. This challenge has always been at the heart of the immigrant experience. For example, listen to the following excerpts from nineteenth century letters sent by Swedish immigrants to relatives back in Sweden:

> Without work, often with work that is hard and painful, he [the immigrant] cannot hope to achieve success....We do not regret our undertaking....From the experiences of others we see that in a few years we can have a better livelihood and enjoy comforts that we must now deny ourselves....One thing is certain, and that is that those who wish to and can work can escape from want; for work and earnings for both men and women are not lacking here.[11]

Third, individual worth is at the center of the American value system. The growth and well-being of the individual is the objective, through freely chosen education, work of one's own choosing, and self-governing processes. Some national cultures, like Japan, for instance, have in the past (it is now changing among the college students) greatly deemphasized individualism and instead fostered the spirit of group centeredness, group-oriented values.[12] One is taught to put the group first,

11. H. Arnold Barton (ed.), *Letters from the Promised Land: Swedes in America, 1840–1914* (Minneapolis: U. of Minnesoata Press, 1975), pp. 24, 92.
12. Hiroko Nishida, "Variations in Value Orientations and Cultural Change in Japan and the U.S.A.: An Intercultural Perspective," unpublished Ph.D. dissertation, U. of Minnesota, 1979.

be it the family or a business corporation. Totalitarian countries of course consider that the individual exists for the government; it is the reverse in democratic, open societies.

Fourth, change and progress were also at the heart of the immigrant vision, and it was assumed that change automatically meant progress. Despite rude awakenings by war in the twentieth century have taught us that change does not necessarily mean progress. Nevertheless, we still cling to that idea, for it still contains considerable legitimacy.

Fifth, a strong strand of pragmatism exists in the American fabric, that is, an emphasis on the workable. If it works, it is good. Abstractions which cannot be demonstrated to operate effectively have little appeal. This applies to all walks of life, including governmental procedures, business methods, and educational processes. We are concerned with, some observers would even say obsessed with, efficiency, and we want something not only to work but to work well. We are problem-solvers, and do not rest while something remains to be repaired. A broken-down wagon, a stalled automobile, or a clogged communication channel in some business we want repaired as soon as possible. People in some other cultures are not so concerned about solving problems as quickly.

Finally, there is an abundance of faith in the common man. It was felt that the unschooled but savvy frontiersman was the person in whom Americans could put their trust. Log cabin origins and good common sense went far. From European experiences, many early Americans deeply distrusted the upper classes, the wealthy, the powerful, and the educated elite who kept the common man in virtual servitude. America provided a safety valve for Europe's common man to find an outlet for his inherent capabilities. Despite a strong strain of anti-intellectualism, America honored education, but education for the masses—and, thus, free public education—was given an impetus which many nations in the world are only just now awakening to.[13]

RELATIONSHIP OF RECEIVERS TO THE SUBJECT

Arguers who desire to be effective need to anticipate the receiver's knowledge of, and attitude toward, the subject being discussed. To communicate on the proper intellectual level and to predict accurately the likely reactions to one's views are marks of an alert advocate.

13. For further discussion of the American value system as it relates to communication, see Edward D. Steele and W. Charles Redding, "The American Value System: Premises in Persuasion," *Western Speech*, 26 (1962): 83–91. For a discussion of cultural bases of persuasion, see Brembeck and Howell, *Persuasion*, pp. 200–24.

One should be careful not to underestimate or overestimate the receiver's knowledge of the subject matter. To use the technical terminology of any given profession or activity when such terminology is probably unfamiliar to the receivers, leads to ineffective advocacy. A speech by a scientist before her colleagues would have to be radically reworded and simplified when given before the general public. On the other hand, every communicator must avoid the temptation to become too simplistic, hence losing the respect and interest of the receivers.

A wise arguer is thoroughly attuned to the important difference between unintelligent and uninformed receivers. A person giving a travelogue on her recent visit to Asia before an audience of university students needs to inform them of the specific geography involved, for if she does not, this intelligent audience cannot be expected to get the most out of her lecture. A person with a high I.Q., new to the college campus, might not understand the directions for getting to a particular building, because the person giving directions erroneously assumes the stranger knows the layout of the campus. A straight-A student might be thoroughly confused with technical football talk or with the intricate terminology of an unfamiliar card game. Arguers ought to be clear in their minds on the difference, then, between unintelligent and uninformed receivers.

Furthermore, arguers ought to be alert to the probable attitude of their receivers toward the subject being discussed. As one author has written: "...knowledge of attitudes is crucial in the prediction of behavior, and that is why their discovery is...the primary function of audience analysis."[14] We are all predisposed to respond in a given predictable manner toward ideas, persons, institutions, objects, or events. Thus, when these hardened attitudes, these stereotypes, become firmly imbedded in our mental machinery, they, rather than facts, govern our reactions. Are the receivers partisans, neutral, or opponents? If the attitude of the receiver tends to be reasonably favorably inclined toward the subject and the specific thesis being proposed, the arguers need only to reinforce those preconceptions. But frequently arguers will have to fight animosity or indifference. Advocates often find it difficult, even in conversation with friends, to keep the discussion going for any length of time on a subject in which the receivers are not interested. If the audience tends to oppose the advocate's point of view, the latter should adjust accordingly, perhaps by putting the strongest argument

14. Cullen B. Owens, "Audience Analysis and Motivation," in James H. McBath (ed.), *Argumentation and Debate: Principles and Practices* (rev. ed.; New York: Holt, Rinehart and Winston, 1963), p. 127.

first and by employing appropriate phrasing and tone. Arguers must put themselves in the receiver's place, must try to understand and appreciate the latter's approach to the subject. Arguers need to show respect for the receiver's attitudes, and must employ tact throughout. If arguers indulge in ridicule, or tear something down merely for the sake of tearing it down, they may experience a perverted sense of pleasure but will greatly reduce the likelihood of winning adherents, and may be impairing their own ethos in the long run.

Open-Mindedness

It would be helpful if arguers could determine the degree of open-mindedness of the audience on the subject being discussed. Obviously it is difficult to determine deep personality characteristics short of putting the receivers through elaborate psychological testing, and even then the results may be suspect. But the prime target for arguers is the uninformed, uncommitted neutrals in the audience, for they are the people who would be most likely to shift their position as a result of a persuasive presentation. Informed, committed neutrals (fairly rare individuals) will unlikely shift quickly, for they will demand an abundance of evidence and argument. Closed-minded, highly dogmatic people, whether for or against something, are also difficult to shift. Occasionally, dogmatic individuals may shift from one extreme position to another, for they feel secure in such firm allegiances; the tentativeness of an open-minded middle-ground position is more threatening to them than a complete reversal of position.

The saliency (significance) of the subject to the receivers is a crucial dimension to keep in mind. How ego-involved are they in the subject? Asking someone to change their brand of peanut butter is likely to be less ego-disturbing than asking them to change their religious affiliation.

Sometimes advocates are in a position to pretest their messages with a group of receivers. For example, a public official or political candidate may send up trial balloons, offhandedly suggesting an idea to see what reactions are forthcoming. Advertisers, especially those engaged in nationwide efforts, build into their procedures a carefully structured and planned testing of advertising appeals to get an indication of consumer reaction before investing in an expensive campaign. College and university students try out ideas on their friends and parents before including certain material in an upcoming speech assignment, and so, too, do even small children before formally requesting something from their parents.

RELATIONSHIP OF RECEIVERS TO ARGUER

Arguers also need to be alert to the importance of the relationship between themselves and their receivers. How well do the latter know the advocate, and is his reputation in their eyes good, fair, or bad? The arguer's knowledge of the material, his honesty and integrity, his sincerity, self-control, and fairness, his confidence and decisiveness, and his sympathetic understanding of the wants and needs of the receivers all speak for him.

As discussed in a later chapter, such factors of ethos refer to the prestige the arguers bring to the communication event, the prestige built up during the presentation, and the arguer's behavior after the event. Many times a question-and-answer period following a speech reveals a serious weakness in the speaker's knowledge or character. For instance, consider the damage done to an advocate's cause, if, following a speech, her lack of facts on an important aspect becomes apparent, or if, after a speech in which she pleaded for "tolerance," she displays much intolerance toward questioners. A clergyman's influence in his community is undoubtedly lessened considerably when he fails to demonstrate during the week the spiritual qualities he urged in last Sunday's sermon.

It is important to realize that receivers may be prejudiced against the subject but not against the arguer, or vice versa. For instance, receivers may have much animosity toward the proposal of socialized medicine but have no ill will toward the advocate; on the other hand, an audience might highly favor the advocate's proposal for lower taxes but might be antagonistic toward the advocate as a person.

The basic objective of arguers is to seek some common ground with the receivers in any given situation. If both have shared college life, skiing in the mountains, similar types of summer jobs, or have visited the same parts of the country, then there is wisdom in the arguers utilizing that linkage. If advocates are parents, they might well share family experiences with a PTA audience. It is important to seek some kind of legitimate identification with the receivers if one expects them to adhere to one's claims.

SUMMARY

Effective arguers need to engage in careful analysis of their receivers and adapt appropriately. Many sources can be tapped in order to secure helpful information about the receivers, both prior to and during the communication event. Arguers might want to discover such demographic data as: nationality and race, age, sex, size of audience, habitat, marital status, educational level, socioeconomic level, occupations, political preferences, religious views, membership in interest groups, and recreational interests. Arguers should be aware of basic universal physiological and emotional needs possessed by their receivers, and should also try to empathize with the dominant value orientations of their receivers. Finally, it is important to ascertain as clearly as possible the relationship of the receivers to the subject and their attitude toward the arguer.

EXERCISES

1. Keeping in mind the factors discussed in this chapter, write a 500-word description of the audience at any public speaking event on campus or in the community that you attend within the next two weeks. It is understood that you will have to make educated guesses about many factors. Notice the audience reactions, such as laughing, applauding, reading, or sleeping, which would give some indication of their attitudes and interests. Begin with a brief paragraph in which you explain the speech setting: the speaker, occasion, place, time, and purpose.

2. Prepare a 500-word persuasive paper on some subject, such as the role of student government at your institution. First, compose it for a student audience, then rewrite it for an audience of faculty/administrators or the general public. Identify your appeals in the margins, noting the differences in how you approach the subject.

3. Collect advertisements from newspapers or magazines and analyze their appeals in an informal classroom discussion.

4. Collect a demographic inventory of your classmates. Did such a precise cataloging reveal anything new and possibly startling that you had not noticed before, even though you thought you knew your classmates? Turn in your inventory to the instructor, and share your impressions in an informal class discussion.

5. Write a 1,000-word paper in which you compare and contrast how five textbooks treat the role of audience analysis and adaptation. Discuss the quantity of space devoted to it, what points are discussed, and the varying emphases on the selected points.

12 Arguer: Source Credibility

OVERVIEW

A basic premise in communication is that the higher the credibility of the source of the message, the greater the likelihood the message will be accepted. Arguers whom we trust and respect will be more likely to get us to adhere to their claims than will arguers for whom we have limited trust and respect. In other words, the source of the message is also a source of proof in the claim-making process. Although not so central to argumentation as it is to the wider field of persuasion, source credibility is of crucial importance to the arguer and needs to be understood.

The ancient Greeks and Romans discussed this as ethical proof, as the *ethos* of the speaker. In the last two decades an impressive number of careful experimental studies—not only in speech and communication but in such related fields as social psychology, psychology, sociology, journalism, and business—increasingly have focused on this phenomenon, verifying with greater precision the general wisdom of the ages, and generating new insights. Instead of referring to the many detailed experiments relevant to communication,[1] this chapter attempts to synthesize the findings in a clear and simplified way.

Instead of using the term *ethos*, contemporary literature in the field uses "source credibility." The term "credibility" comes from the Latin *credere*, meaning "to believe," and we are familiar with many words which spring from that origin, such as "creed," and "credentials." When something is not believable, we say it is "incredible." In our context here we are concerned with the believability, the credibility, of the arguer who is the source of some claim.

The source might be not an individual but a newspaper, a magazine, an organization, or an institution. We subscribe to newspapers or magazines, or listen to radio or television news programs, because we have built up a respect and trust for those sources of information. We build up (or fail to build up) trust and respect for what a religious organization or a business corporation tells us. Of course, the mass media have confused the concept of a "single" source, for we realize that more than one person is contributing to what a particular radio newscaster is telling us: people who report the news from the field, those who edit the report, and the scriptwriter, to name a few. When we see a brief television commercial, we know that multiple agents have had a hand in its production, such as a camera crew, copywriters, make-up people, artists, production teams, and directors. Thus, the degree to which we believe the newscast or the commercial is really a reflection of the degree to which we believe that particular network or station, or even the whole media industry. Given that the media, especially television, have the power to create images of political leaders, it becomes increasingly important that we understand the rhetorical power of source credibility. But our concern here is not with the big business of image-making via mass media, our focus is more on interpersonal and public-speaking contexts.

We need to rely on authorities in this complex society, as we discussed in the earlier chapter on evidence. We buy a particular used car because

---

1. For a summary of early studies in ethos, see Kenneth Andersen and Theodore Clevenger, Jr., "A Summary of Experimental Research in Ethos," *Speech Monographs*, 30 (1963): 59–78. An excellent, concise summary of more recent experimental findings in source credibility is the heavily documented chapter in James C. McCroskey, *An Introduction to Rhetorical Communication* (3rd ed.; Englewood Cliffs, N.J.: Prentice-Hall, 1978), pp. 67–85. Also very good are Kenneth Andersen, *Persuasion: Theory and Practice* (2nd ed.; Boston: Allyn and Bacon, 1978), pp. 235–63; and Winston L. Brembeck and William S. Howell, *Persuasion: A Means of Social Influence* (2nd ed.; Englewood Cliffs , N.J.: Prentice-Hall, 1976), pp. 251–67.

we trust the former owner who wants to sell it to us. We decide to read a particular book because a respected friend recommended it. We believe that a particular food is good for us because a noted nutritional expert said so. Certainly one central factor in whether we accept their claims is the degree to which we respect and trust them. Conversely, when we are the claim-maker, others will accept our contentions by the same criteria.

When credibility is not present, minimal acceptance of claims is probably the result. We speak of the "credibility gap" between the President and the public, industrial giants and the public, teachers and students, parents and children, and between former friends. That is, there can be a considerable gap between what one party (usually the more powerful party) says is true and what another party finds to be true. For example, the government says we have no troops in a certain country, but reporters discover that we have; a corporation claims that its product is not armful, but independent investigators demonstrate that it is. When the recipient of the message no longer trusts and respects the sender of the message, no positive influence is engendered. Until that "gap" is bridged, meaningful communication is difficult if not impossible.

Perception

It is important to realize at the outset that source credibility is not something possessed by the communicator, it is something *perceived* by the receivers. Whether we like it or not, we are judged by what others perceive us to be. It is the audience's perception of the qualifications of the speaker. A speaker may have three college degrees, ten years of relevant work experience, and unimpeachable honesty, but if the audience does not know this or does not value those particular factors very highly, then that speaker may well have low credibility as far as that audience is concerned. Obviously, some other audience, one which knows and values the listed factors, may well grant the speaker high credibility. So an advocate might have low credibility with one audience and high credibility with another one. That is hardly very mysterious, for we encounter it daily in a host of informal communicative situations. You praise Professor X, but your friend thinks she is miserable; you cannot stand a particular news commentator, but your friend admires him greatly. The two of you, as separate audiences, obviously perceive quite differently the qualities of those communicators, and would be influenced or not influenced by them accordingly.

But we ought not to put all of the stress on the audience dimension, for the speaker *does* possess factors which another speaker may not possess. One speaker has three college degrees, the second has none; the first speaker has ten years experience, the second has two. Obviously these facts are the raw material on which an audience builds an impression (if they know the facts). Thus it is probably more accurate to look at source credibility as an interaction between qualities possessed by the communicator and the audience's perception and evaluation of those qualities. That is not contradictory, it is complementary, and we secure a fuller, more complete view as a result.

But the pragmatism of any rhetorical situation is that it is the audience's perception and evaluation which determines the degree of adherence to an arguer's claims, so it is reasonable to stress the audience dimension.

This chapter will explore the various components of source credibility, the various categories of source credibility, and then summarize helpful admonitions for students who would desire to strengthen their credibility in argumentation situations.

COMPONENTS OF SOURCE CREDIBILITY

Source credibility is usually thought of as having three major components: expertness (the intellectual dimension), trustworthiness (the moral dimension), and dynamism (the social dimension). While different terms are used by different experimenters and writers, the above three broad components, despite objections by some people,[2] house all the factors with which we are concerned in source credibility.

Expertness

This focuses on the qualifications, the skill, the creativity, the innovativeness, the knowledge, the experience of the arguer. In short, we want to know the degree of *competence* of the rhetor. If the audience perceives the arguer as having a high degree of competence in the *subject at hand*, then the arguer's power to influence is increased. As we have noted in an earlier chapter, a person who is an expert in one field is not necessarily an expert in a second field; an expert on gourmet cooking is not necessarily competent in transportation issues. An audience wants to

---

2. For instance, see Jack L. Whitehead, Jr., "Factors of Source Credibility," *Quarterly Journal of Speech*, 54 (1968): 59–63.

know something about the general native intelligence and ability of the arguer: "Is he a bright person?" "How savvy is she?" "Is she a gifted individual?" "Does he have a reputation for being a thoughtful, logical person?" More specifically, how well informed is the arguer on the subject at hand? Someone might, after all, be basically intelligent but uninformed on the specific subject being considered. The audience will want to know what general education and special training the arguer has had to increase his competence. What specific course of study or training in skills has she had? What kinds of experiences has the arguer had which have further developed her expertness? How successful has he been in previous similar tasks? How long has the person been associated with the subject at hand? Someone who has worked in the legal profession for forty years would be considered more knowledgeable on a legal subject than a young person who had just been graduated from law school.

This concept of the value of seniority is built into many aspects of life (for example, becoming chairperson of legislative committees), because it is assumed that the longer the person has been associated with the subject at hand, the more informed and more competent she is. (Of course, we need not dwell on the many instances in which we have found this to be a false premise.) Business and all sorts of institutions base their reward systems on seniority, the premise being that the longer the person has been with the company or institution, the more competent and valuable she is, hence her salary and other rewards ought to be increased. Likewise, an audience "rewards" an arguer who demonstrates long association with his subject by more readily accepting his claims.

Trustworthiness

This moral dimension of credibility is more general and more difficult to pinpoint than expertness. How much faith do we have in the arguer's ethics, in being a "good" person? Is she dependable, honest, frank, sincere, fair, reliable, open-minded, earnest, simple, dedicated, courageous, mature? Can she be relied upon to keep confidential material to herself? Does she think of the welfare of others? Does she reflect an abundance of goodwill toward her audience? In short, how much can we *trust* this person? Some scholars use the term "safety" to depict this quality of trustworthiness, in the sense that such a person is one in whom we would feel "safe" to place our confidence.[3] While many people are

3. See Brembeck and Howell, *Persuasion*, p. 257.

poor judges of sincerity and some of these other qualities, their perceptions nevertheless are extremely important.

We perceive people to have a high degree of trustworthiness if they have a background of having demonstrated such qualities over a long period of time; in other words, if they have a good track record. Some especially trustworthy people in our lives may be our grandmother, a religious leader, a local grocer, or a close friend; we have grown to trust them. If an arguer holds a prestigious station in life, either in the particular job he holds or in the general respect he has engendered, we assume he has earned the trust of many people along the way and, hence, is worthy of our trust as well. It is a fact of life, however, that one misstep, one instance in which one failed to show impartiality, for example, is difficult to correct. Indeed, it may take years to regain the confidence of people because of a single instance of dishonesty or of not keeping information confidential.

Dynamism

A person campaigning for public office, for example, needs to convince the electorate that she possesses not only expertness and trustworthiness but also that she has the social engineering ability to work with people, ideas, and situations to solve community problems. She must convince people that she has the ability to "get the job done." A campaign slogan such as "Leadership you can trust" succinctly combines expertness and dynamism in the term "leadership," and trustworthiness in "trust." The job description of most public positions includes the ability to solve community problems, and if someone can project an image of being able to see a problem through to its resolution, that person will have increased credibility with most people. This image would include such qualities as aggressiveness, assertiveness, forcefulness, stamina, ambition, enthusiasm, energy, and boldness. Such a person is a hard worker, is willing to tackle anything, is a go-getter. Such a person is charismatic. Sometimes the term "showmanship" is included, but that is somewhat peripheral.

Dynamism can be manifested by such verbal and nonverbal means as a rapid rate of speaking, by energetic bodily action and gestures, or a vigorous tone of voice. But it is also manifested by a general spirit and attitude which reflects the above qualities, and by having a past record of achievements.

It is interesting to note that when we associate dynamism with negative overtones, we tend to link it with trustworthiness; that is, we just can't "trust" an excessively aggressive, fast-talking salesperson, for example. When we associate dynamism with positive overtones, we link it with expertness; that is, we feel that such a person is indeed capable of doing what needs to be done.

An additional ingredient in the social dimension of credibility is *likability*. It is the sociability, the friendliness, the warmth of the person. Such a person is cheerful and humorous, is "fun" to be with. She is courteous and kind, and shows an interest in us. She is good-looking (he is handsome). We might purchase something from a salesperson, for instance, not because of her expertness or trustworthiness (these may be largely unknown anyway), and not because of dynamism, but simply because we "liked" her. We often purchase some product, for example, an article of clothing or a bicycle, mainly because we "liked" the salesperson. We "buy" the ideas of arguers often because we "liked" the person.

These social, moral, and intellectual components of source credibility are of course interrelated; we separate them here in order to see each more clearly. A person may rate high in one or more components, but low in the others. For example, we may decide not to take our car to Mechanic X for repairs, for while we acknowledge that he is an expert mechanic, we have heard that he is prone to fix things that really do not need fixing (we do not trust him), he is slow in completing his work, and, besides, he is a grouchy, unfriendly person. Which of the components is most important will depend of course on the variables in each communicative situation, but expertness and trustworthiness are generally the two most important, especially when the subject matter is of considerable importance, and the audience is mature and perceptive. The ancients asserted that an effective rhetorician was "a good man speaking well." We can be more specific: "An effective arguer is one who reflects expertness, trustworthiness, and dynamism."

CATEGORIES OF SOURCE CREDIBILITY

Categories Based on the Agent Factor

One of the ways in which credibility is analyzed is to approach it from the standpoint of who the agent is who is making the statements about the arguer's qualifications designed to enhance the credibility of the arguer. That is, does the arguer present information about herself, or does someone else do it? If it is the former, it is *primary*, or direct, credibility; if the latter, it is spoken of as *secondary*, or indirect, credibility.

Primary credibility   When the arguer is unknown to the audience, or if the audience is misinformed about her, then the arguer may need to identify her qualifications. The arguer may announce in a straightforward manner: "I studied small engines for three years at Central Technical Institute, and have worked on them for fifteen years, so I think I know my subject rather well." A more subtle manner might be to say: "When I was graduated from Harvard. ..." Indicating relevant and meaningful relationships with other important people is an acceptable means of building credibility: "I studied for three years with the famous physicist, Professor X." However, one must avoid inappropriate and excessive name-dropping. One could indicate one's experience, the special training one has had, the positions one has held, and one's special skills. One could mention how long one has been interested in the subject, how much research one has done on it, the special information one has secured, and how hard one has labored to solve the problem. How long one has been employed in a particular position might be important to emphasize. One would be wise to indicate how one's goals, values, background, and ideas mesh with those of the audience. Age, education, cultural heritage, religion, race, traditions, and habits might be mentioned. We tend to believe people from our own socioeconomic background or those on a higher rung on the socioeconomic ladder. If the subject being discussed is a highly controversial one, then similar attitudes toward it are more important than the other aspects of common ground. Establishing such legitimate common ground with the audience should also be supplemented by showing a genuine concern for their well-being. One also would want to mention people and organizations which hold views similar to ours.

Obviously it is very important that one mentions these things about oneself in an appropriate manner and spirit, for being boastful or brazen would no doubt reduce one's credibility. But if done gracefully, accurately, and in the spirit of informing the audience, one may well enhance one's credibility. It should be realized, finally, that what may be appropriate for one audience may be inappropriate for another.

Secondary credibility   As mentioned above, when some person other than the arguer is the agent of credibility-enhancing statements about the arguer, this is spoken of as secondary or indirect credibility. In a formal speaking situation this may be the person who introduces the speaker. That is, the introducer will usually survey the speaker's training, expertise, experience, and accomplishments, will usually give some testimonial about the speaker's trustworthiness, and will link the introducer's prestige with the speaker. Thus, the speaker has the benefit of support from another person, usually someone who has high ethos with the audience, before even saying anything, or at least is assured that the audience will be told some highly favorable, factual information about herself. Sometimes the sponsor of an event is in itself an indirect testimonial. If the League of Women Voters, for example, sponsors a speaker, this suggests that it regards the speaker as a person of high credibility, or else it would not have associated itself with her. Sometimes advance information about the event is mailed out, which would give the speaker's credentials. A book publisher's biographical sketch on the back of a book jacket highlights the credibility of the author.

In the advertising field, manufacturers frequently rely on some famous entertainment figure to give testimony for their product: "Ms. X, the famous actress, likes our breakfast food." It is the use, then, of some prestigious person to support a particular commercial claim, in this case: "Our breakfast food is a good product, and you ought to buy it." It adds strength if the testifier's prestige is closely related to the product or subject; for example, a famous swimmer giving a commercial for a swimsuit. In the advertisement the person may utter the testimonial directly: "I always use Brand X swimsuits," or "I have eaten Y breakfast food for ten years." Sometimes only the person's name or picture is used alongside the product.

Categories based on the spatial dimension

When the arguer's credibility is affected by rhetorical factors within the communication transaction itself, that is, the quality of the message and its presentation, as well as the influence of the audience, occasion, and media employed, then this is referred to as intrinsic credibility. When the credibility is affected by factors external to that particular communication transaction, that is referred to as extrinsic credibility. Thus, it is the spatial dimension of being inside or outside of a particular communication episode which is being called into play to categorize the credibility.

Intrinsic credibility   If the ideas, values, motive appeals, and purposes are seen as respected and powerful ones by the audience, the arguer's credibility is likely to be enhanced. If the evidence is impressive and the reasoning is sound, the credibility of the arguer is likely to be increased. Receivers hostile to the arguer may respond favorably to strong evidence and thus the arguer's prestige may improve in their estimation. Strong evidence strengthens credibility, especially if the arguer has low credibility with the audience prior to the presentation, for the audience is more likely to scrutinize the evidence and reasoning; whereas a person with high credibility can probably get by more easily without such strong evidence. Also, strong evidence strengthens credibility particularly if the evidence is new to the audience. Citation of one's sources of evidence also may help. It is noteworthy that an increase in credibility caused by high-quality evidence and reasoning is especially effective in the long term. It should also be mentioned that omissions of certain evidence and arguments and appeals may affect the audience's perception of the arguer's credibility, either positively or negatively.

Organization and language can also affect credibility. Clear organization enhances it, as does language which is appropriate, clearly understandable, and which is not militant, opinionated, or offensive. The use of conventional grammar and good spelling has a positive effect, although with some readers these may not be so important.

Delivery in oral argumentation can definitely affect credibility. Fluent delivery, an energetic but controlled rate of speaking, a calm voice, a confident manner, and an appropriate earnestness can enhance one's credibility. When one's expression show that one has thoroughly prepared one's statements, one's credibility can increase. An arrogant, supercilious manner and a "know-it-all" attitude will lower one's credibility with most receivers. Direct eye contact, natural gestures, relaxed posture, and neat grooming will be an asset with most receivers. Physical attractiveness enhances credibility (witness the use of movie stars in commercials.) Being tall sometimes seems to help; being overweight does not. Experiments using both male and female advocates and respondents seem to confirm that men are somewhat more creditable than women (but an attractive woman is more creditable than an unattractive man). Demonstrating fairness, sincerity, and flexibility will enhance credibility, as will open-mindedness. In this regard, it may be wise to admit one's differences with the receivers on some points, for this will indicate one's willingness to be open. Answering questions from the receivers in a competent, confident, and tactful manner will add to your credibility.

In addition to delivery, language, and organization, the media of communication will also affect the arguer's credibility. If a television camera is covering one's speech, or if one's claims were reported in a television or radio newscast, one's credibility would probably be enhanced. If one were to appear on a radio or televison program, one's credibility would be heightened. In short, most people assume, correctly or incorrectly, that a person's views would not be selected for inclusion in the mass media unless the views and/or the person were not newsworthy. Hence, an arguer's claims gain in credibility simply by being carried by the mass media. Even just having one's name appear in a book, pamphlet, or any other publication, gives one added prestige.

Even the setting and occasion of a communicative event can affect the credibility of the arguer. Having respected dignitaries sitting on the platform behind the speaker gives the latter increased credibility, as might the presence of the American flag or other revered artifacts. If the occasion is an important one, such as a Fourth of July celebration, the speaker's credibility is heightened simply by the fact that he was chosen to speak at such an auspicious occasion.

Special characteristics of the receivers and the relationship between the receivers and arguer, and between the receivers and subject, can be extremely important in affecting the credibility factor. For instance, how the receivers perceive the arguer's power to reward or punish them can be an important consideration. Furthermore, credibility of the source becomes especially important when the receivers are relatively uninvolved and hence quite willing to take the word of the arguer. For example, even a moderately prestigious source might sway uninvolved receivers on a controversial issue such as abortion; whereas even a highly prestigious source might be ineffective with receivers who were strongly committed to a position on abortion. A person of high credibility would be more successful than a person with low credibility in using a strong appeal to the fear motive. If the subject matter is of great importance to the receivers, then even the high ethos of the arguer will bring about only a slight shift in attitude among the receivers. Individuals vary in the degree to which they may be influenced by the source's credibility. Some, but not all, experiments have concluded that closed-minded people in the audience tend to be more willing to accept source credibility as a form of proof. That type of mind set, apparently, is more dependent on argument from authority than is an open-minded one.[4]

In attempting to increase respect from an audience, arguers may in some situations focus on a few opinion leaders in the audience who will

4. Andersen, *Persuasion*, p. 257.

subsequently have influence over the others in any decision-making which might follow the presentation. It is the familiar "two-step flow" theory associated most often with mass communication, whereby the media aim at important opinion-makers in the society, hoping that those key people will influence positively those with whom they come in contact. These respected opinion leaders spread their perceptions of the arguer's credibility to their peers in the audience, and thus can have much influence. Sometimes these opinion leaders are quite unaware of their influence.

Obviously there can be no set formula to suggest in the creation of favorable credibility in the minds of the receivers, for too many variables are operating. But the communication act does give arguers an important opportunity to enhance their credibility with those particular receivers. Depending upon their effectiveness, their credibility can be raised, lowered, or remain unchanged.

Extrinsic credibility   The image of the arguer perceived by the receivers from sources outside of the actual communicative event is labeled extrinsic credibility. The factors which contribute to the building of this image could be many and varied. The receivers may have had some previous experience with the arguer or may have been given information about the arguer. These facts and impressions may or may not be valid, but in either case they would be operating. The arguer may have been endorsed by someone else, which will make an impact on the perceivers. A whole host of factors immediately prior to the communication act could have an influence for enhancing or reducing credibility, even such things as how the speaker walked up onto the platform, his general demeanor, and at whom he smiled. The audience might have had information on the speaker's educational background, what he has published, his attitudes and positions taken on controversial issues, and the religious, social, political, interest groups to which he belonged. We tend to give prestige according to our values and associations; that is, "athletes" will have a high credibility if we value that group in society, low if we do not. "Mechanics," "university students," "housewives," "gamblers," and any other group we may have ready-made opinions of, and, hence, perceive their credibility accordingly. We build up an expectation about people on the basis of these predispositions, either favorable or unfavorable, and then we read or listen selectively as a result. Extrinsic credibility may be of considerable help in securing an audience, for people will make the effort to come to hear someone they perceive of as possessing high credibility; they will willingly put themselves in the presence of the message. We buy books frequently because of the prior reputation of the author; likewise we go to public speeches, or listen to a conversation because we have allocated high credibility to the communicator.

Categories based on the time dimension

These factors which we have discussed using the spatial labels of intrinsic and extrinsic are sometimes approached from the temporal dimension, that is, on a time continuum. The extrinsic factors which arguers bring to a communicative event are referred to as their *initial* credibility, that is, their reputation prior to a speech or written message. It is the image which they have built up in the minds of a particular audience over the past days, weeks, or even years. It is this selective perception, based on their existing attitudes, on which the audience makes their judgments.

After being affected by the intrinsic factors during the presentation, the credibility which exists at the end of the presentation is referred to as *terminal* credibility. It may be higher or lower or the same as the initial credibility, depending upon the effectiveness of the presentation. Student A might have been originally impressed with Professor X's reputation, but after today's poor lecture the student reduces greatly his opinion of her credibility. The terminal credibility, then, is the result of the initial credibility interacting with the intrinsic factors. The terminal credibility is the extrinsic ethos of the arguer's next presentation.

This time dimension categorization is helpful, since in attempting to measure credibility in experiments, it is reasonable to do so through before and after tests. That is, the audience will be asked to rate a speaker's credibility before the speech begins, and then again immediately after the speech, thus obtaining measurements of the initial and terminal credibility, and determining the effectiveness of that presentation. The terminal credibility could be measured at some later time also, but many other intervening variables then have to be taken into account. Much of the experimental literature, thus, rather naturally speaks of initial and terminal categories.[5]

The point to be emphasized is that a speaker's perceived credibility is fluid, it is changing constantly during any presentation. So the speaker's task is to try to improve, or at least maintain, her credibility throughout

5. See McCroskey, *Introduction to Rhetorical Communication*, pp. 71–83.

the presentation. One cannot rest on one's reputation, for an audience's image of the arguer is constantly being reviewed and revised.

The development of credibility, from initial to terminal credibility, depends on the interaction among four "images" of the arguer: (1) the "real" person, which is really an abstract concept, which is the expertness, trustworthiness, and dynamism possessed by the arguer; (2) the arguer's image of herself, derived from her own introspection and from what others tell her; (3) the audience's image of the arguer; and (4) the arguer's perception of the audience's image of her credibility, as far as it is possible to secure it in terms of accuracy and completeness. The arguer tries to modify her image according to the need of the moment, but if she erroneously analyzes (2), (3), and (4), then she will arrive at a distorted image and probably will be less effective. If all four images are similar, then the arguer is on solid ground.

GENERAL CONSIDERATIONS

To increase the likelihood of making source credibility work favorably in one's argumentation, one needs to make a genuine effort to improve one's expertness, trustworthiness, dynamism, and likability. In other words, one needs to obtain proper education and training, secure meaningful experiences, develop sound moral values, refine personality qualities, and improve one's communicative abilities. Obviously, that is a big order. But what could be more important than strengthening one's own integrity and increasing one's own self-worth? We must not seek to improve our credibility by artificial pretenses, by surface image-altering, which would no doubt eventually be discovered anyway; we must, instead, *be credible*, not just *appear* to be.

But while we stress the importance of the genuine development of the above virtues, we must also stress, as we did at the outset of this chapter, how important it is for the receivers to *see* these virtues. Otherwise, one's effectiveness in making claims will not be significantly strengthened by the source credibility factor.

There obviously are no guarantees that high credibility will be utilized for good ends by any particular arguer (but of course we can only hope that it will be.) Unfortunately, arguers with high credibility might well utilize it to achieve immoral or questionable ends. For example, an habitual liar may be admired by a circle of peers for his fluency, and this prestige helps him sway them to his unhealthy point of view on various subjects.

We should remind ourselves that source credibility is simply one of many variables affecting the effectiveness of an arguer in any given communicative transaction. Over a long period of time the quality of the message rather than the quality of the source is more important in changing attitudes of receivers. That is, over a period of time, dissociation occurs between the source and the message, and the latter takes on more significance. This is referred to as the "sleeper effect."[6] In some situations demonstration is more effective than credibility, so the vacuum cleaner salesperson, for example, does not comment on the mechanism, but says, simply, "Let me show you how the cleaner picks up this mess."

Finally, we need to emphasize that more research is needed. Experiments in source credibility are more numerous and more reliable in some areas than in others. For example, there are few experiments in intrinsic credibility, and those that do exist are inconclusive; it is difficult to create and alter as desired in experimentation. It should also be noted that many of the experiments in source credibility use college students as the subjects, who are not necessarily a representative cross section of the population. But we can take comfort that the past two decades have produced a significant quantity and quality of research, so that our statements about source credibility can now be made with greater precision and assurance.

SUMMARY

Source credibility can be an important contributor to the strength of an argument. The three major components of source credibilty are expertness, trustworthiness, and dynamism, which might be thought of as intellectual, moral, and social dimensions. These qualities, as perceived by receivers, can play a significant role in the arguer's success in proving contentions. One way of categorizing source credibility is whether the arguer is making comments about herself (direct or primary credibility) or whether someone else is making the statements (indirect or secondary credibility). If the source credibility is affected by the message and its presentation, it is spoken of as intrinsic; if the factors are external to the transaction, then it is extrinsic. Finally, the credibility which the arguer has in the minds of the receivers prior to a communication transaction is termed initial credibility, and what the receivers think after the presenta-

6. McCroskey, p. 84.

tion is spoken of as terminal credibility. Much research during the past two decades has enabled us to make statements about source credibility with greater precision and assurance than previously, but more research is needed in order for us to refine our statements and insights.

EXERCISES

1. On a scale from 1 to 7 (1 is low; 7, high) rate separately the trustworthiness, expertness, dynamism, and likability of three people, for example; (1) an associate at your place of work (past or present), (2) some public official, (3) some professor or classmate, and so on. Tabulate and total the ethos "score" for each person. Give this tabulation to the instructor and include a 500-word essay in which you briefly summarize why you gave the specific ratings that you did.

2. Before a speech is given on campus or in the community, state your preconceived image of the speaker's ethos. What occurred during and immediately after the speech that altered (postitively or negatively) or reinforced your prior image? Discuss in a 500-word essay or share your analysis in an oral report to the class.

3. Study the campaign literature (billboard ads, newspaper ads, radio and television commercials, and pamphlets) of someone running for public office. Analyze the candidate's material, both printed and pictorial, noting the relative emphasis on trustworthiness, expertness, dynamism, and likability. Share your observations in an oral report to the class, bringing whatever visual aids would be available.

4. Together with four other classmates, analyze the expertness, trustworthiness, dynamism, and likability of a national or state political figure. In a panel discussion before the class, reveal and account for the similarities and differences in your analyses.

5. Prepare a five-minute speech in which you praise some person for whom you have great respect. It might be a close friend, a member of your family, a campus leader, a community leader, an athlete (or musician, scientist, doctor, grocer), someone recently deceased, or a famous figure in our nation's history. Organize the speech around the components of expertness, trustworthiness, dynamism, and likability.

13 Organizing Argumentation

INTRODUCTION

To have good ideas and good evidence is only part of the story for one engaged in argumentation, for it is also extremely important that these materials are organized effectively. Wise arrangement of claims and data is crucial, just as an army commander must know how to deploy his troops and equipment if he is to utilize their maximum effectiveness. It might be contended that the difference between noise and music is that the latter is the arrangement and structure of a multitude of isolated sounds. Humans need to hear and see patterns. For example, we choose to create constellations in the heavens, such as the "big dipper"; that is, we bring to these isolated stars some kind of meaningful pattern with which we can identify. We link them together to form entities. Likewise, all of the myriad bits of information which we may gather on some subject, like stars in the heavens or isolated sounds or unorganized troops, are diffuse and difficult to "see" and are utilized ineffectively until we arrange them into some pattern, some form. Humans bring order to facts. We impose arrangement on them.

This chapter will focus on organization in three different senses. First, it will help strengthen one's command of the basic techniques involved in briefing and outlining arguments. Second, it will explore the various formats from which one might choose when organizing one's case. Finally, it will look at organization in a macrosense, that is, it will clarify the various types of debate formats through which argumentation might be put into practice.

BRIEFING

Research has shown that logically and clearly ordered messages aid the receiver's comprehension and retention of the information.[1] Good organization becomes even more important when the ideas are more complex. Fewer studies have focused on the effect of organization on attitude change, but it is safe to contend that disorganized presentations weaken the credibility of the arguer, and, lessen the likelihood of securing the desired change of attitude. Admittedly, if recipients are highly motivated, they may be challenged by disorganized material to create some structure and hence get more involved than if the organization was laid out neatly for them, but it is unlikely that many recipients will be that highly motivated. Clear organization aids not only the recipient but also gives the presenters inner confidence, a sense of having come to grips with the subject. The more important the subject is, the more concerned we are to win adherence from our audience, the more important it becomes to organize our arguments and data well. To become better organizers, we need to have a firm command of briefing.

Nature and Purpose of a Brief

A brief is an arrangement of our reasons for making some claim. It is an overview of an entire case which presents all of the arguments on a given proposition in such a manner that the conclusion is first stated and subsequent points are reasons for accepting the conclusion. A "complete" brief includes the evidence upon which the claims rest, and the sources of the evidence. A "skeleton" brief omits the evidence and its documentation, leaving that to the arguer's note cards. The complete brief includes more time or space than would be permitted in any given

1. Arlee Johnson, "A Preliminary Investigation of the Relationship Between Message Organization and Listener Comprehension," *Central States Speech Journal*, 21 (1970): 104–07; J. Michael Sproule, *Argument: Language and Its Influence* (New York: McGraw-Hill, 1980), p. 252; Richard D. Rieke and Malcolm O. Sillars, *Argumentation and the Decision Making Process* (New York: John Wiley & Sons, 1975), p. 151.

debate or essay, or more than would be necessary to convince a particular audience. The brief is an intellectual framework, much as a blueprint is a framework for an architect. A "traditional" brief structures only one side of an issue, much like a lawyer's brief arranges the arguments for one side of the controversy. A "full" brief includes both sides of an issue. It has been wisely emphasized that one really does not understand one's own case until one thoroughly understands the case of the opposition.

A brief differs from the general outline in that the latter seeks to divide a subject into its parts, whereas a brief arranges reasons. Since division automatically creates at least two parts, every subdivision in an outline must have at least two points—a rule no doubt remembered from high school. But since only one reason may be operating to defend some contention, a subdivision in a brief may consist of only one point. This will be illustrated shortly. An outline often is made before work has begun in order to obtain a general framework and limitation to one's project; but a brief is made only after all of the information is in, in order to view and test the linkage between claims and reasons. The outline also is constructed as an aid to presentation, taking into account the need to adapt to an audience. The brief is not concerned with audience adaptation, for it is a pool of information, a storehouse of material, an inventory which is arranged in a logical manner, and from which the arguer selects what is desired for any particular argumentative occasion. A brief is understandable to anyone who sees it, whereas an outline, which may be in more abbreviated form, may be understandable only to the person constructing it.

The following short "skeleton" brief of the affirmative case on a proposition of policy should be adequate to facilitate a clarification of the rules of briefing, which will follow.

RESOLVED: That the University of Sleepy Hollow should replace all intercollegiate athletics with an expanded intramural sports program, for

NEED
STEP

I. The present athletic arrangement is unsatisfactory, for
   A. Athletes have to slight their studies, for
      1. Practice sessions are too time-consuming.
      2. Trips are too time-consuming.
   B. Athletes get preferential treatment over other students, for
      1. Scholarships for the athletes are numerous.
   C. It is too expensive, for
      1. Equipment is expensive.
      2. Travel to other universities is expensive.
   D. Athletics have become merely public entertainment.

PRACTI-
CALITY
STEP

II. An expended intramural sports program would be practical, for
   A. It is financially possible.
   B. It has been tried successfully elsewhere.
   C. It has wide support.

BENEFIT
STEP

III. An expanded intramural sports program would be beneficial, for
   A. Participants would not have to slight their studies, for
     1. Fewer practice sessions would reduce the time spent.
     2. Elimination of trips would reduce the time spent.
   B. All students would get equal treatment, for
     1. Lucrative athletic scholarships would be abolished.
     2. Whatever scholarships would be given would be open to all students.
   C. It would be less expensive, for
     1. Less elaborate equipment would be needed.
     2. Travel to other univerisites would be eliminated.
   D. Athletics would blend into the educational function of the university more appropriately.
   E. Additional benefits would also be forthcoming.

Rules for Briefing

Rule #1: The proposition should be placed at the head of the brief. In our illustration this is the resolution: "That the University of Sleepy Hollow should replace all intercollegiate athletics with an expanded intramural sports program." This is the conclusion of, and is a distinctive aspect of, a brief, in that one really begins with one's conclusion, and everything else which follows is simply in support of that proposition.

Rule #2: A complete brief should contain an introduction, a body, and a conclusion. In our illustration which is shortened to conserve space, we have omitted the introduction and conclusion, and actually have only a skeleton body.

Rule #3: The introduction, usually written after the body of the brief has been completed, should contain the following topics:

(1) A succinct comment on the timeliness and significance of the proposition; that is, a clarification of why this subject is being discussed, why a case for such a proposition is being presented.
(2) A concise statement on the origin and history of the issue. Obviously, that has to be very short, for it is intended only as a sketchy backdrop for the discussion of the issue. The arguer should try to be objective in the selection of the items, but the necessity of selecting only a few items out of the vast history realistically means that the arguer's point of view will be apparent. The audience should be aware of that. No

matter how often textbooks admonish the arguer to be objective in the introduction, it would be unrealistic not to expect the arguer's bias to appear in the selection of facts.

(3) Definition of terms. This would include not only those key terms in the proposition but also any additional central terms and concepts which will need to be clarified, in order for the debate to progress profitably. A special interpretation of the proposition by the arguer needs to be defined.

(4) Statement of any admitted (conceded) or irrelevant matter. This excludes from the debate unnecessary items, and disposing of them will permit closer concentration on those factors which are at issue.

(5) Expression of the issues. This is done in question form, for example: "Is the present athletic arrangement unsatisfactory?" This is very important, for it becomes the organizational structure for the rest of the brief.

Rule #4: The conclusion at the end of the brief summarizes the main points, concludes with an affirmation or denial of the original proposition, and may include a call for action.

Rule #5: Arrange the individual items with uniform symbols and indentations. This is illustrated in our example, and no doubt is familiar to the readers from their experience with outlining.

Rule #6: Every statement should be made in the form of a complete sentence. This permits a clear and full understanding of what is intended to be asserted. In contrast, an outline may contain abbreviated phrases or even single terms.

Rule #7: Each statement should include only one point; that is, avoid complex and compound sentences. Our illustration includes only such simple sentences, and perhaps readers at first thought it was rather simplistic and abrupt. But the important concern in a brief is that the points being made are clearly and appropriately arranged.

Rule #8: In the body of the brief each statement for which there is a subpoint should be followed by "for," which is a shortened version of the longer expression "for the following reason(s)." This indicates its relationship with the successive supporting statements. A helpful test of an appropriate linkage is to read the brief backwards, so that the subpoint is read first, followed by "therefore."

Rule #9: Proper subordination and coordination should be demonstrated. The statements labeled with the Roman numerals are on a coordinate level with each other; the statements labeled with the capital letters are on a coordinate level with each other, but are subordinate to the Roman numeral statements. Statements 1 and 2 under A are in a subordinate position to A. It is crucial that the brief shows the proper coordinate and subordinate relationship between points being made. It goes without saying that each subpoint should actually support the statement above it. No confusion or overlapping of points should occur.

Rule #10: The wording should be impersonal. Avoid the first person, such as, "I think ..."; "we assert that. ... "

Rule #11: In a "full" brief the documentation for each point may be placed in the left-hand margin next to the assertion, or in a footnote, or in parenthesis following the assertion. This has of course been excluded in our short skeleton brief.

Rule #12: In a "full" brief it also is customary to include the refutation statements which a debater anticipates making. They should clearly indicate which point is being attacked. This is also excluded in our short example.

Advantages of a Brief

A brief is a vast reservoir from which the arguer may select what is needed in a particular situation. It serves as a guide to the presenter, and, eventually, also to the receiver. It increases the likelihood that the linkages between points are strong and appropriate. It sets up the coordinate and subordinate relationshps between points. It reduces the likelihood that the arguer will omit some argument or some bit of evidence. The ethos of the arguer may be enhanced, for it will increase the likelihood that a more confident and more clear presentation will result. The receiver is more likely to accept the contentions if they are presented with clarity which the brief would foster. The brief helps the arguer see which weak points need to be strengthened. The brief helps the arguer anticipate where the opposition might attack, and thus the arguer can bolster those areas. Whenever new material is secured, it can quickly be placed into the appropriate spot in the overall case; hence the brief becomes the master filing cabinet. That ought to suggest, also, that the brief is a dynamic, growing entity, and the arguer should be quick to adjust it whenever new material or new ideas indicate that a modification is appropriate.

CASE FORMATS

Problem-Solution

In earlier chapters we have fully explored some heuristic questions related to an analysis of problems and solutions in the context of claim-making. Refer again to that discussion, for it is the problem-solution format or, as it is sometimes called, the "needs" case, or the "classical" affirmative case or the "traditional" case. The latter two terms are chosen because the problem-solution format has historically been the most often used; the "needs" label comes from the first step, which is to assert that a "need" exists for a change in the status quo. It is contended that problems exist, that the need is inherent in the status quo, that the arguer has a plan to meet the need, that the plan is practical, and that the plan is beneficial.

The short example we have included earlier in this chapter illustrates this type of format. Glance back to it for a moment. The Need Step (Roman numeral I) is a list of complaints, a list of problems which the arguer contends need to be changed, and implicitly are inherent in the present status quo of intercollegiate athletics. The Practicality Step (Roman numeral II) asserts that the plan, the solution, which in this case is "an expanded intramural sports program," is workable because it is financially possible, has been tried successfully elsewhere, and has wide support (presumably among those who will be affected, such as students, faculty, administration, parents, and alumni). The Benefit Step (Roman numeral III) is a careful point-by-point solution to the Need Step. The Benefit Step should answer each complaint, or else something would be lacking. It simply is superimposed on the Need Step, much as if you placed one hand on top of the other, with each finger of the former "covering" each finger of the latter. It will be noted that, at the very end, item E in the Benefit Step asserts: "Additional benefits would also be forthcoming," which is a standard clause included to point out that indeed one's plan not only solves the complaints but also has additional benefits. For instance, the "expanded intramural sports program," in our example, not only solves the problems cited but also may inspire alumni to give more financial aid to the school.

The problem-solution format is used frequently by all of us in our everyday informal argumentation, whether we are aware of it or not. It is a pragmatic and easily understood format which focuses on what is wrong and suggests how to correct it. It is a format used by many people in government and those running for political office, for their jobs are inherently "problem-solving" occupations. Journalists also are looking for problems in society about which to write, and they are often criticized for focusing too much on the problems and not enough on the solutions.

Modified Problem-Solution

A modified version of this format is one in which the arguer holds that the status quo has certain strengths, a number of good things exist, but certain inherent shortcomings are present, and then the arguer goes on to present a plan, as above. This is less threatening to those who are attached to the status quo, and thus they may give their assent to the proposal more readily.

Comparative Advantages

In the 1960s in intercollegiate debate circles the comparative advantages case increased in popularity,[2] and "by the 1970s it was probably the most widely used affirmative analysis by varsity debaters on the national circuit."[3]

The comparative advantages approach focuses "more on securing future advantages than on solving present problems."[4] It does not emphasize that something is wrong with the status quo but instead contends that a particular proposal will make conditions even better. Its central rationale is, "If the present policy is good, think how much better it would be with the addition of this advantage."[5] It proposes small, incremental changes, small improvements; it adds to the strengths already present in the status quo. It is like contending: "Let's strengthen our already fine athletic program by adding soccer." A meat company has as its slogan: "When you're having a good time, [our product] makes it better!" There is no complaining about the status quo, but there is a claim that new proposals will enrich life even more. The comparative

2. Bernard L. Brock, "The Comparative Advantages Case," *The Speech Teacher*, 16 (1967): 118–23; James W. Chesbro, "The Comparative Advantages Case," *Journal of the American Forensic Association*, 5 (1968); 57–63; John Cragan and Don Shields, "The Comparative Advantages Negative," *Journal of the American Forensic Association*, 7 (1970): 85–91; David Zarefsky, *The Comparative Advantage Case* (Evanston, Ill.: Championship Debate Enterprises, 1970).
3. Austin J. Freeley, *Argumentation and Debate: Rational Decision Making* (4th Ed.; Belmont, Calif.: Wadsworth, 1976), p. 185.
4. W. Scott Nobles, "Analyzing the Proposition," in Douglas Ehninger and Wayne Brockriede, *Decision by Debate* (2nd ed.; New York: Harper & Row, 1978), p. 169.
5. Rieke and Sillars, *Argumentation*, p. 174.

advantages case stresses that its advantages are significant, compelling ones, that they are inherent in the proposal (that is, they come directly from it), and that the benefits are unique to the proposal, that is, they cannot be secured elsewhere.

It is different, not in kind but in emphasis, from the traditional problem-solution case. Its relationship may be thought of in three possible ways: (1) it implies that no problem exists; (2) it implies that the problem is so obvious that there is little point in spending time on it; or (3) it actually is a subltle, indirect way of asserting that a problem exists, for, after all, "If those advantages are inherent, then it might be said that the very lack of those advantages constitutes a 'need.'"[6] Whichever of those views is taken, the comparative advantages case proceeds from what already exists, and hence may antagonize fewer receivers, for the emphasis is not on destroying the status quo but on building on it.

Ideal Criteria

In this approach the arguers set up ideal criteria which they wish to be met, and then proceed to demonstrate that their proposal does indeed meet those criteria. For example, in choosing a new president of the university the search committee might specify that the person to be eventually selected must fulfill to a high degree the following criteria: must have had experience in administration; must have had experience as a classroom teacher; must have published scholarly books or articles; should possess a sense of humor; and should be able to communicate effectively with the public. When the committee finally makes its recommendation, it becomes a collective arguer, claiming that its selected candidate meets all those criteria to an unusual extent. To take another example, suppose Don is looking for lodging in a rooming house while attending the university, and he sets up criteria (perhaps unknown to himself) against which each place he looks at is measured. When he has made his final selection, he presents a case to himself, so to speak, in which he tries to convince himself that the chosen rooming house best meets his prior criteria of: close to the university; near a city bus line; inexpensive; pleasant landlord; and a reasonably good view. This ideal criteria approach is argument from definition, that is, the case is in a sense defined ahead of time, and it is merely a matter of matching some proposal (for example, selection of rooming house or selection of

6. Robert C. Dick, *Argumentation and Rational Debating* (Dubuque, Iowa: Wm. C. Brown, 1972), p. 49.

university president) to that preformed list of prerequisites, indicating how the selected proposal fulfills those objectives. This focuses heavily on value judgments, but also on facts.

The problem-solution and comparative advantages formats also include ideal criteria, but do not highlight them so centrally. The plans that they propose are put forward precisely because they fit, implicitly if not explicitly, certain prerequisites. The "expanded intramural program," for instance, had to measure up to such criteria no doubt as a program which would reach a large number of students, would not involve expensive equipment, would not demand unusual height or weight qualifications of the participants, and would not demand highly complicated skills.

Public Opinion

Similar to the criteria format, another *a priori* format is the public interest or public opinion format, whereby one determines what the public wants, and then proceeds to create a proposal to meet their desires. Public opinion polls are one means available to public officials, who thus create programs to match the results of the poll; and they proceed to justify and to sell the program on that basis. A public official puts forth a plan to preserve intact a particular wilderness area, since recent polls have indicated that people in that state favor such a proposal. "What the people want is what ought to be done," is the rationale behind this argumentative format.

"The people" should be thought of in more limited contexts, too, of course. Suppose two couples are planning to double date. One girl wants to see a certain movie, so her boyfriend tries to convince the other couple that the foursome should go to that movie, because "that's what she wants." His girlfriend in that instance is "the public." She no doubt had various criteria in mind when she made her selection: the movie is a comedy, which she enjoys; the theatre is a nice one; it is not too far away; it is not too expensive; her favorite actress is in the movie. The movie meets her criteria for an enjoyable movie, but the only criterion her boyfriend operates on is "that's what she wants."

Method of Residue

This is the surveying of all possible options, showing how all but one's own are not sufficiently workable or beneficial. For example, after Peter has demonstrated that all the suggested plans for handling campus auto parking are not acceptable, he then comes to the one plan left (for example, underground parking), which is what he advocates as the best option. This leaves the receivers with "this or nothing" option, that is, since all other possibilities have been rejected, this last one is presumably better than nothing. In a sense, physicians do this in their diagnoses; possible causes of the patient's symptoms are checked out and eliminated; the one which survives the scrutiny is the probable cause of the problem. Small groups often arrive at decisions by this route, whereby possible solutions to a problem are examined and discarded until the option that remains is the strongest, the residue; or in selecting a group leader, knowing who they do not want eventually leads to the choice of the person who remains as the one with the least amount of opposition.[7]

Preventive Case

This focuses on the future rather than on the present. It offers a proposal which is designed to prevent some particular problem from occurring. For example, it might advocate a system of flood control to prevent the future inundation of valuable farm lands, or it might urge the creation of a summer athletic program for youths to prevent juvenile delinquency from developing. Its "need" step is a prediction of what will likely be a problem in the future (based in part on its current existence in embryonic form), otherwise it is very similar to the traditional problem-solution format.

Acceptable-to-the-Less-Acceptable

This highlights the audience dimension, for the arguer begins with those points likely to be agreed to by the receivers. Step by step the arguer then moves to additional points on which opposition is more likely to be forthcoming. For example, suppose student leaders want to urge a number of proposals to the university administration. Based on what they anticipate the administration's attitude to be, the students might present their points in the following order: (1) an increased number of study days prior to final examinations, (2) regular student-administration meetings, (3) an enlarged student union building, and (4) lower tuition. This procedure enables advocates to begin with helpful

7. Ernest G. Bormann, *Discussion and Group Methods: Theory and Practice* (2nd ed.; New York: Harper & Row, 1975), p. 254.

common ground with the receivers, strengthening the relationship with them, and tempering the opposition on the more controversial points to come.

Moral Issue

This is a focus which contends that while the status quo is working satisfactorily from a pragmatic point of view, it nonetheless may raise a moral issue. For example, the development of nuclear weapons may be proceeding satisfactorily as far as weapon production is concerned, but it raises serious moral questions for the scientists involved and for government officials who would have to make the decision to use such lethal weapons. Compulsory military training may work well, but some citizens claim that the morality of youth is corrupted by such an experience.

Obviously these kinds of cases are heavily philosophical in nature, and deal with values. Recently it has been urged that propositions of value should be occasionally used in tournament debate instead of only the traditional propositions of policy.[8]

Two-sided vs. One-sided Presentation

Arguers have historically puzzled over the relative wisdom of presenting only their side of an issue or presenting both sides, stressing of course their chosen side. Some interesting research over the years has concluded (although not too conclusively) that in certain situations it is more effective to present both sides, thus somewhat challenging the older view that it is better to present only one's own side of the issue.[9] Specifically, research has suggested that it may be wise to present both sides, if the decision-makers, the receivers, are educated beyond the high school level; if the decision-makers are likely to be exposed to the opposing view anyway, from some other source at some other time; and if the

8. Ronald J. Matlon, "Debating Propositions of Value," *Journal of the American Forensic Association*, 14 (1978): 194–204. See also Joseph W. Wenzel, "Toward a Rationale for Value-Centered Argument," *Journal of the American Forensic Association*, 13 (1977): 150–58. Matlon notes that only once, in 1921–22, has a proposition of value been the national debate topic. A list of the national intercollegiate debate propositions from 1920 to 1976 can be found in Freeley, *Argumentation*, pp. 418–21. The topic in 1921–22 was "Resolved: That the principle of the 'closed shop' is unjustifiable."

9. For concise summaries of some of the research, see Sproule, *Argument*, pp. 253–54; and Kenneth E. Andersen, *Persuasion: Theory and Practice* (2nd ed.; Boston: Allyn and Bacon, 1978), pp. 148, 150–51.

decision-makers are initially opposed to one's point of view. Thus, the audience dimension is a crucial variable.

Some exceptions do appear, however. Research has suggested that it is wiser to present only a one-sided version if the decision-makers will be likely to hear an opposing one-sided speech within a week's time. Another exception is when the decision-makers are highly ego-involved in the decision. In such a situation the receivers will tend to reject opinions differing from their own.

The arguer has to assess carefully each situation and try to determine the relative wisdom of presenting one or both sides of the issue. But it is also important to remember that most social issues have more than two sides, so that a multisided view may, in certain situations, be a wise approach. Obviously, time and space often dictate how fully we will be able to explore points of view which vary from ours, because, after all, the chief purpose of arguers is to present their own central claim.

Climactic vs. Anticlimactic Order

Literary works traditionally build to a climax. Their task is to retain the reader's interest throughout, hence the concept of resolving tensions only at the very end. Up until the last four decades, oral communication seemed to accept that same general climactic approach. Researchers finally began to question that premise, however, and now have different specific admonitions for students of argumentation.[10]

It is suggested that the anticlimactic order, that is, presenting the strongest argument first, is more effective if (1) the decision-makers are likely to be antagonistic to the arguer's point of view; (2) the decision-makers are uninterested in the arguer's case; or (3) the decision-makers are highly ego involved in the subject. It is suggested that the anticlimactic order helps the audience remember the material better, and results in a greater shift of opinion toward the arguer's claim on the most important of the points presented. While there are some conflicting findings on the relative strength of placing the strongest material first or last, research does seem to agree that the poorest location is in the middle. All of this assumes, of course, that arguments can clearly be distinguished as strongest, average, and weakest in terms of their contribution to a given claim, and that their probable impact on the receivers can be meaningfully measured. It also assumes that placing

10. For concise summaries of some of the research, see Sproule, *Argument*, pp. 254–55; and Andersen, *Persuasion*, pp. 171–72.

them in varying sequences can make a significant difference. These assumptions still need to be tested more.

The anticlimactic order operates on the premise of association, that is, that the strongest point early in the presentation will catch the attention and win the respect of the receivers, and that this will then transfer to the following points, making them seem perhaps even stronger than they are. Students, for example, soon learn that it is wise to exert a strong effort at the beginning of each school term, to impress the instructor quickly of their high qualifications, so that this favorably influences the instructor's judgment of their subsequent work.[11]

Closely related to climactic and anticlimactic order are the law of primacy, placing material early in the presentation, and the law of recency, placing material last, that is, the most "recent" position as one looks back on the presentation. The distinction is succinctly expressed by Andersen: "Primacy and recency are matters of placement; climax and anticlimax deal with the psychological or perceived importance of the material."[12]

It is clear that the large number of variables to which we have alluded, such as the subject matter and the receiver's knowledge of, interest in, and commitment to, the proposition, have to be carefully considered in each situation.

Summary of Formats

These varying formats are not so categorically distinct or mysterious as the first look at the list probably suggested to the reader. In fact, most of them might be viewed as modifications of the basic problem-solution format; each of them simply emphasizes one aspect of that overall format. One might view them as follows, realizing that the general percentages given are merely simplistic and indicative and are not to be thought of as being precise. The problem-solution format devotes approximately 50 percent of its focus on the need for a change and 50 percent on the proposal to solve that need. The modified problem-solution format admits strengths in the status quo (about 25 percent),

---

11. Of course, that may boomerang. Instructors may raise their expectations, and if the student does not continue to fulfill them, the instructors may feel that the student is being lazy. Or a student may encounter an instructor who actually judges each effort individually, refusing to be influenced by the quality of earlier work.

12. Andersen, *Persuasion*, p. 172.

then attacks the status quo's weaknesses (about 25 percent), and then devotes about 50 percent of the emphasis to the solution. The comparative advantages approach spends zero percent on the problem, but focuses 100 percent on the solution. The ideal criteria format also focuses 100 percent on the solution, but highlights the criteria which are behind the selection of the solution. The public opinion format also focuses 100 percent on the solution, highlighting the selectors of the criteria. The method of residue focuses 100 percent on the solution step, eliminating unsatisfactory options until the one remaining is selected. The preventive case approach may vary considerably in each situation; it may be 50 percent on the problem and 50 percent on the solution, or it may alter those percentages, depending upon where the arguer feels the stress should be placed. The acceptable-to-the-unacceptable format is even more audience centered, and the amount of time/space devoted to the problem and solution will vary considerably depending upon the particular situation. The moral issues format may focus on either the problem or solution; it may admit that a given aspect of the status quo is working well, but its very success raises some moral issues.

DEBATE FORMATS

A variety of ways exist for structuring a debate program. They might be grouped into six major types: (1) standard debate format, (2) cross-examination debate, (3) heckling debate, (4) direct-clash debate, (5) parliamentary debate, and (6) mock-trial debate. The times listed for individual speakers can of course be modified to meet the demands of classroom, radio or televison, or other progammatic context considerations, wherever the debate takes place, and under what conditions, and for what purposes.

All of the formats have the same overriding objectives of providing a format in which claims can be offered, challenged, and defended in an atmosphere of openness and fairness, in order for truth to be approximated to the greatest possible extent. In training situations, such as in collegiate classroom or contest situations, the added specific objectives are training in such things as research processes, testing of evidence, organizing of material, quick thinking, effective use of language, smoothness of delivery, general confidence of manner, courtesy and tact under stress, and general maturity in dealing with ideas and people.

Standard Collegiate Debate

The format which used to be the traditional one employed in intercollegiate debates in the United States is the following:

First affirmative constructive speech	10 minutes
First negative constructive speech	10
Second affirmative constructive speech	10
Second negative constructive speech	10
First negative rebuttal	5
First affirmative rebuttal	5
Second negative rebuttal	5
Second affirmative rebuttal	5
	60 minutes

This traditional debate format is sometimes used in a variety of modified forms. The *three-person team*, used heavily at the turn of the century, is seldom used today, despite its advantage of allowing for more participants. The *one-rebuttal debate* calls for only one rebuttal speech:

First affirmative	5 minutes
First negative	10
Second affirmative	10
Second negative	10
An affirmative person	5

Another variation is to have *split-team debates*, that is, one member of a given school is teamed up with one member from the second school. This is often done when British debate teams tour the United States; the affirmative team and the negative team will each be composed of one member of the British team and one member of the host United States university. This reduces institutional and international rivalry, but it does make serious teamwork rather difficult, resulting in somewhat lighthearted debates, more suited for an entertainment program than a serious clash of issues.

Two-person debate forums are another good modification for a program with a general audience. A moderator will give a five-minute introduction of the issue, the procedure, and the participants. Then the affirmative speaker and the negative speaker will each present a ten-minute speech (or longer, of course) followed by questions from the audience. A variation on this is for the opening affirmative speech to be only eight minutes, and after the ten-minute negative speech, the affirmative will be permitted a two-minute rebuttal prior to the questions from the audience. This two-person debate forum is well adapted to radio and television as well as to face-to-face audience context. The handling of questions from the audience can be done either by having them stand and state the question orally or having them write the question which ushers would then take to the speakers. Radio or television audiences could phone in questions.

A final modification of the traditional orthodox debate format is the *dialectic debate*. Instead of constructive speeches, each team develops their case through a dialogue:

Affirmative team through direct questions to each other establish their case	15 minutes
Negative team through direct questions to each other establish their case	15
Affirmative team cross-examines the negative team	10
Negative team cross-examines the affirmative team	10
One person on the negative team presents a summary	5
One person on the affirmative team presents a summary	5
	60 minutes

This can be rather interesting for the audience, but the cases are likely to lack coherence and conciseness.

Cross-Examination Debate

Growing in popularity during the 1970s and now the most common one on the debate scene is the cross-examination debate format. Its format is as follows, with slight variations possible in the time allocations:

First affirmative constructive speech	8 minutes
Second negative cross-examines	3
First negative constructive speech	8
First affirmative cross-examines	3
Second affirmative constructive speech	8
First negative cross-examines	3
Second negative constructive speech	8
Second affirmative cross-examines	3
First negative rebuttal	4
First affirmative rebuttal	4
Second negative rebuttal	4
Second affirmative rebuttal	4
	60 minutes

For a general audience situation the following simplified two-person format often is more satisfactory:

Affirmative constructive speech	12 minutes
Negative cross-examines	4
Negative constructive speech	12
Affirmative cross-examines	4
Negative rebuttal-summary	5
Affirmative rebuttal-summary	5
	42 minutes

The purposes are to facilitate the gathering, clarifying, and analyzing of data, the testing of premises, and the exposing of weaknesses in the opposition's analysis, and to weaken the credibility of the opposition. When used well, it can clarify issues and facilitate a direct clash. It trains a person to be not only a set speaker but also a questioner and a respondent. It develops the ability to construct a well-thought-out line of questioning, a series of questions whereby questions arise out of answers given, all leading to some predetermined objective. It fosters quick thinking and quick phrasing; it demands instant analysis and adaptation, which in turn demands thorough preparation. In short, it requires expertise in subject matter, in intellectual analysis, and in communication ability.[13]

The nature of cross-examination debate reflects the kinds of argumentation situations encountered in the courtroom, in legislative hearings, in public forums, in academic debating, in classroom settings, and in everyday situations. Thus, it provides students with very helpful training. But there are potential drawbacks to it. It may limit the number of points that can be covered thoroughly, for it tends to hit the surface of a number of points. Valuable time may be consumed by the lengthy and involved questioning or the evasive tactics of the respondents. It also may inject personality considerations too much into the proceedings, and may tend to honor showmanship and an aggressive spirit.

Heckling Debate

A modification of the cross-examination type of debate is what is called the "heckling" debate. Here the questioning is done during the speech,

13. For a fuller discussion of cross-examination debate, including numerous guidelines for questioners and respondents, see George W. Ziegelmueller and Charles A. Dause, *Argumentation: Inquiry and Advocacy* (Englewood Cliffs, N.J.: Prentice-Hall, 1975), pp. 213–26. See also Freeley, *Argumentation*, pp. 326–29.

rather than after, and the questioners may be either the opponents or the audience. The format is as follows:

First affirmative speaker	10 minutes
First negative speaker	10
Second negative speaker	10
Second affirmative speaker	10

Often there are no rebuttal speeches, but the normal five-minute rebuttal by each speaker might be used. It is customary not to permit questioning during the first three or during the last two minutes of the speeches. It is also common to permit only a maximum of four interruptions during any speech. The second affirmative speaker is not permitted to introduce new arguments during the final two minutes. The questioners (hecklers) should phrase short and relevant questions, should deal only with main points, major faults in reasoning, and significantly weak evidence, and should exhibit good taste even though they admittedly are trying to unnerve the speaker. The major objective is to expose weaknesses in vital areas of the opposition's case, not merely to harass the speaker. Thus, the term "heckle" is misleading, for it tends to suggest meaningless and obnoxious behavior.

Weaknesses of the procedure are that it may intensify conflicts, may get too much into personality factors, and will be less coherent and organized. The speakers cannot possibly have material available to handle every challenge, so they may be totally flustered or may be encouraged to bluff and bluster. On the other hand it is excellent experience to have to respond to a "real-life" situation in having to respond to interruptions; and, actually, it often strengthens the speakers, most of whom discover that being interrupted is not all that threatening, that they are better informed than their questioners, and that listening to the questioner gives one a chance to catch one's breath.

Direct-Clash Debate

For a two-person team the format could be as follows (actually up to five members on each team could be feasible):

First affirmative defines terms, states issues, states plan	5 minutes
First negative reacts to definitions, proposes issues as seen from their perspective, and may propose a counterplan	5

The judge might enter in at this point, giving a point to that side which did the better job. Actually, the judge may halt the debate here or after any future clash over issues if the judge feels that one team has gained a clear superiority.

Second affirmative develops one basic issue	4 minutes
Second negative deals with that issue	3
First affirmative deals with that issue	3
First negative deals with that issue	3

The judge gives a point to one side.

Second negative develops a second issue (Note: the negative and affirmative alternate in initiating clashes on issues)	4 minutes
Second affirmative deals with that issue	3
First negative deals with that issue	3
First affirmative deals with that issue	3

The judge gives a point to one side.

The team that wins three clashes wins the debate, or the judge, as indicated, can declare the winner at any of the intervals noted. The procedure has been compared to a boxing match, with the boxers given points at the end of each round, and indeed one boxer may win by a knockout in any round.

A drawback to the direct-clash debate is that by analyzing each issue by itself, it does not get at the interrelatedness of issues, and, also, it may be difficult to secure the necessary type of well-qualified judges. But it is an interesting format for participants and audience, and by excluding minor issues it helps focus attention on the major ones. It is a procedure which is especially helpful for intrasquad practice. It could be modified by omitting the expert judge, and having the audience score the points or fill in shift-of-opinion ballots at the end of the debate.

Parliamentary Debate

This is patterned after the British parliamentary format in the British House of Commons and in British university Debating Union Societies such as Oxford and Cambridge. A "Speaker" or presiding officer is "in the chair."

First affirmative—proposes a motion	10 minutes
First negative—opposes that motion	10
Second affirmative—seconds the motion	7
Second negative—opposes the motion	7
First affirmative—summing up	5

During the speeches, the chair can interrupt, and the audience can raise questions, as long as the questions are seeking information. Following the conclusion of the above speeches, an open forum period follows in which members of the audience can make statements; usually a time limit of five minutes per speaker is enforced. Also, no one in the audience may speak more than once. As far as possible, speakers for and against the motion are selected alternatively by the chair. After a certain period of time the audience votes for or against the motion.

This British style of debate, which is found, with slight modifications, throughout those parts of the world that once constituted the British Empire, is characterized by a seating arrangement which is significant for the debating process. The debating chambers are fairly small, with rows of benches facing each other, with the Government benches to the right of the Speaker, and the Opposition benches to the left. The style of speaking is conversational and informal, and compared with American debate, is more witty, literary, and philosophical. British university debating is more reliant on humor, emotion, and is more concerned with pleasing the audience; it does not have the teamwork, the extensive evidence, logic, and seriousness of the American debating teams.

Mock-Trial Debate

A typical format would be as follows, with all roles being filled by students:

A judge gives background and clarification of procedure	3 minutes
Plaintiff's attorney outlines his case	3
Defendent's attorney outlines her case	3
Plaintiff's attorney calls his three witnesses, and questions each one for four minutes	12
Defendent's attorney may cross-examine each witness, asking each one a maximum of three questions	6
Defendent's attorney calls her three witnesses and questions each one for four minutes	12
Plaintiff's attorney may cross-examine each witness, asking each one a maximum of three questions	6
Defendent's attorney sums up and makes final plea	3
Plaintiff's attorney sums up and makes final plea	3
	51 minutes

After instructions from the judge, the jury votes.

Audience may discuss.

It is obvious that this format is especially good for prelaw students, but it is an interesting variation of debate for many other students as well. It dramatizes the clash of ideas, and enables claims to be made and challenged within a realistic, specific case context.

SUMMARY

This chapter has examined briefing of arguments, the various case formats which the arguer might use, and the many formats that might be used when planning a debate program. The nature, purpose, and advantages of a brief were surveyed, and rules for briefing were listed, using a sample skeleton brief. The many potential case formats included the following: problem-solution, modified problem-solution, comparative advantages, ideal criteria, public opinion, method of residue, preventive case, acceptable-to-less-acceptable, moral issue, two-sided vs. one-sided presentation, and climactic vs. anticlimactic order. The various debate formats included: standard collegiate debate, cross-examination debate, heckling debate, direct-clash debate, parliamentary debate, and mock-trial debate.

EXERCISES

1. Take careful and thorough notes on a speech given by some advocate on campus or in the community. Afterward, reconstruct a detailed brief which shows the framework of the case which was presented. Evaluate the strengths and weaknesses of the case.

2. Analyze a television news interview program, such as *Issues and Answers*, and note the types of questions asked. Do clear lines of questioning emerge? What techniques are used? Also evaluate the responses. How evasive were they? Summarize your observations in a 500-word paper.

3. Construct a five-minute speech in which you advocate a point of view on a subject of significance to you and your classmates. Give the instructor a brief of your presentation. Be prepared to respond to questions from the audience for two minutes following your speech.

4. Attend a presentation by your school's debaters, be it some inter-school contest, a public program, or an intrasquad practice. Reconstruct the case as clearly and as thoroughly as possible. Give the instructor a brief of both the affirmative and negative cases. Write a 500-word evaluation of *one* of the sides, citing both strengths and weaknesses.

5. In the *Journal of the American Forensic Association* are found transcriptions of the final rounds in annual National Debate Tournaments. Using that source, study the handling of data and arguments, and also study the judge's comments. Write a concise 500-word summary of your observations.

14 Attacking Arguments: Refutation

Introduction
Overview of Refutation
Attacking Evidence and Reasoning
Special Methods of Refutation
Summary
Exercises

INTRODUCTION

As was discussed in the first chapter, we live in a society which values highly the notion that truth is more likely to be approximated if opposing views can be freely and openly expressed. Rooted in the ancient Athenian tradition of the democratic, open society, we encourage rather than suppress the expression of opposing views. We labor in the faith that truth will spring from the uninhibited clash of opposing views.

People who have made a habit of looking at both sides of every issue, of being at home with the give-and-take of refutation and rebuttal, are much less fearful of ideas that are different from their own and are much less likely to be unduly influenced by charismatic and compelling persuaders. Some people try to hide from ideas that are contrary to their own; which, even if it were desirable, is not possible in today's world of mass communication. Looking at all sides of an issue develops an open-mindedness toward, and a sense of tolerance of, contrary views, as well as toward people of different persuasions. We are helped to realize that those who hold views contrary to ours are not necessarily villainous people.

Throughout this chapter the term "opponents," or "opposition," is frequently used. It is important to understand the significance of this terminology in order to clarify the vast difference between opponent and enemy. Watergate, with its enemy list, reminded us how dangerous it is to democracy to think of those who oppose us as enemies. If they are indeed enemies, this seems to permit a person to use any kind of means to counteract them; opponents demand that our means are just, and that even if we do not agree with our antagonists, we respect their right and responsibility to differ.

Argumentation does not take place in a vacuum, for opponents are present, will usually attack some of the claims put forth, and then the original claim-maker will engage in counterrefutation, and on and on. Whether this exchange takes place in the debating chambers of Congress, in the courtroom, in an intercollegiate debate, in the dormitory, in the classroom, around the kitchen table, or on a date, the process of refutation is central to the flow of the communicative exchange.

It is the purpose of this chapter to help students gain a fuller understanding of this process of refutation. After presenting an overview, we will survey the attacking of reasoning and evidence, and then discuss some special methods of refutation.

OVERVIEW OF REFUTATION

Definition

The term refutation comes from the Latin *refutare*, meaning "to repulse." In argumentation, we endeavor to "repulse," "attack," "weaken," "destroy," "block" the claims of other people. We try to cast significant doubt on, show the inadequacies of, their arguments, so that an audience of decision-makers (which may or may not include our opponents) will lessen their adherence to the claims of others. Rebuttal, or resubstantiation, refers to the rebuilding of one's case which has been attacked by the opponent. Since refutation usually takes place within a broad context of two clashing cases, actually, both tearing down and rebuilding, refutation and rebuttal, are constantly going on. Exposing weaknesses in the opposition's case is generally more effective than presenting a new counterargument, for the latter depends on winning acceptance for its data and reasoning.[1] The previous chapter, on organizing argumentation, approached argumentation from the perspective of the initial claim-maker in an argumentative context (the affirmative case in debate); this chapter approaches it from the perspective of the secondary claim-maker (the negative case). But as the initial claim-maker will come back with counterrefutation and rebuttal, this chapter is pertinent to both arguers. Essentially, then, we define refutation as the attempt to weaken or destroy an argument with which we disagree, and we may or may not rebuild our case after it has been attacked.

When to refute

Whether in informal argumentative situations or in a formal debate, whenever one disagrees with what has been said, one may be moved to engage in refutation. Usually one would want to launch one's attack as soon as possible. Debaters are admonished to bring their refutation early into their presentations, for it reduces more quickly the impact of the claims of the opposition. Two standard procedures in debate are to begin one's speech by refuting what the previous speaker said and then go into one's own case, or to weave one's refutation into one's presentation at the appropriate places. The latter is usually more powerful and more damaging, but also more difficult. At times, one actually may want to save one's refutation for the end of the presentation. Obviously each situation is different, and in informal argumentative situations, as well as in formal debate, one will have to determine in each instance just when in the exchange it is more appropriate to insert one's refutation.

Research has reinforced experience in making clear that refutation which comes before the attack is significantly effective.[2] That is, preexposure to a weakened form of argument, like preexposure to a weakened form of a disease (for example, diphtheria inoculation), helps to reduce its impact. Hence, the term "inoculation" is used to describe this preventive approach in refutation. One seeks to weaken an attack by alerting the audience to it before the opposition launches it. In a debate the first affirmative speaker may say: "The negative team will no doubt claim that unemployment is not at a serious level, and admittedly it is not in certain isolated areas, but I can assure you that it is an enormous

1. Vernon E. Cronen, "The Interaction of Refutation Type, Involvement, and Authoritativeness," In Jane Blaknenship and Hermann G. Stelzner (eds.), *Rhetoric and Communication* (Urbana, Ill.: U. of Illinois Press, 1976), pp. 155–70.
2. See James C. McCroskey, *An Introduction to Rhetorical Communication* (3rd ed.; Englewood Cliffs, N.J.: Prentice-Hall, 1978), pp. 39, 64–66, 111.

problem in the nation as a whole. Just listen to these figures, and listen to this testimony. ..."

In some situations a debater may find it wise to withhold refutation until the opponents have overextended themselves, until they have fully exposed their arguments and evidence. Some nations have historically used this as a military technique with great success. Russia, for example, has allowed an invading army to penetrate deeply into their territory until, inevitably, the invaders far outdistance their supply lines and become cut off, isolated, from the source of their matériel. At that point the Russians have successfully counterattacked. By encouraging the opposition to expose fully its arguments and evidence, advocates get a clearer and fuller view of what it is they have to refute, and can proceed to attack with more precision and confidence. One lets the opposition's own momentum throw them off balance. One avoids a head-on confrontation until they are exposed, weary, and isolated, then one picks the time and place to attack. One lets them contribute to their own defeat. This procedure may be particularly helpful in argumentative situations which extend over a period of time, say, weeks or months, such as a campaign to get certain concessions from one's employer or parents.

Know the Target Audience

Since proof is whatever moves the audience to adhere to one's claims, it becomes crucial in refuting claims, as well as in making original claims, to know one's target audience. This may or may not include the antagonist. If one is trying to change the mind of one's roommates, then they are the target, but if two senators are debating, they are trying to win over other senators, not each other. The impact on the specific decision-making audience is the test of one's success. If one is trying to refute claims made by one's parents, or one's employer, one has to know what will impress *them*. In a debate tournament, it might help if one knew the basic attitudes of the judge. If the audience is composed of many people, one would find it an advantage to possess some general insights into their interests, experiences, education, and preferences. During an oral presentation of one's arguments, one will want to observe carefully nonverbal (as well as verbal, of course) messages from the audience, so one can estimate more accurately how well one's refutation is succeeding.

Know One's Case

Excellence in refutation depends not on some superficial verbal manip-
ulation but on how well one has done one's homework, how well one has
immersed oneself in all aspects of the issue. There is no short cut. In
order to engage effectively in the spontaneous cut-and-thrust of refutation, one must know one's material thoroughly.

Know the Opponent's Case

It is of fundamental importance that one knows the opponent's case as
well as one knows one's own. The clash of debate in legislatures or in
informal contexts increases in excellence and significance if both sides
are conversant with each other's case. It is built into college debate
training programs and tournaments that the participants have to debate
both sides of the proposition, not to lessen their commitment to truth
but to increase their knowledge of all sides of the subject. Knowing the
opposition's arguments increases one's confidence, stimulates quicker
rejoinders, and strengthens the overall presentation of one's case. Of
course, one may occasionally encounter a trick case in a debate tournament, or a surprise twist in other argumentative situations, but even so,
one will be able to adjust more effectively than if one did not thoroughly
know the opposition's traditional arguments. Realistically, one may not
know their case in total, but at least one generally will not have to
contend with *major* surprises.

Select Only the Important Material to Refute

If the opposition makes numerous points, one would be wise to
concentrate the refutation on only those few which are the most
important, according to one's best judgment or according to the emphasis given by the opposition. The assumption is that by weakening the
strongest pillars, one weakens the whole structure of the opposition's
case. For example, suppose Ann's roommates want her to join them in
going to a particular movie for three or four reasons but *mainly* for the
purpose of enjoying some light entertainment. Ann points out that the
suggested movie is a heavy psychological drama, and would hardly be
light entertainment; hence their major reason is destroyed. (Of course,
they may well invent other strong reasons.) In an argumentative
situation time may not permit an advocate to cover everything, and,

anyway, one may convince the audience more effectively by helping them focus on only the few major points. Time and energy spent on a "shotgun" approach may be time and energy wasted; it may well be wiser to use a "rifle" and destroy a few important targets. Also, one may want to group related points in order to refute many with one timesaving reply. It strengthens one's refutation by highlighting that the arguments one is dealing with are the most important ones in the opposition's case.

A significant variation on this admonition, however, might be noted in passing. In certain situations one may want to avoid direct confrontation with their major points, and may instead prefer to nibble away at various points until it suddenly becomes apparent that one has eaten into their case to a significant extent, much as a fisherman eventually discovers that nothing remains of the bait on the hook. This eliminates early confrontation, and may weaken the opposition sufficiently so that when one strikes at a major point, they will not be prepared to counterattack.

Preview What One Plans to Refute

In formal educational debate, if not in informal argumentation, it is helpful to state what it is one feels is necessary to refute, and then proceed to deal with it. For example, one may assert: "In order to refute the opposition's case it is necessary to show that they have reasoned entirely from authority, and that the authorities are too few and too biased." Then one proceeds to support that charge. Sometimes the opposition will have gone over their case rapidly, so one's precise pinpointing of what one plans to refute helps to clarify one's structure for the judge and audience as well as for oneself.

Blocking and Charting of Arguments

Some clear blocking of arguments in a meaningful diagram form is something which debaters usually find very helpful, for they can see where they ought to put their chief refutational efforts. Of course, it should not stifle one's creative and spontaneous refutation during the argumentative exchange. In the course of a debate the participants often construct flow-charts so they can see quickly the ebb and flow of claims and refutation:

Opponent's claims	My refutation	Their rebuttal, etc.
1. ————————	1. ————————	1. (perhaps nothing said)
2. ————————	2. (perhaps omit)	2. (no need to comment)
3. ————————	3. ————————	3. ————————————

Sometimes the first two columns could be sketched out prior to the debate for practice purposes in order to sharpen one's refutational points. One of course would need a system of abbreviations to enable one to record much material in a small space. This process of tracing the flow of the arguments helps one to see what needs to be done, what one has done, what damage one has inflicted on the opposition's case, and what weak areas one might continue to exploit.[3]

Summarize What One Has Refuted

In an argumentative context which takes place over a considerable period of time it is helpful to utilize frequent, concise summaries. Especially in a situation such as a multiday conference, a legislative debate, or a lengthy court trial the decision-makers need to have summaries to remind them just what refutation one has accomplished. Debaters are trained to conclude their speeches with summaries so that the judge gets a final overview of what the debaters feel they have done to the opposition's case. Also, frequent internal recapitulations are helpful not only for the judge and audience but also for the arguers, so they can remind themselves what they have refuted and what remains to be done. Even in informal dyadic argumentation it often is a good idea to remind the opposition what specifically one has done to their contentions. Such explicit summary statements help to ensure that the opposition and audience understand what one feels the impact of one's refutation has been; one cannot be sure that they would, if left to arrive at their own judgments, see that so clearly.

Reflect Ethical Values

The earlier chapter on ethics attuned us to the importance of ethical values in argumentation in general. When engaged in the specific process of refutation, we need to be especially concerned with our commitments to such values as honesty, fairness, courtesy, and tactful-

3. For mechanical procedures in handling refutation during a debate, see George W. Ziegelmueller and Charles A. Dause, *Argumentation: Inquiry and Advocacy* (Englewood Cliffs, N.J.: Prentice-Hall, 1975), pp. 204–10.

ness, for we may be tempted, in the excitement and heat of the exchange and in our desire to win, to lower our ethical standards. Sometimes it may be ineffective listening on our part (one may try to quote the opposition in order to be accurate with one's refutation), or a matter of choosing our language more carefully, such as softer phrasing: "Perhaps Ms. A didn't have time to study these examples. ..." More than likely, however, it often is a question of our basic attitudes, so we need to develop proper humane sensitivity to the psychic welfare of our opponents. To be able to hit hard without being discourteous to the persons involved is the mark of a mature and responsible arguer.

Multiple Approaches

In our discussion of methods of refutation which follows, do not assume that there is only one method which ought to be used in any given situation, for it usually is wise to rely on multiple methods. Thus, get into the habit of thinking of the plural rather than the singular, for multiple approaches will often be blended together. An arguer, like an army, usually attacks on many fronts. It is also important to stress that there is no one best method of refutation, for the many variables of each situation will determine which method would be the strongest to employ.

ATTACKING EVIDENCE AND REASONING

Faulty Evidence

To charge the opposition with having faulty evidence is a standard basic approach to refutation. By referring back to the chapter on evidence, we can simply summarize the points made there. That means that arguers could levy their challenge in one or more of the following directions.

1. One might accuse the opposition of presenting *inaccurate* information. If they stated that a given university had an enrollment of fifteen thousand students, one might point out that the true figure is only ten thousand.
2. One might accuse the opposition of presenting an *insufficient amount* of evidence, either too little or none at all. One might point out that when the opposition backs up an assertion with only one quotation, that is hardly enough support.
3. The evidence presented might be impressive in quantity and fully accurate, but it might be *irrelevant* to the claim being made. For

example, suppose the son argues that he should be given the family car next Saturday night because he did a good job of cleaning his room yesterday. The parents may say that that has nothing to do with whether or not he should have the car; it is irrelevant.

4. The evidence might be *outdated*. If one's opponent contends that the owners of professional baseball are losing money, and for substantiation we are given figures from twenty years ago, we would rightly challenge the lack of recency of the evidence.

5. One may claim that the evidence presented is *biased*, and hence untrustworthy. Suppose someone claims that Restaurant Z is an excellent place to eat, and it is then discovered that that person is part owner of that restaurant. One would reduce one's reliance on that person's testimony, and hence reduce the likelihood of accepting the advice.

6. Somewhat related, one may point out that the person presenting the evidence is *unqualified*. Suppose the person is contending that the American Revolution was the work of a small group of hotheads. One might question whether that person is sufficiently grounded in the study of that period of American history to be able to make such an assertion.

7. One might contend that the opposition has presented misleading statistics. They might have used the mean rather than the median, and if these varied greatly, that might well give a distorted picture.

8. An alert and informed person will be able to note when the opposition has *omitted* key evidence. In short, it is important to point out not only the faulty evidence presented but also the omission of significant evidence: "It is interesting to note that you have completely ignored the President's energy proposal of last month."

Faulty Reasoning

To attack the soundness of the opposition's reasoning, one would be dealing with the components discussed in the earlier chapters on reasoning. We will summarize those considerations here, but readers may wish to refer back to those chapters for more examples and elaboration.

1. One might contend that the opposition is engaging in faulty generalizing. They might be accused of formulating hasty generalizations: "You have concluded rather quickly that fraternities are irresponsible, before you have really studied the whole picture of fraternity life." One might hurl the challenge that the opposition has arrived at their conclusion on the basis of an insufficient number of instances:

"When you asserted that all lawyers are crooks, you gave us only the example of Ms. X." One might question the accuracy of the quantifier: "You claimed that *most* students favor retaining intercollegiate football, but I question whether you can prove that the majority actually do, for I have information which suggests otherwise." One might point out that the opposition has exaggerated in their conclusion, that is, they ended up saying that "an incredible number" of senators are alcoholics, whereas earlier they had talked of only "a few" being alcoholics. One might assert that the opposition used instances which were not typical: "The senior class valedictorian was cited by the high school superintendent when the latter claimed that the senior class was an especially intelligent group." "You do not account for the following fact. ..." A defense attorney, for example, might point out that the prosecution's hypothesis, that the suspect is guilty of robbing a bank, does not account for the fact that the suspect could prove he was in a different city at the time of the robbery. One might raise doubts about the opposition's claim by suggesting a plausible alternative hypothesis. For example, the "noisy" behavior of the students in class is not evidence of disrespect toward the teacher but, rather, their enthusiasm for the subject matter. One might accuse the opposition of falling into the fallacy of unnecessary complexity and suggest some simpler hypothesis to account for the facts. One might point out that the opposition has shifted wording, whereby a person originally spoken of as a "tardy" student becomes a "weak" student in the conclusion. Finally, one might indicate that the opposition is showing bias in its selection and handling of material, that their previously held notion—that construction laborers are all lazy—was governing the selection of examples and the handling of other information in order to back up the preconceived notion.

2. One might accuse the opposition of faulty reasoning by comparison. One might contend that the two things being compared are not similar in the essential aspects. One might point out that the opposition has relied only on reasoning by comparison and has not corroborated their claims by other reasoning.

3. One might challenge the opposition's reasoning by connection, which one will recall includes arguing from cause and arguing from sign. This might involve pointing out that the opposition has committed the post hoc fallacy, that the alleged cause is not strong enough to produce the result, and that other causes are being overlooked, or that attention is being given only to recent precipitating causes, ignoring long-range background causes. One might point out that the opposition is erroneously claiming a causal connection when it is only a sign indicating an associational relationship between two events.

4. One might focus one's attack on the opposition's deductive reasoning. One might point out weaknesses in their categorical, disjunctive, or hypothetical syllogisms. Refer back to the earlier chapter on deductive reasoning for details on what might be challenged.

Faulty Analysis

One might accuse the opposition of faulty analysis of the issues. One might focus on attacking the warrants, the assumptions that tie together the evidence and the claims. One might assert that the warrant is not the likely one, or that the warrant simply is not true. One might assert that the warrant has too many exceptions, too many improbables, to be accepted. One might argue that additional or different criteria are necessary. One might attack the value judgment which is implied in the warrant. One might contend that the definition of terms is unclear. One might assert that the opposition is evading certain key issues, or is focusing on relatively minor issues. One might claim that the conclusion is illogical, irrelevant, inconsistent, or unimportant.

Expose Pseudo-Reasoning

One will want to be alert to counteracting pseudo-reasoning displayed by the opposition. Refer back to that chapter to recall the specific things to watch for. Sometimes, publicly mentioning the inappropriate behavior might be sufficient to weaken the opponent in these areas.

The person engaged in refutation, then, might attack the evidence and reasoning, might claim faulty analysis, and might expose the pseudo-reasoning of the opposition. In addition, a number of special methods of refutation might be used; the remainder of the chapter will discuss these.

SPECIAL METHODS OF REFUTATION

The special methods of refutation have been divided into three somewhat arbitrary categories: (1) those methods which focus primarily on the proposal made by the opposition; (2) those which charge the opposition with some deficiency; and (3) those which create a uniquely awkward position for the opposition.

Methods Which Focus Primarily on the Proposal Made by the Opposition

Attack the proposal   One may contend that the opponent's plan is far too drastic, that whatever problems exist can be corrected by minor repairs rather than introducing a new and perhaps complicated and dangerous innovation. One might also adopt what is termed in debate the "even if" strategy, whereby one asserts something like this: "*Even if* a need exists, which I do not believe, the plan that the opposition has presented will not solve the problem." This permits one to focus one's attack on the proposal, and still make it clear that one does not agree that a problem exists. For example, suppose Harvey contends that a multi-story parking ramp should be built on campus to solve the parking problem. Marcella thinks such a proposal is very unwise and wishes to focus her attack on it; yet she also wants to make clear that she does not grant the premise that a serious parking problem exists, so she asserts: "*Even if* a serious parking problem existed on campus, which I do not believe is the case, the plan for a multistory parking ramp is extremely unwise."

Present a counterplan   In some situations, and often in formal debate contexts, one may want to present a counterplan as a basic approach to one's refutation. This means that one will agree that a need for change exists, but then assert that the opposition's plan to solve the problem is unworkable or undesirable. One then follows up with one's own proposal, which one contends is a better one. After clarifying one's plan, one then of course has to defend it by showing how it is workable and how it meets the problem. For example, suppose a dormitory resident contends that the dorm food is poor, and that the residents should picket the cafeteria. Gerald agrees that the food is bad, but suggests a different course of action, that is, he urges that a group of five residents should go talk to the head resident. In a formal debate, suppose the affirmative team's case holds that the United States' supply of energy resources is dangerously inadequate, and that the United States should explore and develop Alaskan oil resources more rigorously. The negative team agrees that current energy resources are dangerously inadequate, but urges a more rigorous development of coal resources, contending that it is a more workable solution and that it is more likely to solve the problem.

It is important to caution ourselves that showing the weakness of the opponent's proposal does not necessarily mean that ours is any stronger. Tearing down someone else's plan does not necessarily build up our plan—unless those are the only two options. Showing conclusively that Candidate A is not a worthy candidate for office does not necessarily mean that one has shown that Candidate B is worthy, but if they are the only two candidates, then Candidate B is probably selected by default. To demonstrate that a Ford does not meet one's needs, does not prove that a Chevrolet does—unless one has limited oneself to those two options. We should not delude ourselves into assuming that our plan is strong simply because we have demonstrated that the opposition's plan is weak.

Method of residue   As we discussed in the previous chapter, when one eliminates all possible options except one, that which remains is the residue. One may wish to refute by pointing out that the opponent's proposals are all unworkable or not sufficiently beneficial, and that therefore the remaining possibility, one's own proposal, is the only possible course of action. One should make sure that the options listed do indeed exhaust the possibilities, so that one's proposal is truly the residue. One will need to bolster one's contention with proof, of course, as it seldom would be sufficiently convincing merely to assert that one's proposal is the last remaining option; one will want to show why it is a strong option as well.

If one has to engage in counterrefutation against the method of residue, one could assert that there are other options which have been overlooked; one of the rejected options is stronger than contended; and the residue, the supposedly last and best option, is not so satisfactory as claimed.

Weaken proposal through amendment   In legislative debate, one refutational strategy sometimes followed is to weaken the opposition's case by offering an amendment, which will decrease the likelihood that the bill would pass. For example, suppose a member introduced a bill to give oil companies a tax exemption so that they will be encouraged to explore for additional oil resources. A legislator proposes an amendment which will exclude offshore explorations, knowing that that amendment will greatly reduce the possibility of the bill passing. Thus, the person "refutes," not by picking apart the opposition's case but by loading additional baggage onto it, which will weaken it and make it less attractive.

Trend toward an undesirable goal   One might adopt the posture whereby one admits that the opposition's suggestion is not so bad in itself, but then contend that it is a step in the direction of a very undesirable end. This is sometimes called the *slippery slope* tactic. For example, one may admit that it might not be a bad idea for the community to establish a municipal liquor store, instead of permitting a private one, in order to control the atmosphere and obtain revenue for the community; then one warns that it is a step away from free enterprise, that we would be sliding down a slippery slope toward socialism. Hence, the municipal liquor store proposal should not be adopted. *If* legitimately done, without raising spurious, fear-arousing images and without employing inappropriate name-calling, this technique can be an effective approach. After all, it is wise and responsible to visualize what today's action will lead to in the weeks ahead and years to come. To warn against a step in the wrong direction, however small it may be, can be an important contribution, just as warning people not to take the wrong fork in the road, for they will end up far from their hoped-for destination.

Wrong time, place, occasion, or place   One might seek to weaken the opposition's case by virtually agreeing with its substance, but attacking it on the procedural ground that this is the wrong time for the proposal, or this is the wrong place for it, or this is the wrong occasion, or its implementation is being rushed. For example, suppose one agrees that restricting intercollegiate athletics at one's university would be a good idea, but not this year, since the school has very good football and basketball prospects. One might agree that the plan for eliminating cars on campus is a good plan in general, but not for your university in particular. One might agree that getting a political official to speak at school functions is a good idea, but not for a graduation ceremony, where an educator would be more appropriate. Finally, one might admit that a vigorous recruitment program for one's university is a good idea, but that it should not be entered into too rapidly, for needed dormitory space is not yet available. In short, one does not necessarily attack the substance of the opponent's proposal; instead, one attacks procedural considerations, such as time, place, occasion, and pace.

Praise motives, but ...   A somewhat indirect method is to praise the motives and efforts of the opposition while one attacks their proposal. For example, suppose Gretchen's parents want to send her to an expensive, private women's college in some distant state. Her brother Peter praises his parents for desiring an excellent education for his sister, for their willingness to pay a lot money, and for the effort they put into examining many colleges before making their selection. But he then proceeds to argue that his sister really prefers a nearby, inexpensive, tax-supported university, that his sister is not the type to get the maximum benefit from a private women's college, and that it is a waste of money. Often one's "opponents" are willing to abandon their proposal if their good motives and hard work are recognized and praised. Imagine how the above parents might bristle if their son presented only his negative claims, without the accompanying praise. The absence of praise often suggests that the original arguer has questionable motives (parents want the prestige of a child associated with a famous college) and has not given it enough thought. This approach, of softening one's refutation, assumes the genuine use of praise, not misleading flattery.

Methods Which Charge the Opposition with Some Deficiency.

Attacking motives   Suppose an alderman is advocating building a hospital in a new location. The issue is debated publicly on its merits for a few weeks, and then it is discovered that the alderman owns some of the land in the proposed location. Arguers point out that he will stand to reap a sizable income through the sale of the property; in short, the alderman's motives are attacked, it is asserted that he might be primarily concerned with private gain rather than the public's health. One will recognize that this approach to refutation is perilously close to the fallacy of *poisoning the well*, that is, implying that the proposal is unsound because the source of the proposal is questionable. Also, it raises the issue whether it is ethical to question the person's motive. So, obviously, here we are suggesting a responsible attack on the person's motives, for why the person is proposing something is indeed often an integral part of the proposal. But even if we are proceeding legitimately, we know that motives are extremely difficult to ascertain accurately, and the risk of misinterpreting a person's motives and of causing that individual much harm is indeed high. After all, we often cannot describe accurately our own motives, much less someone else's. Furthermore, multiple motives frequently are operating, and the above alderman might well have both his private gain *and* the public welfare in mind, and the first need not cancel out the second. In short, attacking motives is an extremely hazardous approach, but it certainly can be a responsible and legitimate method of refutation if used with great care.

Oversimplification   In some situations one may contend that the opposition is seriously oversimplifying the issues. One asserts that the opponents are being incomplete and are avoiding the complexities which are present. For example, suppose someone contends that Chan soon should go on to graduate school after she gets her B.A. degree. It is said that it is merely a question of her desire to do so and her achieving a high enough academic record. She agrees that those two factors are important, but she contends that many more factors need to be considered, such as: (1) Will I have enough money? (2) Will I have to delay getting married? (3) Will my husband-to-be agree to the sacrifices to be made? (4) Can I move to another city easily at this stage of my life? (5) Am I clear enough in my future goals to make the most of graduate work? (6) Are there jobs available in my field even if I complete graduate studies? Thus, she "refutes" not by disagreeing with the two original points but by indicating that a host of interrelated factors make it a very complex issue, which the opposition has not taken into account.

Inconsistency   If the opposition fails to be consistent on significant points, it can weaken their position considerably if this is pointed out to the audience. Those two conditions—that an inconsistency actually exists and that it is significant—must be present to make this a responsible tactic of refutation. Readers will recall that the chapter on pseudo-reasoning warned of the irresponsible use of charging inconsistency, as a type of *ad hominem* argument. But if advocates do not display consistency, they need to be exposed. For example, suppose in the presence of a student audience a university official claims that tuition should be lowered, and a couple weeks later that same official, speaking to a group of nonstudents, claims that the university needs to keep the tuition at its current level in order to remain financially solvent. That official obviously has to be called to account, and if someone were to point out the inconsistency, that would greatly weaken the official's credibility. As this example suggests, refutation through the charge of inconsistency often depends on analyzing argumentative situations over a period of time, though it often is present within a single presentation.

It may take an especially alert observer to catch inconsistencies, and students will want to improve their ability to do so.

If one were to counter the charge of inconsistency, one could claim that one's opponent misinterpreted one's remarks, that one was not too clear in phrasing one's true position, or that times and conditions have changed so that the shift in one's position was justified.

Avoiding issues   To point out that the opposition is avoiding important issues can be an effective way to weaken their case. One could even agree that what they have presented is sound, but then indicate that they have been silent on one or more key issues. For example, suppose someone presents an impressive case for reinstituting compulsory military training to ensure the necessary number of personnel in military units; but one points out that nothing was said about such key issues as the likelihood that such action would only stimulate other nations to increase their preparedness, too, so that nothing would be gained; and such a compulsory program has the potential of weakening our democratic freedoms. Whether one went further and suggested that such omission was intentional depends on whether one could make such a claim legitimately . Throughout one's speech, if the arguing is in a formal context, or throughout the debate or over a period of time if such is the context, one might entrench one's refutation by repeatedly referring to the continued silence of the oppositon of those points, if they did not respond to one's attack.

Irrelevancies   One might weaken the opponent's case if one could show that no matter how impressive their claims might be, the case is simply irrelevant to the controversy being debated or irrelevant to the needs of the audience. The opposition might present an impressive case for the need to increase the number of teachers, but that might be considered quite irrelevant if the issue being debated is how to decrease the staff and trim the school's budget in light of decreasing enrollment. A more subtle method of asserting that some comment is irrelevant is simply to ignore it. Some parents and teachers have been known to use that technique.

Methods which create uniquely awkward position for the opposition

Point-by-point refutation   This is often cited as being the most effective method of refutation, for it deals point by point with the opposition. It can give a sense of overwhelming the opposition if done thoroughly and well. College and university debaters are often encouraged to utilize this procedure, for it lessens the likelihood of omitting any point, and of going off into divergent directions. The debate judge and audience feel that debaters have indeed stuck to the opposition's case and have covered everything. Having the advantage of following the same organization as the opponents, it is clear both to participants and to an audience.

There is, however, an important caveat that needs to be expressed here, for inexperienced debaters sometimes merely end up *restating* what their opponents said without really *refuting* it. There obviously is a difference. A nondiscriminating audience may be misled, but an experienced judge or alert audience will not be. The main concern here is to warn students not to mislead themselves into thinking that they have refuted something when they have merely restated it.

Formulate a dilemma   To present two options both of which are undesirable is to create a dilemma. Readers will remember that in the chapter on pseudo-reasoning they were warned against constructing false dilemmas, but we must acknowledge that some dilemmas may indeed be responsibly and appropriately constructed in order to weaken an opponent's case. If the two options created are the only two possibilities, if they are mutually exclusive, and if they are not spurious, then such a device does have the merit of sharpening the available options, and puts the onus appropriately on the opposition. In addition to an "either/or" format, the "if/then" structure is a common one for framing a dilemma, whereby both consequences are untenable: "If she votes for price controls, then she will alienate the producers; if she votes against price controls, she will alienate the consumers." When three undesirable options are presented, it is called a *trilemma*, but some texts prefer to use the term dilemma to include "two or more" undesirable options.

The traditional metaphor to depict the two undesirable options inherent in a dilemma is to refer to them as the "horns of a dilemma." If one has to attack a dilemma, one may "take the bull by the horns," showing that one or both of the alternatives is not undesirable, or "slip between the horns" of the dilemma by adding an option which was not mentioned.

Extend the analogy   One effective means of refutation is to use the figurative language of the opposition and extend it so that it aids in strengthening one's position. Suppose one is in a committee meeting in which the relative merits of various candidates for a job are being discussed. One member says that Candidate X should be selected, for she is "a real exciting fresh breeze." Another person counters with the comment that "fresh breezes have a way of dying down by evening"; that is, she does not have the qualities for performing consistently well over a long period of time.

Reductio ad absurdum   In an earlier chapter readers will recall we discussed this as a form of pseudo-reasoning which ought not to mislead us. With that in mind, we can still suggest that to push the opposition's case to the extreme, so that it is absurd, can conceivably be done within the bounds of appropriateness and responsibility. But one must also realize that people may be alienated by, rather than amused by, one's attempt to ridicule, so that it can boomerang. One seeks the underlying general principle of the opponent's contention, and by extending it to an extreme application, one demonstrates the absurdity of the opposition's claims. Suppose a grocery store contends that under no conditions are animals allowed in the store. Does this mean that a blind person who depends on a seeing-eye dog can never go in the store, and thus must presumably starve? Possessing simplicity, directness and ridicule, the approach of *reductio ad absurdum* can be powerful refutation if used properly.

In the above example an unusual specific instance was used to challenge the general principle, but often argument from analogy is employed in *reductio ad absurdum*. For example, suppose someone contended that football should be abolished, since five or six players in the nation are killed each year and about one hundred are seriously injured. This is refuted by asserting that such a contention is like saying that bathtubs should be abolished because each year many people are seriously injured and even killed by slipping in them. The underlying principle is that dangerous things should be abolished, but the refutation is based on the contention that in some areas of life we have to live with the danger because of the importance of the object, in this case, the importance of bathtubs in our lives.

If one has to counterattack *reductio ad absurdum*, one could do so by contending that the analogy is a weak one, that the specific instance is an unusual one which does not negate the general principle, or that the extension is irrelevant, unjustified or unfair. One also might show that the general principle attacked is not the real central one in the argument, or that no real damage was done to one's case, that the ridicule was simply harmless amusement.

Turn the tables   When one accepts the opponent's premise or evidence, but draws a different conclusion, one is "turning the tables." This process of refutation, if legitimately done, can be a strong weapon. Suppose Candidate A presents a long list of his accomplishments over many years for the betterment of the community as evidence for why he should be elected mayor. This is countered by agreeing that his list of past contributions is indeed impressive, but then it is asserted that this indicates that he deserves a rest, that the community should not give him the additional burden of being mayor. One uses the same evidence for coming to the opposite conclusion, one turns the table.

For another example, suppose a group of citizens argue that increased racial disturbances in the community indicates that schools should be segregated, whereas this is refuted by saying that such an increase in disturbance only indicates that the races should be kept together in the schools to help them to learn to live together in harmony. Thus, one agrees with the evidence, but draws a contrary conclusion. If the opposition has not carefully thought through the issues, one will likely be more successful in turning the tables.

If one is engaging in counterrefutation, endeavoring to turn the table right-side up again, one generally would contend that the new interpretation is not sound, and indicate why one thinks not. One also might want to underscore that the opposition has agreed with one's evidence.

Questions   Occasionally one's refutation may have greater impact if one communicates one's attack through questions rather than declarative statements. For example, one might state: "Can you imagine Country X sitting idly by in the presence of our reinstituting compulsory military training?" Sometimes college and university debaters try to overwhelm the opposition (and the judge) with an endless series of questions, such as those touching on the practicality of the affirmative plan: "Who will manage the program?" "How much will it cost?" "What if it isn't accepted?" "Why will it work here?" A flood of questions primarily to confuse and intimidate is hardly a responsible use of questioning, but if used judiciously and appropriately, they can be a strong tactic, for they will force the opposition to follow one's lead and deal with what one wants them to. If they cannot answer satisfactorily, then one has succeeded in discovering weak areas in their case.

SUMMARY

Refutation is the attempt to weaken or destroy the arguments with which we disagree, and usually is accompanied by an attempt to rebuild our case, which has been attacked in the ebb and flow of arguing. It is important to know when to refute, and to become thoroughly familiar with one's audience, one's case, and the opponent's case. One should select the most important points to refute, preview and summarize one's contentions, and, in formal debates, it is helpful to block and chart the arguments. One should conscientiously adhere to ethical values, and realize that multiple approaches to refutation are available for use.

Attacking the evidence and reasoning is the fundamental tactic for the person engaged in refutation. In attacking the evidence, one could call attention to many factors: the opponent has inaccurate information, has too little data, has outdated material, has biased information, uses misleading statistics, or is omitting significant data. In attacking the reasoning, one might accuse the opposition of faculty generalizing, faulty arguing from comparison, faulty argument from cause and sign, and faulty deductive reasoning. One also might contend that the opposition has made a faulty analysis of the issues, and one also will want to expose any pseudo-reasoning employed by the opposition.

There are many special methods of refutation which one might use, assuming one is responsible in so doing. Some methods focus primarily on the proposal made by the opposition, such as attacking the plan, presenting a counterplan, using the method of residue, weakening their proposal through amending, pointing out that the proposal represents a move toward an undesirable end, indicating that the time, place, occasion, or pace are wrong for the suggested proposal, and responsibly praising the motives of the opponents while attacking their plan. A second group of special methods of refutation charge the opposition with some deficiency, such as attacking their motives, or accusing them of oversimplification, inconsistency, avoiding issues, or of including irrelevancies. The third group of special methods create uniquely awkward position for the opposition. These would include point-by-point refutation, posing a dilemma, extending analogies, *reductio ad absurdum*, turning the tables, or raising a number of questions.

EXERCISES

1. In a summer issue of the *Journal of the American Forensic Association*, study the final-round presentations of the National Debate Tournament. Identify and evaluate the refutation methods. Concisely summarize your findings in a 500-word essay.

2. Prepare a five-minute speech in which you refute a speech given earlier in the term in your class (or some other speech given on campus). Use some of the special methods of refutation. Turn in an outline of your speech, and clarify what special methods you used.

3. Interview one or more members of your school's varsity debate squad and find out how they usually go about their refutation during intercollegiate tournament debating. Do they have certain techniques which they rely on more than others? Share your findings with your classmates in an informal discussion.

4. Write a 500-word essay in which you refute some editorial in a newspaper or magazine. Attach the editorial to your essay, and indicate your methods of refutation. You may want to condense and adapt your essay, and send it in to the newspaper or magazine as a letter to the editor.

5. Together with four or five classmates, attend a persuasive speech on campus or in the community. Each of you should focus on a different precise method of refutation and develop an attack on the speaker's arguments. You and your classmates should then share your refutation in a panel discussion in front of your class.

15 Language in Argumentation

INTRODUCTION

People making claims can employ a variety of instruments, such as real objects (showing the alleged murder weapon in a courtroom), visual creations (a cartoon), or nonverbal actions (gestures, sit-ins, or marches). But the chief instrument is language, and that is the focus of this book and specifically of this chapter. Language is not an end in itself, but is a means to an end. In argumentation it is a means, a vehicle, an agent to enable people to make and react to claims. Thus, language should not draw attention to itself, but to the claims, to the substance, just as messengers should not draw attention to themselves but to their message.

It is important at the outset to remind ourselves of the fundamental axiom that meaning resides not in the words themselves but in the minds of people, the user and the receiver. There is no inherent relationship between the word and its referent; a word simply represents something, "stands for" something. Meaning is given by people to the words; the words do not by nature possess some meaning. The term "table" in English means a familiar piece of furniture on which we place things; the German word *tisch* means the same thing. People speaking English and German have arbitrarily designated those respective terms for the same object. Thus, a different set of phonemes are used to refer to the same thing. If there were an inherent relationship between a word and its referent, then presumably one word, one set of phonemes, would be used universally.

Furthermore, it is important to emphasize that meaning is determined by context. Suppose we ask, "What does the term 'bear' mean?" If we say it in the context, "There goes a big, black bear," it means one thing, but if we say, "I can't bear to watch this movie any longer," the meaning is considerably different. The context clarifies and determines the meaning.

We should strive for breadth in vocabulary. This is of course a lifetime enterprise, not limited to college days or to a course in argumentation. The more we read and the more we experience, the more we work at expanding our vocabulary and the more effective we will become in our argumentation. Quantity of ammunition certainly is not the only important factor in warfare, but quantity is indeed one central factor, and as each nation seeks to have more armaments than an opponent has, so persons engaged in argumentation should see to it that their vocabulary arsenal is stock-piled.

But we need more than just an impressive abundance of words. Arguers should acquire flexibility in using their available lexicon, should be able to choose words and word arrangement freely and easily, depending upon the situation. To have an excellent command of only one style, is to hobble oneself, for life places us in an incredible variety of situations and we need to adjust our vocabulary accordingly if we wish to be effective.

The eternal circular linkage between language and thought has been summarized in the familiar assertion: "As we speak, so we think; as we think, so we speak." Language affects thought, and, in turn, thought affects the language we use. The immense significance, then, of using language wisely in argumentation should be clear.[1] To use it wisely, we need to look at it closely, and that is what this chapter intends to do. It will focus on word clarity, definition of terms, word overtones, figurative language, and word arrangement.

---

1. For a recent discussion of language as it relates to argumentation, see J. Michael Sproule, *Argument: Language and Its Influence* (New York: McGraw-Hill, 1980), pp. 29–55.

CLARITY

Lack of clarity in argumentation is a state of affairs to be grappled with constantly. If our comments are imprecise, indistinct, or obscure, our effectiveness is automatically decreased. Vagueness, then, is something we all need to control. It may well reflect the arguer's lack of vocabulary or lack of command of the subject. Furthermore, to possess clarity suggests that the arguers have respect for the subject, for the audience, and for themselves. Exceptions can at once be thought of; that is, occasionally a government official, parent, teacher, or student will find it important, and justifiable, to be vague, but such instances of an intentional lack of clarity ought not to distract us from the importance of achieving maximum clarity. To aid in increasing our clarity, we will focus on the subjects of ambiguity, relative terms, concreteness, simplicity, specificity, technical vocabulary, word economy, and the process of definition.

Ambiguity

Sometimes lack of clarity is the result of a term or phrase having too many meanings, that is, the expression is ambiguous. More precisely, no term or phrase is ambiguous in and of itself, but the context makes it ambiguous, just as context makes words clear. Semantic ambiguity occurs when a term has more than one possible meaning. For example:

INVESTIGATOR ASKING A PERSONNEL DIRECTOR OF A FIRM: "How many people do you have broken down by sex?"

PERSONNEL DIRECTOR: "Alcoholism is more of a problem for us."

Obviously the confusion comes from the two possible meanings of "broken down" in that context. The questioner meant "categorized," whereas the respondent took it to mean something like "morally damaged," or "degenerated." Ambiguity can be used intentionally for humorous effect, and it also can play an interesting role in poetry. But it is of paramount importance that arguers seek to reduce ambiguity, if they are serious about getting their claims accepted. *Syntactic* ambiguity will be discussed later.

Relative terms

Sometimes the lack of clarity comes from the use of terms which carry within them the potential of being in varying locations on some continuum.

1ST STUDENT: "It sure is cold today."
2ND STUDENT: "I don't think it is."

How "cold" is "cold"? To a skier or someone accustomed to living in an area which habitually has temperatures below zero degrees Fahrenheit, "cold" is something different from that experienced by a person accustomed only to living in Hawaii. "Cold" and "hot" are obviously terms on a continuum. Suppose Semore says, "George is a poor student." Jan strongly disagrees, pointing out that George is getting Cs in all of his classes. Semore responds, "That's what I mean. He's a poor student." To Jan "poor" meant doing failing work, but to Semore "poor" meant doing something considerably below A. As a struggling, budget-squeezing student, Barb may define a "rich" person quite differently from her wealthy friend. When a customer asks the grocer if the eggs are "fresh," his response is "sure," but the two people probably are placing "freshness" on a different point in a continuum. Thus, when the degree of something is in doubt, lack of clarity and lack of understanding may occur in argumentation, and it is important to use relative terms with care and sensitivity.

Concreteness

Another continuum, a vertical scale, on which terms can be placed is what is called the "ladder of abstraction," where the most concrete term is at the bottom, and the most abstract term at the top. For example:

Wealth
Personal possession
Transportation vehicle
Automobile
Dodge Omni
"Oliver" (the name one gives one's Omni)

At the bottom, the specific car one owns and calls "Oliver" is a very concrete item. It can be placed in a higher level with all other Omnis, or higher yet in the category of automobiles, or transportation vehicle, or personal possession, or in an abstract category of "wealth." To talk at the higher levels of abstraction may produce lack of clarity in the mind of the receiver, so the general guide advocated by many in the field of communication, especially the general semanticist school, is to make the language come as close as possible to the thing being discussed. One can make one's language more concrete by giving examples, creating analogies, or giving specific instances. For example, the abstraction of "democracy" might be discussed in part by talking about the more concrete, specific procedure of the "secret ballot"; the abstract notion of "efficiency" might be discussed in part by focusing on "careful use of time." One should bring one's language as close as possible to the five senses, so that, for example, the term "noise" might be replaced by the more concrete term "shouting," and the abstract term "beautiful" might be changed to "reddish."

Of course, one should quickly recognize that the situation, audience, and other well-known variables in any communication event help to determine whether or not a high level of abstraction is appropriate. After all, if one's focus is really meant to be on the abstract level of "personal possessions" then to come down to such a concrete term as "Dodge Omni" might be inappropriate. The key here is to become proficient at working with all levels on the ladder of abstraction and to be able to sense what degree of abstraction the communicative context calls for. After all, at times the arguer has to talk about highly abstract concepts such as democracy and efficiency, and to come down the ladder would inappropriately shift the focus. This flexibility, this command of all levels of abstraction, is a mark of the effective arguer.

Simplicity

A familiar and fundamental admonition is to use simple, plain, direct language; avoid elegant big words. While it is good to try to stretch out in search of a wider vocabulary, that does not mean artificially seeking big words simply to try to impress. Don't try to be profound; *be* profound, and the words will take care of themselves. If a term is new to our active vocabulary (our passive vocabulary is that which we, as receivers, understand), it may well come through as awkward and inappropriate, at least it will be so detected by the sophisticated receiver. Thus, instead of impressing people, it merely reveals our weak vocabulary. Even if we have control over the elegant terms, pompous words only serve to reveal pomposity, and unless we desire to communicate that, then there is not much point in using those terms. Inexperienced college debaters unfortunately become enmeshed in this process, and need to be particularly careful to avoid the pitfall. Excessively elegant terminology often becomes circumlocution, talking around a subject; and results in a lack of clarity. We need to acknowledge, however, that the subject and the occasion are important variables, and elegant vocabulary would be more appropriate to a large ceremonial banquet than to an informal debate in a small room before a small audience. Formal, elegant attire may be appropriate to the opening night at the opera, but hardly to the local swimming pool.

Specificity

The arguer needs to determine the degree of specificity to be employed in the choice of language in any given situation. Most of the time it is wise to follow the familiar admonition to "be specific," to avoid generalities which may make something unclear. But actually, one cannot assert that specificty has any inherent virtue not possessed by generalness.

For example, suppose a classmate asks Susan, "Where do you live?" She would probably respond by giving her specific address, "7236 Jackson Lane." Suppose Susan goes skiing in a distant state during winter vacation and someone there asks her, "Where do you live?" She probably would respond with the name of the city or state from which she came. Suppose she goes to Europe during the summer, and someone asks her, "Where do you live?" She probably would respond, "America." It is a horizontal continuum:

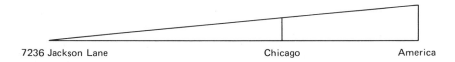

7236 Jackson Lane   Chicago   America

The answers varied in degree of specificity, because each was adjusted to what was expected in each communicative situation. We cannot say that the more specific the response, the better. To the European inquiry Susan hardly would respond, "7236 Jackson Lane."

If Guillaume went to a hardware store and asked for a "thingamajig," he might have a lengthy conversation ahead of him. Knowing the specific term obviously would be a real advantage. If we are talking about "freshmen" or "collies," it would be better to use those terms rather than the more general ones of "college students" or "dogs." If a mother is trying to get her children away from the television set to come to dinner, she is likely to be specific if the menu is to their liking ("The hot dogs are ready"), but general if it is not ("Dinner is ready"). She adapts to the situation.

Technical terminology

Engineers who talk in language which only other engineers can understand are on safe ground if the audience is only engineers, but not if the audience is made up of the general population. In this increasingly specialized age, any field has a horrendous number of subareas, so that one engineer may well find it difficult to understand the specialized language of another engineer. An economist, plumber, dentist, or farmer likewise have technical terminology which needs to be adjusted if they are communicating with someone outside of their group.

Each of these groups, and any coherent grouping of people on the basis of occupation or interests, such as football players, lawyers, construction workers, restaurant employees, or teenage gangs, will develop not only a formal technical terminology but also an informal vocabulary, which is usually called "shoptalk" or "jargon." The campus lingo of "credit hours," "recitation sections," and "prerequisites," so familiar to college and university students, would leave an outsider puzzled. The special terminology students learn in an argumentation class, such as "rebuttal," "burden of proof," or "post hoc fallacy," would likewise fail to be clear to other students who have not studied the same subject matter.

Whether informal or formal, these specialized vocabularies have the advantage of permitting rapid, brief, and precise communication with "insiders," but create puzzlement, lack of interest, and perhaps disgruntlement in "outsiders." An irresponsible arguer may intentionally employ technical terminology to impress or overwhelm the general audience in an effort to win their uncritical assent, since they cannot grapple with the terminology sufficiently to challenge the arguer's statements. Obviously this intentional effort to embarrass, confuse, or intimidate the audience is to be strongly deplored. So it again comes to the central point: know when formal and informal technical language will be appropriate in any given communicative situation, and use it responsibly.

Economy

A trustworthy guideline in argumentation is to use as few words as possible to get the job done. A personnel director of a company is expected to hire only the number of people necessary to run the company efficiently. If fifty people were hired instead of the necessary forty, so that ten were sitting around with little to do and even getting in the way of the others, the personnel director would be creating an unfortunate atmosphere. Likewise, if an arguer uses fifty words instead of the necessary forty, and ten words are doing little and even getting in the way, then the arguer is indeed unwise. "Make each word work," is a helpful guideline. Students sometimes mistakenly believe that quantity is the same as quality, that the more words, the better. They praise themselves when they turn in a three-thousand-word paper, when the instructor asked for a two-thousand-word paper; they pat themselves on the back when they talk for twelve minutes, when the instructor had assigned a seven-minute speech. In most cases these excessive lengths reveal only the student's lack of command over the subject and lack of care in preparation. Verbose, wordy people delude themselves, and unsophisticated receivers, into believing that an endless stream of words means a strong argument. Often it is a cover-up for a weak case, and, even more often, wordiness contributes to lack of clarity.

DEFINITION

Importance

This discussion of the cautions to exercise in the use of langauge brings us to the importance and helpfulness of clear definitions. Much of the cut and thrust of casual, everyday argumentation revolves around definition of terms:

1ST PERSON: "What d'ya mean 'lazy'? Why, my cousin is one of the hardest working people I know."

2ND PERSON: "Well, I mean he's slow to do things that must get done; he's always fooling around with insignificant things."

1ST PERSON: "Oh, well, I certainly don't call that 'lazy.' He's one of the most active guys I know."

At the outset of any formal intercollegiate debate, a clear definition of terms by the first affirmative speaker is a basic expectation so that the debate can proceed along agreed-upon meanings for key terms. In any claim-making situation such as an editorial or essay, the careful arguer takes time to define the key terms.

In many situations the arguer creates what is known as an "impromptu" ("stipulated") definition, in which the arguer constructs a specific definition for the immediate task at hand. Thus, an editorial writer might say, "In this editorial I define 'insensitive' to mean. ..." This is usually helpful, unless the definition is so unusual, such a departure from the conventional defintion, that its very uniqueness makes it difficult for the receiver to follow the argument. Unfortunately, some college debaters create trick definitions designed to throw their opponents off guard, so that they will be unable to adjust their case in the short time available. It is indeed unfortunate when such definitions are used simply to confuse and distract rather than to clarify the clash of issues.

Methods

Various methods might be employed in creating definitions. Arguers might cite a synonym, a word which means close to the same thing—there being no such thing as a total duplication of meaning. The dictionary concludes many of its entries by giving some synonyms: for "incessant" the synonym "continual" is included by one dictionary. Defining in this way is direct and simple, and is often sufficient, but in some situations it may not be adequate, especially if the synonym is no more clear than the original term. A second method is to define by authority; that is, "Webster's dictionary defines ... ," or, "As Albert Einstein once defined it, ... " One might define by example, that is, cite a specific case, an illustration of what is meant. One might give an explanation, as did the dialogue above to help clarify what was meant by "lazy." One might define by classification (sometimes called analysis), whereby one puts the term into a class and then differentiates it from other members in that class. For example, one might say, "Doctoral candidates are those graduate students who have successfully passed their Ph.D. preliminary examinations." One might define by comparison and contrast. For example, a "yard" of dirt might be defined as about twenty bushels or six wheelbarrows; that way, customers can visualize the quantity by comparing it to some measurement with which they are familiar. One might choose to define by negation; that is, state what one does *not* mean by the term: "When I say that college football teams should be investigated, I do not mean to include intramural teams." One might define by etymology, that is, giving the root derivation of the term, which often clarifies it, except for the obvious caution that words, over time, may change in meaning. For example, in trying to clarify the term "holograph" it is helpful to point out that it is derived from the Greek term *holographos*, which is a combination of *holos* ("entire") and *graphein* ("to write"), so that it refers to a document, such as a will or letter, which is wholly in the handwriting of the person whose signature it bears. One might define by function: "A thermometer is an instrument which tells the temperature." Finally, in oral argumentation one can define by showing; that is, one can show the pistol said to have been used by the accused person, thus clarifying the nature of the alleged murder weapon.

Cautions

It is necessary to include some cautions to be aware of when one attempts to define. Avoid circular definitions, that is, using the term-to-be-defined in the defining term. For example, "Brotherhood is when the people of a given group think of themselves as brothers." Since it is assumed that the defining term is understood by the receivers (otherwise there would be no point in using it), one needs to make sure that it is indeed understood by them. Question-begging definitions should be avoided; that is, one should not assume in the definition the very thing which one is supposed to clarify. One's definition should be as specific and as full as the situation seems to demand. Watch out for the "persuasive definition," whereby arguers create a definition to make a term mean what they want it to mean and not what it is generally understood to mean. For example, suppose Beverly asserts, "A real teacher is one who facilitates discussion, who gets the students to do most of the talking." Knowing that Mr. X is a good lecturer but a poor discussion leader, Beverly shifts and narrows the focus to an area which fits her persuasive case, that is, that Mr. X is a poor teacher. Finally, be alert to equivocation—the inappropriate shifting in meaning of a term in the process of making some claim. That is, using a term to mean one thing in a premise and something else in the conclusion must be avoided, and must be detected if one's opponent does it.[2]

OVERTONES

Connotation

It is one thing to try to define words carefully, to clarify their *denotation*, that is, their "core" meaning, their dictionary meaning, which is a widely shared meaning. But we also need to be alert to the *connotation*, that is,

2. For a fuller discussion of definitions, see Douglas Ehninger, *Influence, Belief, and Argument* (Glenview, Ill.: Scott, Foresman, 1974), pp. 37–49.

the suggested meaning, the peripheral association, the emotional overtones which words can communicate, which may reveal a private
meaning which could vary depending upon the attitudes, values, and
experiences of the receiver. For example, the term "college student"
probably is a term which, to most of us, has positive overtones, but to
someone else it may connote young people who are too lazy to do
manual work or who are excessively too conceited. Connotations are
somewhat fluid, and change as experiences vary. Suppose an elderly
neighbor of Joe's had always held the latter, negative views about "college
students," but after observing Joe for four years the neighbor no longer
thinks of college students as lazy, conceited, or disrespectful. The
connotation has shifted, but the denotation has not changed, for a
college student still is a person who attends an institution of higher
learning. Arguers need to be reasonably sure that the terms, especially
the key terms, they use connote the same thing to the receiver that they
do to the user.

Honorific and derogatory terms

Words which carry heavily favorable connotations are called *honorific*, or
commendable, terms, and those which have heavily unfavorable connotations are *derogatory* terms. Such terms are emotionally loaded. Lewis
calls himself "cautious," but someone else calls him "cowardly"; we are
"firm," they are "obstinate." One person is a "statesman," another is a
"politician." Our government has an "information agency," other countries have "propaganda agencies." Someone has suggested that the
difference between "news" and "gossip" is whether one tells it (news) or
hears it (gossip). Think of the difference between "discipline" and
"repression," "obedient" and "kowtowing," and "cooperative employee"
and "yea-sayer." These strongly loaded terms may unnecessarily and
erroneously create two polar positions, and generate too much emotion,
too much of a desire to be totally negative or totally positive.

Glittering generalities and name-calling Honorific terms may result in gratuitous flattery or glittering generalities, and derogatory terms
may result in unfair name-calling. If misused, honorific and derogatory
language generates undue emotion, excitement, awe, or hatred, which
can impede reasoned and sober consideration of the subject under
consideration. They can be an obstacle to clear thinking, and contribute
to the creation of strong assertions without substantiation. But it should

be stressed that the problem is the abuse and not necessarily the use of these strong terms, for at times the situation may indeed call for loaded language.

Heavily connotative language can communicate swiftly, colorfully, and concisely the attitude and mood of advocates. Their intensity of feeling is thus openly shared, and this may well be as important as, or even more important than, communicating the advocate's point of view. Intense feeling and clear reasoning are not necessarily incompatible. There are times when generalities such as "justice," "harmony," or "equality" need to "glitter," for all too often life has tarnished them. For example, Martin Luther King, Jr.'s, classic "I Have a Dream" speech is loaded with such glittering generalities, and few observers would contend that he inappropriately used them in that historic and emotional setting.

Name-calling can be grossly unfair and inaccurate to the person, institution, or concept so labeled. Furthermore, the stigma attached to such labels lingers a long time afterward. For instance, suppose one says, "That neighbor's kid is a real troublemaker." Once so labeled, the worst possible interpretation is put on everything that youngster does from then on. How often have we caught ourselves putting people into stereotyped categories, into narrow pigeonholes, and then continue for years to think of that person only in terms of that label? "She's a tightwad." "He's a jock." "That couple are a pair of real old fuddy-duddies." Perhaps later experiences permitted us to see those people in a different light, we perceived additonal sides to their characters, and we felt embarrassed, stupid, and apologetic for having applied such narrow labels to them for so long. The same holds true for honorific labels, too. "She's a real angel." "He's a real friend." Experience may lead us to change these evaluations. But most labeling is probably derogatory in nature, and often can be incomplete, inaccurate, unfair, and misleading. It can end further thoughfulness, as it seems to have "closed the case"; that is, one thinks one has the person or situation sized up, and so needs to give no further thought to it. But if labeling is done accurately and fairly, it can be a succinct summary of some person, product, or situation, and can be helpful in focusing attention on a central characteristic.

"God" and "Devil" terms   God and Devil terms refer to a two-valued orientation, whereby our language reflects what we highly value and what we strongly dislike. We may treasure such things as "democracy," "liberty," "equality," "justice," and "integration." We may strongly dislike "inefficiency," "tyranny," and "Fascism." Much can be ascertained about arguers by their God and Devil terms, for their value commitments are clearly revealed.

Neutralizing language   In general, one needs to neutralize one's language as much as possible, to search for terms which fall in the middle of the two extremes. One might neutralize one's expressions also by including two somewhat contrasting terms as sort of boundary lines, indicating that one's position is somewhere in the middle. For example, one might suggest that one wants to be "firm but just," or wants to do a task "rapidly but not hastily." Of course this leaves the arguer open to the accusation of being "wishy-washy" and of artificially trying to occupy some middle ground, but it also can reveal sensitivity to different values, to different boundary lines within which one can take a stand.

Extreme quantifiers and intensifiers

Another way in which we load our language is by using extreme quantifiers—that is, terms such as "all" or "every"—and extreme intensifiers—terms such as "absolutely" or "certainly." One needs to choose one's quantifiers with care; terms such as "a few" or "some" and "probably" or "possibly" may be more accurate intensifiers. This is not meant to encourage qualifying everything one says but simply to stress the importance of framing one's contentions with as much accuracy and fairness as possible. It will prevent needless disagreement, for, frequently, the heat of a controversy is greatly increased because one of the participants uses an immoderate term. If it is wise to try to prevent disease, so it is wise to prevent unnecessary disagreement, especially if this can be accomplished by simply choosing one's words with care.

Slanting

Finally, we may load our expressions by including only material favorable to our point of view and omitting material opposing our position. This slanting of our message by such selection and omission obviously presents an incomplete and distorted version which is often difficult for receivers to perceive, unless they are extremely well-informed and sophisticated people. If intentionally done to try to give a half-truth, to give a warped, distorted view, then this process of *card-stacking*, of selecting only those points favorable to one's point of view, is strongly discouraged. In some contexts, of course, such as in a court of law where prosecutor and defense attorney are, by definition, presenting only their side of the case, the process of card-stacking is open and understood. Likewise, when one goes on a job interview, it is understood that one would be telling the interviewer only one's strong points. But be alert to its abuse.

Euphemisms

When certain terms are considered too blunt, harsh, painful, or offensive, people sometimes substitute a more acceptable term, a euphemism. We substitute "sanitary engineer" for "garbage collector," "misstatement" for "lie," and "passed away" for "died." Instead of facing up to the harsh realities of "retreat," we bring in all kinds of peripheral considerations to show that it really is a "strategic withdrawal." While we may sometimes ridicule others who attempt to cover up or avoid the embarrassment or pain of a situation by relying on euphemisms, when we ourselves are faced with a similar situation, for example, a death in our immediate family, we soon discover that we, too, use these softer terms. It often is no more than an appropriate adjustment of the language to the situation. But sometimes it is carried to an outlandish extreme, and we must remember to control it.

Slang

Slang has many characteristics, one of which is the ability to communicate emotional overtones, and hence we will briefly consider it here. It is a colloquial, informal lexicon which may be appropriate in certain contexts, but quite inappropriate in others. In conversational argumentation with close acquaintances, it might be useful; in a formal public debate in a large auditorium before a public audience, it would probably be quite inappropriate. Slang is a transitory vocabulary, frequently appearing and waning within a few years, central to our expressions, for example, in high school, but shockingly childish by the time we are seniors in college. Potentially outdated, offensive, immature, or unclear slang may be a negative component in our language arsenal. But it also can be vibrant, vivid, colorful, innovative, humorous, refreshing, and direct, and as such can be an asset. Again, the arguer needs to decide on the appropriateness of using it in each particular situation.

Clichés

In some instances, originally vivid overtones to terms and phrases have become washed out. Heavily used terms get worn out, and trite expressions should be avoided if one does not want to bore one's audience. Clichés suggest that the arguer has a limited vocabulary, is unimaginative and dull. Effectiveness is accordingly reduced. This is always a difficult area in college essays, for a young student obviously has not heard the expressions as often as an elderly professor, who proceeds to scribble "trite" in many places in the student's essay, and doesn't see why they are trite. Gradually we all acquire a reasonably good grasp of overworked platitudes and phrasings, and learn to avoid them.

FIGURATIVE LANGUAGE

Humans have a tendency to think in images, and figurative language is a vehicle that enables us to do so. Figurative language is not a stylistic gimmick nor a decorative feature, such as the frosting on a cake. Instead, it might be compared to the drop of coloring placed in the cookie mix, which pervades the whole. Figurative language is inherent to the message; it is part of the thought itself. Figurative language is a rich resource for the arguer, and we need to examine it closely in order to extract fully its potential wealth.[3]

Types of figures of speech

A *simile* states a comparison between two items (objects, concepts, actions, qualities, or situations) by using an explicit linking term such as "like" or "as." For example, we might say that someone "runs like a rabbit," thus transferring the known quality of swiftness from the rabbit to the person. A closed simile is one in which the specific item being compared is indicated, such as, "She is as beautiful as a queen," which explicitly indicates that the quality of beauty is the queenly element being transferred (rather than such things as poise, charm, arrogance, or haughtiness). An open simile, "She is like a queen," leaves unspecified the precise quality being compared. An *analogy* is an extended simile

3. For a stimulating discussion of the importance of analogy and metaphor in argumentation, see Ch. Perelman and L. Olbrechts-Tyteca, *The New Rhetoric: A Treatise on Argumentation* (Notre Dame, Indiana: U. of Notre Dame Press, 1969), pp. 31–410.

and develops the comparison more fully for the purpose of explanation or illustration. This has been discussed in an earlier chapter. A *metaphor* on the other hand is a compressed simile, whereby the "like" or "as" connectives are omitted, and the comparison is implied; hence, it is usually more subtle than a simile. The comparison is made in an abbreviated fashion; thus, for example, a fast runner on the track team may acquire the nickname of "Rabbit-Legs," or we may refer to freeways as "lengthy parking lots."

In these metaphors, analogies, or similes there are two terms: the term about which one is speaking (the runner) and the term to which it is being compared (the rabbit). The first term is referred to as the primary term (also as the tenor, the X term, or the literal term), and the latter is the secondary term (also the vehicle, the Y term, or the figurative term). One of the terms might be omitted, and the receiver has to supply it.

Special figures of speech should be clarified. *Personification* is the treatment of things, animals, or abstractions as if they were human. Following are examples of each: "The trees waved good-bye in the wind." "The lizard voiced dissent over our presence." "Mother Nature took good care of our rose bushes last winter." The last instance, giving an abstraction concrete human form, is called "reification," that is, giving substance to abstractions. Another example of it: "History will judge whether or not we were right." Strangely, some textbooks call reification and personalizing a fallacious process; such unimaginative analysis is rather unproductive. *Oxymoron* [ox-si-mor´-on] is the joining of two items which are seemingly contradictory: "thunderous silence," "heavy lightness," "overwhelmed by insignificance." *Metonymy* [ma-ton´-a-mē] is the substitution of a term for another closely related term. For example: "The White House said yesterday … ," which substitutes the President's place of residence for the President himself. We say that "the pen is mightier than the sword," whereby "pen" is substituted for "literature" and "sword" is substituted for "warfare." *Synecdoche* [si-nek´-da-kē] is when the part is spoken of as if it were the whole. For example, a farmer employs "hired hands"; the part of the human used in farm work, the hands, is chosen to stand for the whole person. Likewise, the mayor claims he will get the best "brains" in the community to solve the transportation problem; here the portion of the anatomy used in thinking, the brain, is substituted for the whole person. We speak of our daily "bread," to stand for the general term "food."

It is the interaction between the primary and secondary term, almost a chemical process, which creates the new image. For example, we have used the sentence, "The trees waved good-bye in the wind." The verb "waved" initiates the personification, suggestively comparing the tree to a human being, but one could not very well say, "The rock waved good-bye in the wind." The interaction between "waved" and "rock" simply does not have the right physiology to permit a metaphorical creation. So one cannot say that the mataphor is *in* the verb "waved"; it is in the intereaction between the verb "waved" and the subject "trees," helped by the prepositional phrase "in the wind," which gives some context.

Role in problem-solution analysis

In the portrayal of social problems and their solutions, an arguer often employs familiar metaphorical themes. The medical metaphor is heavily used, as problems are spoken of as "ills" of society or are called the "cancer" of society, and the arguer is put in the role of a doctor coming to "cure" them. The theft metaphor is used when the problem is depicted, for example, as "our liberties have been stolen from us," and the arguer is the person "restoring" the stolen item. The cleansing metaphor is used by many candidates for public office who want to "clean up the mess" in city hall. The fix-it metaphor is utilized in asserting that "the machinery of government has broken down," and needs to be "overhauled." The edifice metaphor is present when we hear of how "the foundations" of society are "crumbling." The "light-dark" metaphor is frequently used, as we hear of the "dark night" of the previous administration (or regime) whereas with the coming election (or revolution) we are promised the "dawning of a new day." Nature is also relied on in such expressions as the "avalanche" or the "flood" of angry dissent from the population. The journey metaphor is used, as we hear of the "obstacles" on the "rocky road" we are encountering; the arguer promises to remove those obstacles and to make smooth the pathway. The sea metaphor is used by arguers defending the status quo, when they warn us not to "rock the boat" or "make waves"; arguers wanting to change the status quo accuse current leaders of "drifting" on a "rudderless" course. Football metaphors urge us to "hold the line" against inflation, and the weaver metaphor is part of our lament that the "fabric" of society is being "torn" by inequality. In short, the sources of metaphors are endless for an arguer who is trying to solve society's problems.[4]

4. For a fuller discussion of the role of metaphor in problem-solution analysis, see J. Vernon Jensen, "Metaphorical Constructs for the Problem-Solving Process," *Journal of Creative Behavior, 9 (1975): 113–24.*

Effects of figures of speech

They can capture attention by their arresting nature; they may shock or startle; they may illuminate with the suddenness and brightness of a flashbulb. They can simplify the complex and make concrete the abstract; they can compress substance greatly; they can foster visualization and conceptualization. They can pass judgment; that is, they can praise or deprecate. They can heighten emotion and reveal the degree of intensity of feeling of the arguer. They can bring in humor easily. They involve both intellect and emotions by appealing to both mind and senses, by providing a fresh way of looking at, and feeling about, any given subject. They can make material highly interesting, understandable, compelling, and memorable. The metaphorical themes selected tell us much about the arguer as well as about the subject matter. Appropriate and judicious use of figures of speech may increase the ethos of the arguer in that they suggest a person with a lively imagination, who is well-read, and who has wide experience. (in order to see the necessary relationships.)

But if used inappropriately, figures of speech can produce decidedly negative effects. By their very power they may cause much mischief. They might obscure rather than clarify. They can insinuate an idea into the mind of the receiver with the ease of subliminal advertising, with all of its potential dangers. Our attitudes and outlook can be subtly and firmly molded and controlled. Deep-seated, unexamined attitudes and beliefs can hide, and grow fat, in figures of speech. Our thinking might become ossified, so that we narrow our outlook and weaken our ability to see variations and additional options. For example, it has been common (as it was during the American Revolution) for a country to express its relationship with its colonies in the family metaphor, that is, the "parent" and the "offspring." This communicates that the "mother" country has dominance and power over the immature colonial "child," which ought to be dependent and obedient, subservient to the will of the parent. Once that language becomes embedded in the discourse, that mental image and conceptual framework become entrenched, and it is difficult for those in the mother country to grant independence to the child.[5] Metaphors can perpetuate two-valued thinking; in the above example, the parents are "good" and the children are "bad" or "immature."

---

5. For an analysis of the family metaphor in the American Revolutionary War rhetorical context, see J. Vernon Jensen, "British Voices on the Eve of the American Revolution: Trapped by the Family Metaphor," *Quarterly Journal of Speech*, 63 (1977): 43–50.

Arguers might also be trapped by their own image-making in the sense that if they portray themselves as the "doctor" coming to heal the "wounds" of society, they find it difficult to understand how anyone could be so misguided and ungrateful as to reject their ministrations, as most people would be unlikely to reject the advice of a doctor on medical subjects. The metaphor can be crucial in defining situations; for example, it makes quite a difference whether we view the drug user as a sick person (calling for treatment) or a dangerous deviate (calling for imprisonment).

Guidelines for using figures of speech

Use figures of speech sparingly, like the coloring in the cake frosting is used sparingly. A tiny drop can color the whole message. Excessive use simply becomes boring, even ludicrous, and the novelty and vividness soon wear away. The familiar warning to avoid mixing one's metaphors still is a good one to remember. For example, a politician "sitting on the fence with his ear to the ground" creates an unrealistic image. Keep in mind that figures of speech are more appropriately used in certain situations and contexts than in others. Although it is sometimes effective to continue to develop a particular figure of speech at some length, many times it would be wise not to linger too long on it but, instead, to blend into a related image. Do not force the creation of figures of speech, let them come naturally. Finally, enter into the metaphor freely, but also be able to step outside of it; do not be carried away by it. One should be alert, then, to the presence of figures of speech when one is using them and when one is receiving the message of some claim-maker, and one should realize the potential for good and for mischief which this vivid form of language possesses.

WORD ARRANGEMENT

Syntactic ambiguity

In the section on ambiguity, we postponed the discussion of syntactic ambiguity, for it relates directly to word arrangement. Suppose one wrote for a hotel reservation: "We'd like a room for two people with a bath." To remove the confusion (and, unfortunately, also the humor), one would move the prepositional phrase "with a bath" next to the noun it is intended to modify, that is, "room." Thus the sentence would read:

"We'd like a room with a bath for two people." Syntactic ambiguity is caused not only by such misplaced modifiers but also by dangling participles ("Running across the street, the car struck him"), and by unclear referents for pronouns. Elliptical constructions, that is, shortcut expressions more frequently encountered in conversational situations, also contribute to lack of clarity. For example the statement: "He liked the movie better than Mary," would have its clarity improved by adding the omitted terminology: "He like the movie better than Mary did," or "He liked the movie better than he liked Mary."

Parallelism

The balance of terms, phrases, or clauses can set up a rhythm which catches attention, communicates a message clearly, and leaves an indelible impression on the receiver's memory. Francis of Assisi's familiar prayer illustrates this:

"That where there is error—I may bring truth,
That where there is despair—I may bring hope,
That where there is sadness—I may bring joy."

Balancing of infinitives and adverbs in the following creates a helpful rhythm: "To study diligently, to work conscientiously, to play vigorously, all go to make a well-rounded person." A special kind of parallelism is *antithesis*, whereby contrasts are constructed for the purpose of clarifying or emphasizing. President Kennedy's famous admonition illustrates this: "Ask not what your country can do for you, ask what you can do for your country." This involves a sort of refutational thrust, just as Biblical admonitions assert: "Ye have heard an eye for an eye, ... but I say unto you. ..." The "but I say unto you ..." sets up a bridge, rhythmically binding together the two expressions.

Repetition

Advertisers depend on repetition; it is the lifeblood of their profession. They operate on the assumption, proved valid by years of experience, that repeating their claims over and over again will eventually capture and hold a sizable number of consumers. Political and religious leaders likewise depend on repetition to win and hold adherents to their beliefs. Keep in mind the cautions we expressed about repetition in the chapter on pseudo-reasoning. But here we are focusing on the more narrow concern of word arrangement, of repeating words and phrases, not ideas. In the above prayer of Saint Francis, repetition contributes greatly to its effectiveness. An arguer might assert: "We must not overlook the widows; we must not overlook the orphans; we must not overlook the aged." The idea obviously could be expressed in fewer words: "We must not overlook the widows, orphans, or aged." But repetition helps to focus attention, serves as a helpful transition, and aids the memory. In other instances the repetition of a key term or phrase throughout a presentation may help to keep the receiver's mind on the central point. Excessive repetition, that is, redundancy, obviously should be avoided, and each of us needs to determine the appropriateness of repetition in each given situation.

Questions

Arguers ought to be flexible in framing their assertions, using not only declarative or imperative sentences but also the interrogative form. Questions have a way of involving the receivers in a compelling way, for a query invites a response. Questions sweep receivers into a commitment, even if their response is a silent one. A question in which the desired answer is built in is termed a *rhetorical question*. For example: "Do you want foreign countries to dictate to us what the price of oil should be?" Obviously, the arguer knows that the audience's response would be a resounding, "NO!" On the other hand the declarative statement: "We do not want foreign countries to dictate to us what the price of oil should be," simply does not invite audience involvement. Thus, making one's claim via a rhetorical question may in some situations be quite effective. However, if overused, if used to distract, or if used to excite the audience unduly, then the rhetorical question may be unwise or even somewhat irresponsible.

Slogans

The arranging of words into slogans to propagate a claim is a significant phenomenon. Organizations of all kinds often depend on slogans in their public relations efforts. Commercial advertisers live on them. Relying heavily on billboards, newspapers, handbills, and magazines with their limited space, and on radio and televisions with their limited time, advertisers construct their appeals in short, succinct utterances, that is, slogans. Candidates for public office have slogans at the center of their campaigns. Large demonstrations utilize slogans to focus attention on their demands: "Yankee, Go Home," "Down with the Gang of Four," "No Nukes," "Ban the Bomb." Buttons and bumper stickers are familiar on the American scene.

The purpose of slogans is not to further thoughtful consideration of the subject at hand but to stimulate into action those people who already are committed to a claim (which, presumably, has previously been thought through), or to sweep the fence sitters into the camp of believers. Sloganizing is not inherently bad or good, but depends on the context. In certain situations a vivid, simplistic slogan may be very helpful, and in other situations it may be shameful and dangerous. Terse, attention-catching, memorable, and often witty, slogans can be powerful for both good or ill. All too often, unfortunately, they work against careful thoughtfulness.[6]

Transitions

Clearly and smoothly phrased, transitions are the cement which holds an argumentative speech or essay together, and as such they are extremely important. They may be a paragraph, a sentence, a phrase, or a single word, but whatever the form, they link together the various segments of the presentation. They can summarize and forecast; that is, they are bridges leading from the past into the future: "So much for the advantages, now let us consider the disadvantages. ..." They tell receivers where they have been and where they are going. Transitional signposts can also provide enumeration, such as "second," "fourth" or "finally." They can facilitate comparison, such as "similarly" or "likewise"; they can provide contrast: "however" or "on the other hand." Transitions can lead us into specifics: "for example" or "for instance." "Consequently" or "therefore" can indicate cause-and-effect relationship, as can the following: "Why do these deplorable conditions exist in our community? I'll give you three reasons." The importance of transitions far exceeds the small amount of space or time that they occupy. Clarity, brevity, and variety are guidelines in using them. The degree of informality in phrasing will, of course, depend on the context.

6. For an analysis of nonrational discourse in the late 1960s, of which sloganizing was a part, see Franklyn S. Haiman, "The Rhetoric of 1968: A Farewell to Rational Discourse," in Richard L. Johannesen, *Ethics in Human Communication* (Wayne, N.J.: Avery Publishing Group, 1978), pp. 108–21.

SUMMARY

The role of language in argumentation is indeed a central one. To achieve better clarity and effectiveness, arguers need to be more fully aware of semantic ambiguity, relative terms, concreteness, simplicity, specificity, technical vocabulary, and word economy. How to define terminology more effectively is important for arguers who wish to maximize clarity. Words have suggestive overtones as well as denotative meanings, and thus it is important to better understand what is involved in honorific and derogatory terminology, glittering generalities, name-calling, "God" and "Devil" terms, neutralization of language, extreme quantifiers and intensifiers, slanting, euphemisms, slang, and chichés. The power of figurative language is important for arguers to better understand, that is, to distinguish the varying types of figures of speech, to see more clearly the presence of metaphorical themes in problem-solution analysis, to be cognizant of the effects of figurative language, and to have command of basic guidelines in the use of figurative language. Finally, it is important for arguers to see more clearly the role of word arrangement, that is, to understand syntactic ambiguity, and to see the potential power of parallelism, repetition, interrogatives, slogans, and transitions.

EXERCISES

1. Write a 500-word summary of what you did last week, or a description of something. Then shorten it to 300 words, and then to 100 words without altering the central message. Turn in all three versions, and include a 100-word statement about what this exercise in word economy taught you.

2. Listen to, and study the printed version of, Dr. Martin Luther King, Jr.'s speech, "I Have a Dream." Analyze the figurative language and his use of balanced phrasing (parallelism). How many times did he repeat, "I have a dream today ..." ? Include in your analysis some evaluative statements about the degree of effectiveness of these factors.

3. Carefully note the use of "God" and "Devil" terms in the daily newspapers, news magazines, or newscasts on radio and television. Evaluate their appropriateness and effectiveness. Did they help to persuade you without your first noticing it?

4. Examine your storehouse of name-calling labels that you have come to apply to various people. Select five individuals (use fictitious names), list the main labels you have come to associate with them, and then discuss the accuracy and fairness of your stereotyping. Have some of these labels shifted noticeably recently (either positively or negatively), as you came to know the people better? Summarize your findings in a 500-word essay.

5. Select the jargon (shoptalk) of a particular trade (plumber, carpenter, or painter), profession (doctor, lawyer, teacher), general occupation (waitress, construction worker, manager), sport (hockey, soccer, tennis), or other recreation or hobby (skin diving, amateur radio, fishing). In a 500-word essay clarify what the chosen items mean in that context and why the term has probably come to be employed in that way (you may have to guess if the etymology is not clear). To provide context, you may want to begin the paper with a brief narrative in which you include and underline the terms you intend to analyze.

16 Oral Presentation of Argumentation

Importance of Oral Presentation
Improving Vocal Factors
Improving Nonverbal Visual Factors
Modes of Delivery
Rehearsing
Summary
Exercises

IMPORTANCE OF ORAL PRESENTATION

One's personality may be clearly revealed in one's written work, but not so inevitably or fully as in oral communication. For instance, hearing speeches by journalists, novelists, or textbook authors, whose works we have only read, may have shocked us because they seemed to be far removed from the people we had imagined them to be on the basis of their writings. Indeed, sometimes a veritable tiger in print may be a gentle lamb on the platform, or vice versa. Frequently, people who seem to be very tolerant and objective in their writings (perhaps the result of hard work and many revisions), may impress us as being aggressively authoritarian when we meet them in person. Since our focus in this textbook is on oral argumentation, it is important to look carefully at the presentation of the oral dimension.

Communicating orally has many potential advantages. As one author recently summed it up: "The comparative advantage of the combination of the audible and visible codes over the audible code alone and over print seems reasonable, especially in terms of persuasive effect."[1] The

1. Andersen, *Persuasion*, p. 227.

message can be made more interesting and vital. It can be adapted more effectively to audience reactions. It can appeal to both the ear and eye of the recipient, and can establish a personal bond between sender and receiver. That delivery is very important has been substantiated by a number of studies. The importance of effective delivery in the careers of various leaders in our society has been frequently analyzed, and numerous experiments have corroborated that fluency in delivery is important in facilitating the changing of attitudes favorably toward a message, in enhancing understanding of the material, and in increasing the speaker's ethos.[2] It is even more clear that poor delivery decreases effectiveness, for if what the recipients see and hear is unpleasant or unattractive, they will be less inclined to react favorably to the message and the sender.

Unfortunately, there have been individuals who have so over-emphasized delivery that the implication is that what counts most is not what you say but how you say it. This conclusion has made "good delivery" suspect, and justifiably so, for it suggests a prostitution of content, a focus on vain, insincere, artificial performing. Obviously, emphasis on good delivery should in no way detract from the importance of sound substance, for it is the content that must be kept in the spotlight. But to witness the tragedy of a highly informed and thoughtful person, who has a truly important message, stumble through an embarrassingly ineffective presentation is a sorrowful experience indeed. It is matched only by the tragedy of hearing a shallow, uninformed person win plaudits only because of polished delivery. Surely no oral communication program or argumentation course at a respectable college or university would take pride in encouraging the covering up of inadequate substance with polished delivery. This has been denounced throughout history and should continue to be denounced.

In fact, beginning speakers must be cautioned against being unduly impressed should they be praised for "excellent delivery." Many times smooth speakers may impress and tantalize their listeners so that the latter give immediate, positive response through laughter, applause, or comments of praise. But afterward, the audience may realize, in their more thoughtful moments, that the speaker's content was superficial and inadequate. This in turn may well cause them to reverse their opinion of the speaker, turning from praise to ridicule. The speaker, like the court jester of old, is dismissed from their minds when the

---

2. For a summary of some studies, see McCroskey, *An Introduction to Rhetorical Communication*, pp. 183–88; and Sproule, *Argument*, pp. 256–58.

"entertainment" is concluded. But these second thoughts are seldom if ever relayed to the speakers, so they go on mistakenly believing that they are more effective than they really are. Thus, as we elaborate in this chapter on the importance of good delivery, it is with the understanding that the subject is approached with the above warning in mind.

IMPROVING VOCAL FACTORS

Attention should be focused at the outset on some of the problems involved in, and some of the methods arguers might employ to improve, the vocal aspects of their speaking.

Articulation

In the haste and tension of a speech, sounds may be inadvertently added or omitted. A sound may be substituted for another, or may be inverted (for example, irrelevant becomes irrevelant). Perhaps the most common difficulty is the general distortion caused by the lethargic or uncoordinated movement of the jaw, lips, and tongue.

Accurate, precise, and energetic articulation is very important to effective oral communication. A number of suggestions on improving articulation may be of help. Slow and accurate oral reading, frequently engaged in, and conscientious oral rehearsal of one's prepared speech will aid greatly in improving articulation. So may going through sets of specially arranged exercises. One can energetically manipulate the jaw, lips, and tongue with exaggerated precision, much as athletes energetically stretch and flex their muscles in practice sessions.

Any serious problems in articulation, rhythm (stuttering), or voice quality should be taken to trained speech therapists. For any student needing professional help, making use of speech clinics on campus is an extremely wise decision, for such an opportunity may not come again so easily or inexpensively.

Pronunciation

Closely allied with articulation is pronunciation, which is concerned not only with the proper formation of the desired sound but also with the socially accepted conventions of syllable division and stress. Suppose a person pronounces the name of the famous Swiss city as "Gen´e-va," with the heaviest stress on the first syllable. We would say that that person has mispronounced it, for in the English spoken in the United States it is generally accepted that the syllable division is "Ge-ne´va," with the major stress on the second syllable. For some strange reason, many speakers fail during rehearsals to check the dictionary on pronunciations of words about which they are uncertain. One's mispronunciations suggest limited language ability and a failure to do one's homework, which will likely decrease one's prestige in the minds of one's listeners. On the other hand the ill effects of occasional mispronunciations ought not to be exaggerated. Experienced speakers have learned to avoid becoming unduly agitated by occasional slips, and even to use them as a source of humor.

Pitch

Pitch refers to the highness or lowness of the voice as perceived by the listener. It is determined by the frequency and degree of intensity of vibration of the vocal folds in the larynx; the length, thickness, and tension of the vocal cords; and by the resonation in upper throat, nasal or mouth chambers that may heighten or weaken certain overtones.

Everyone has their own optimum pitch, that is, the pitch level at which sounds are most easily produced and most richly resonated. The objective is to permit this optimum pitch to be revealed in one's oral communication activities without strain—to become one's habitual pitch.

During informal conversation most people employ a healthy and pleasing pitch variety, but under the formality and tension of speaking before groups many people lapse into a wooden monotone, thus sharply reducing their effectiveness. Variety in pitch helps to clarify meaning, to communicate the speaker's emotional values, and to make a more interesting and pleasant experience for the listener.

Thus, one should do all one can to develop an appropriate pitch variety. To achieve this, it is important to be emotionally relaxed, physically rested and healthy, and confident of one's material. One must try to have a sense of conversing with one's audience rather than reciting a monotonous string of words. One should practice pitch variety by reading material with heavy emotional overtones such as anger, fear, envy, love, and so on. This kind of material helps one to forget oneself and to focus on the material. Reading conversational material, even the comics, is helpful, for it demands much pitch variety to portray the characterizations.

Volume

Another important vocal element in the speaking process is the degree of loudness with which the sounds are uttered. Loudness is an objective, quantitative element, which is expressed in terms of decibels. A whisper is approximately twenty decibels, ordinary conversation approximately sixty decibels, and loud speech approximately eighty deicbels. Loudness is perceived differently by different listeners, depending upon their hearing capabilities, their distance from the source, and the intervening elements with which the projected sound has to contend (such as wind, solid objects, and competing noises). Nothing is more disheartening than to realize that an important statement, or a whole speech, is being missed by a sizable portion of an audience merely because the volume is too low.

Speakers, therefore, have to be sensitive to the size of the room, the acoustics in the room, the nature and location of their listeners, and any intervening distractions. Although mechanical amplification has increasingly come to the aid of the public speaker, frequently it is not available or is not working properly. Thus, one would be wise not to depend on having it and to discipline oneself to think in terms of projecting one's voice to the back of the room.

Many speakers begin sentences at an appropriate level of loudness, but unconsciously reduce it gradually to an inappropriate degree toward the end of sentences, because of inadequate breath supply or control. Listening to a tape recording of one's speech may help one to detect this and to improve one's volume level.

Rate

Another important vocal element for oral communicators is rate, that is, the speed at which they speak. All people have their own characteristic rate, depending on their personality traits, their thought processes, the coordination of their speech musculature, and their speaking habits developed over the years. A quiet, passive person would probably speak more slowly than an impetuous, dynamic person. Thoughtful individuals usually measure their words more carefully and hence speak more slowly than one who is not so sensitive to making accurate and meaningful statements. Free and fluent use of articulators enables a person to speak more rapidly than one who has to put more effort into the muscular coordination needed for articulation. Furthermore, a person who has had to compete with five siblings for eighteen years perhaps has come to speak more rapidly than some one who was an only child. Professors who have spent twenty years lecturing slowly to enable students to take full notes often carry this slow rate over into their other public speaking by force of habit. College and university debaters have to guard against an excessively rapid rate, born out of the necessity of saying as much as possible in the very limited time allocated. They become trapped by this one rate, and it often carries over inappropriately into their other speaking, so that a former debater can be spotted immediately by a perceptive listener.

The vast majority of speakers will find that their communication will be more pleasant to listen to , more clear, and more comprehensible if it is not too slow or too fast, and if it is appropriately varied. Many inexperienced speakers speak too rapidly, mainly because of excessive tension. Subconsciously trying to get the ordeal over with as soon as possible, they race along much faster than their normal rate. The excessive rate frequently leads to lack of breath control; distorted articulation; lack of pitch, volume, and stress variety; and lack of conversational directness. Hence, learning to control one's rate can lead to many related improvements and can help to make a better speaker.

Pausing   Since the rate of delivery of a particular speech is dependent not only on the degree of speed with which the sounds are uttered, or on the prolongation of the sounds, but also on the frequency and duration of silence between utterances, we also need to focus attention on the role of the pause. Most inexperienced speakers simply do not pause enough. They speed along as if a moment of silence was an admission of some failure. Radio announcers, who depend solely on their voices to hold their audience, rightly consider silence a major foe. But speakers whose audiences see them can welcome pausing as a potentially helpful ally.

"Pausing" is here to be thought of as a purposeful, meaningful, sometimes planned (most, of course, are unconscious and a result of experience and habit), period of silence, which is highly important to more clearly and firmly communicating the message. A pause is well-organized silence. It can be as eloquent as any spoken word.

The speaker needs to think in terms of speech phrases, most of which would be shorter than long subordinate clauses, and even shorter than some simple sentences. Certainly the speaker should abandon the notion of pausing only at the end of sentences. Many experienced speakers frequently employ speech phrases of from three to five words, but obviously no mathematical rule is appropriate here.

A number of benefits flow from appropriate use of pauses. The material can be made more clear and emphatic. A natural, conversational style is more likely to be developed. Frequent and appropriate pauses can help one, literally, to catch one's breath, and the resultant improved breath control can lead in turn to less tension and clearer articulation. Furthermore, speakers who dare to confront silence usually win a certain admiration from their audience. As any teacher knows, a pause catches the attention and focuses wandering minds, usually more quickly than will words. Also, expectancy is heightened, and significance is built up for the key term or phrase to follow. After an important assertion, experienced speakers often will inject a pause to permit the statement to be fully absorbed by their listeners. Furthermore, a pause immediately preceding a key phrase can often aid retention of it.

Rate variety   Not only should one gain control over the number of words spoken per minute and the frequency and duration of pauses, but, just as important, one should learn to vary the rate appropriately from paragraph to paragraph, sentence to sentence, and from phrase to phrase, depending, for one thing, upon the content. When relating a personal anecdote or other material easy for the listeners to grasp because of its simplicity or interestingness, one should speed up. When the material becomes more complete, more difficult, and less familiar, one should slow down. Major contentions should be expressed more slowly than subordinate supporting material. Key phrases should be expressed more slowly than less important ones. Words or phrases difficult to pronounce, and a sequence of awkward sound combinations should be uttered more slowly.

Rate variation also should be appropriate to the audience. A younger audience would perhaps desire a faster rate than an older one. An audience with a high intelligence level, able to comprehend more quickly, would be able to contend with a faster rate. A transitory audience, that is, where people wander in and out (an outdoor soapbox type of situation), forces speakers to increase their rate in order to hold the listeners. Those who cannot see the speaker, such as a radio audience, demand a faster speed from the communicator to hold their interest. Also, listeners whose command of the language employed by the speaker is not strong, such as a group of foreign students, appreciate it when the speaker's rate is considerably slower than normal.

Stress

A final vocal factor that includes many of the forgoing vocal elements and is extremely important for an oral communicator to master is stress. Anything that helps to contrast a word or phrase significantly to the material around it will tend to stress, that is, highlight or call attention to, that word or phrase. Perhaps we can illustrate the multiple components of stress by stretching our imaginative powers for the moment and picturing a huge medieval castle surrounded by a moat. We stress terms usually by raising the pitch, increasing the volume, and prolonging the vowel, thus enlarging a house into a castle. Then, by pausing before and after the stressed material we isolate it with a moatlike encirclement. Sometimes, of course, we achieve stress by lowering the volume to a whisper. Actors and experienced public speakers are fully aware of the importance of appropriate stress variety. But inexperienced speakers frequently present their material as if every idea were of equal weight, as if all words were created equal. As a result, their presentation becomes less interesting, less clear, and less meaningful than it would otherwise be.

IMPROVING NONVERBAL VISUAL FACTORS

When we deliver messages in person, we do so not with just our voices but with our whole being. Facial expressions are extremely important.[3] Our posture, motions of head and body, and gestures of arm and hand serve as allies or foes, as reinforcers or detractors, depending upon how well we use them.

Widespread use of visual cues

We are all aware that in a great many situations human beings consciously employ nonverbal visual cues in order to transmit their message vividly and economically to their audience, whether it is one person or many. A football official signifies an infraction of a rule by using a specific gesture that can be immediately understood by the thousands of people in the stands. Words would not suffice. A policeman directing traffic may rely on shouted commands and a whistle, but he also depends on specific gestures that tell the drivers to stop or proceed.

3. See Erwin P. Bettinghaus, *Persuasive Communication*, (3rd ed., New York: Holt, Rinehart and Winston, 1980), p. 128.

Firemen, truck drivers, factory workers, military personnel, and radio station personnel have their special gestures.

A deaf mute relies entirely on visual means to communicate, and gains command of the intricate sign language that has been developed, complete with sentence structure and syntax. Many American Indian tribes had highly developed sign languages; less involved ones are used today by Boy Scouts, sororities, and other such organizations. As remarkable as these sign languages may be, they are severely restricted in that their vocabulary is limited, the recipient needs to see the sender, and nothing else can be done with the hands when communicating.

The more closely we associate with others, such as with our family, with people at work, or with friends, the more likely are we to rely on mutually understandable nonverbal cues in place of speech. Whenever silence must be kept, whenever the audience cannot hear, whenever privacy is desired, and whenever insufficient time is available for audible statements, nonverbal visual cues are a fundamental requirement for communication. Thus, the range and variety of communicative situations in which human beings *consciously* use nonverbal visual cues are indeed great and highly significant.

We perhaps are less aware of the incredible amount of communication we do *unconsciously* by numerous nonverbal visual cues. A football player unknowingly gives away the direction of the coming play by a slight head movement or a shifting of his weight. A salesperson's arrogant swagger tells the prospective customer to be on guard. A shuffling walk suggests illness, laziness, remorse, or peevishness. A weak handshake negates a cheery, "So nice to see you." A mother tells her child she loves him, but her cold demeanor tells the child something else. A dinner guest may effusively praise his hostess's food, but the fact that he only pecks at it tells her another tale.

Visual cues should be purposeful

One should use visual cues in some definite reinforcing role. They should make a meaningful contribution. In other words, they should be specific and definite, not random and vague. Carefully controlled, they should clearly communicate to the audience via a complementary visual medium a specific message. Aimless gesturing is merely confusing. One should not gesture just for the sake of gesturing, but for a specific purpose.

Visual cues should be fully executed

A visual cue should not be halfhearted or incomplete. Hand gestures should be approximately at waist level where they can be seen, and thus communicate their intended message. Motions should be entered into with sufficient vitality. A halfhearted gesture loses its communicative value and may even be more of a liability than an asset. It is the "follow-through" concept, as any golfer knows, which is so important. If the motion is worth doing, it is worth doing fully and well.

Visual cues should be spontaneous

Visual cues should come forth naturally, not in a forced, artificial, or mechanical manner. They should be smooth and gradual (unless abruptness is called for), so as not to call attention to themselves. Indeed, it has been said with a good deal of truth that the best gesture is the one not seen; that is, it so naturally complements what the speaker is saying that the listener is virtually unaware of it, but unconsciously absorbs its reinforcing power. Some inexperienced speakers complain that gesturing feels "unnatural." This rests on the assumption that it is more natural for the human being not to gesture. The reverse is true, for human beings do indeed naturally employ parts of their body to accompany the noises emanating from the larynx. Excited people illustrate this very clearly, as they uninhibitedly "let themselves go," with natural gusto. For example, visualize the actions of the athlete excitedly complaining to the official about some decision, a joyous cheerleader applauding some action in the game, an anxious parent severely admonishing a child for some ill-advised act, or an agitated supervisor bemoaning some foolish action of a subordinate. Whereas it is true that part of the process of maturity is learning to subdue the excessive gesturing of the child or the emotionally upset person, for healthy human beings some gesturing with some parts of their body is defintely natural when they communicate. After all, an unhealthy, severely depressed person sits disconsolate and "unnaturally" immobile. An effective speaker, then, should learn to gesture with spontaneity, tempered only with wise and appropriate control.

Visual cues should be diverse

Many human beings develop certain habitual physical moves and tend to use them excessively, usually without realizing it. For instance, most baseball players go through certain habitual movements when stepping up to the plate, such as scraping the ground with their cleats, tugging at their belt, touching their cap, swinging the bat a few times, or rubbing part of the face. Likewise, speakers may excessively and unknowingly scratch behind their ear, rub their chin, or smooth their hair, which become as characteristic of them as their own voices. Most professors have their unique, and sometimes colorful, gestures, which often make for interesting dormitory imitations and jokes. Using the same hand gesture for a multitude of different purposes soon strips it of its distinctive communicative value. We all need to be sensitive to the value of employing a rich variety of gestures if we really want them to be meaningful reinforcements.

Visual cues should be economical

One should employ only those gestures that are needed, and only those that make a specific contribution. One should avoid excessive movements which inevitably lose the communicative value they might have had at the outset. Some flamboyant, energetic speakers use gestures too extravagantly. They wave their arms or pound their fists so excessively that the gestures become serious distractions, or even ludicrous actions, virtually meaningless in their repetition.

Visual cues should be coordinated

The visual cue should be properly timed so as not to come too soon or too late, resulting in a meaningless or even humorous situation. The gesture should be well coordinated with all parts of the body, so that spontaneity and naturalness is enhanced by proper timing and coordination.

Visual cues should be appropriate

The personality of the speakers will govern to a large extent the type and frequency of their gesturing. A quiet individual, for instance, will probably gesture less frequently and energetically than will a flamboyant extrovert. Women are perhaps expected to gesture with less forcefulness and more refinement than men. An emotion-packed subject would call for more gesturing than an informational report on a less highly-charged issue. Younger people in the audience would perhaps respond better to more gesturing than would older people. In a large room with a large audience, vigorous and expansive gestures would be more appropriate than in a small audience situation. A solemn occasion would call for less gesturing than a joyous occasion.

Significance of visual cues

Having looked closely at some of the many possible conscious and unconscious cues we as communicators transmit to our audience, we could almost become neurotic, fearing that some miscue might negate our whole message. Although we need to be sensitive to these cues, to become overly anxious serves no wise purpose. One should realize that the audience absorbs the general overall communicative effort, of which visual cues are only a part. Healthy sensitivity, not irrational obsession, should govern one's approach to the utilization of visual cues. Also, one should realize that all cues are not equal. Some carry far more potential for good or ill than do others.

Cultural diversity in visual cues

Visual cues are culture-bound, that is, they are arbitrary and not necessarily universally employed, contrary to assumptions of a number of decades ago. Modern research in this area operates, then, on the premise that these body movements are learned rather than instinctive. People from varied cultural and subcultural backgrounds use visual cues in different ways, thus "our gesture language which is meaningful to us is as unintelligible to another culture as our verbal language is."[4] The "OK" gesture in the United States is an obscene gesture in some countries. In admonishing a small child not to do something, we shake the index finger forward and backward, whereas in other countries they would move it from side to side. In the United States we beckon someone to come by extending the arm, palm up, and moving the index finger or all fingers upward and toward the summoner, and pulling the gesture back toward ourselves. But in many countries the same request is communicated with palm down and the fingers and hand curving downward and toward the summoner, similar to our gesture telling someone to go away. We clasp our hands over our head as a symbol of

4. Mary Key, "Gestures and Responses: A Preliminary Study Among Some Indian Tribes of Bolivia," *Studies in Linguistics*, 16 (1962): 98.

victory, but in the Soviet Union such a gesture means friendship. The possibility of serious misunderstandings is readily apparent.

MODES OF DELIVERY

Various modes, or methods, of delivery are available to a public speaker. A person may be called upon without notice to give some remarks, to give an impromptu speech. In situations in which one has been given the opportunity to prepare, one may choose to speak extemporaneously, to speak from a prepared manuscript, or to speak from memory. All methods of presentation have distinctive characteristics, advantages, and disadvantages, which the following discussion will endeavor to clarify. Also, it should be recognized that the four categories are not mutually exclusive, for they may be used in combination.

Impromptu Speaking

Definition   An impromptu speech is one given with no advance notice and with little if any advance preparation. Lawyers jump to their feet to object, legislators plunge into the give-and-take of debate, or a national political figure has to respond immediately to questions from reporters. At a party one may suddenly be called upon to tell about one's recent trip to Washington, D.C. In a history class one may be asked to list the causes of the American Revolution. One's supply and command of information on the topics may vary considerably. One's trip to Washington has filled one's mind with exciting and vivid experiences, so it is a question of knowing what to exclude. One's mind is less filled with information on the causes of the American Revolution, especially as it has been a week since one read the assignment. Thus, the extent to which one can be impromptu depends on the degree of information at one's disposal. But the above examples have in common one characteristic: at the moment one was called on, no precise preparation of the chosen subject had taken place.

Utilization   Many experienced speakers who are advanced in years may no longer spend much time preparing their speeches. A religious leader, for instance, who has spent a lifetime in theological study and sermon preparation may give a highly meaningful, well-organized speech on some religious subject with very little advance notice or preparation. Because of the pressure of time, many busy people in public life gather their thoughts together only while being introduced by the chairperson, and yet proceed to give an excellent presentation simply because they are so thoroughly informed on the subject and experienced in speaking on it. But this is not to lead readers to assume that they can go and do likewise. In fact, the purpose in stressing these cases is precisely because so many inexperienced speakers point to these examples and say, "If they can do it, why can't I?" Perhaps one may be able to when one has attained a certain station in life, but college and university training appropriately focuses on helping students to prepare as well as deliver speeches.

Extemporaneous speaking

Definition   Speaking extemporaneously means that speakers have thought through and organized their material, but the exact language to be employed comes at the moment of delivery. They usually speak from notes or an outline. The advance preparation may mean a sketchy outline rather hastily put together. On the other hand it may mean a speech very thoroughly developed.

The term "extempore" has shifted in meaning and connotation through the centuries. An ancient Latin term, it originally meant an unpremeditated speech, both in thought and language, much as we have defined an impromptu speech. Also, it had a somewhat derogatory connotation. But during the first half of the nineteenth century it acquired a more favorable connotation. It came to mean a speech that was unpremeditated only in the language employed, but one that had been carefully thought-out and structured. It is obvious, then, that when modern textbook writers quote people earlier than the nineteenth century on "extemporaneous" speaking, the person quoted was really talking about what we today call impromptu speaking. Unfortunately, most contemporary dictionaries still define "extemporaneous" in its prenineteenth century meaning.

Utilization   Extemporaneous speaking is perhaps the most widely used of all the four modes of delivery. Most clergy, business and labor leaders, political officials, teachers and college and university debaters use it most of the time. The kind of speaking assigned in most speech classes in colleges and universities is extemporaneous. To learn to speak well extemporaneously will also aid one in the other modes of presentation as well, so it is extremely important to note the advantages, disadvantages, and means of improving the use of the extemporaneous method.

Advantages   The advantages are many. When done well it means that the speakers have given full and careful thought to their remarks and have done wheatever research is necessary. A well-defined organizational structure reduces the likelihood of wandering. Yet it may be adjusted to meet the immediate speaking situation, and freedom and freshness of language is retained. The speaker is able to adapt to audience reactions and to develop an intimate rapport through conversational directness. It is the mode of delivery which will most likely link the minds of speaker and listener in a clear and meaningful communication experience. Speakers develop considerable confidence knowing that they can handle the extemporaneous method. Often the audience is much impressed, for they feel they would have considerable uncertainty and tension with the extemporaneous method. Speakers gain experience in thinking on their feet, and of phrasing as they go along.

Disadvantages   If not done well, extemporaneous speaking can cause many problems. It may result in lack of precise phrasing, in considerable repetition, and too much stumbling and hesitation. Important information may be unintentionally omitted, and irrelevant material may be added on the spur of the moment. Organization may become loose, subpoints may be overemphasized, and major points may be underemphasized. The speech may run overtime, as the speaker warms to the audience response and the general excitement of the moment.

Suggestions for improvement   When faced with the actual event of the extemporaneous speech, one should not feel obligated to adhere slavishly to one's outline or present a carbon copy of one's structure. Many inexperienced speakers become frustrated and discouraged when they do not present their material exactly as it is in their outline. As a result, they lose confidence during and after the speech. They somehow feel they have failed. Such should not be the feeling, for extemporaneous speeches should have considerable flexibility. Furthermore, the audience will not be aware of the speaker's modifications.

During the speech one should use notes that are aids, not hindrances. Use them well. Many people like to have their outline or notes on four-by-six cards (some prefer smaller ones, some larger). They should be large enough and yet easy to handle. Especially if there is no rostrum, these cards, unlike a sheet of paper, permit freedom of gesture. Make notations large and clear so that they can be seen at a glance. Little scribblings that may be readable at the time they are written may not be comprehensible when one nervously tries to understand them during the speech. By all means, one should feel free to use one's notes. Inexperienced speakers often furtively glance at their materials as if they were cheating by doing so. Speakers who attempt to ignore their notes usually lunge back to them with a gasp, or fidget through a prolonged pause while they search for their train of thought. One should become accustomed to using the notes openly and with no sense of guilt. Certainly one ought to feel free to read prose or poetry quotations, or statistical material. At the same time, of course, one should abide by the maxim of not using notes too much, but of maintaining eye contact and a sense of direct communication with the audience. The general guideline, then, should be to use the notes sparingly but unashamedly.

While speaking, one should try to be conscious of audience reactions and adjust accordingly. If animosity is apparent, try to calm it. If interest is sagging, try to stimulate it. If the audience seems puzzled, try to clarify the material. Thus, the opportuntiy for adaptability and flexibility in the extemporaneous method may be used to the utmost.

Speaking from manuscript

Definition   A third mode of delivery is to speak from a prepared manuscript. It is important to stress the word *speak*, for we are concerned here not with *reading* from manuscript, which is considerably different. Generally, the latter involves presenting something written by someone else, so that a departure from the prepared material would be to do an injustice to the author. Some instances would include the recitation of a poem, or the reading of a short story or famous oration. On occasion, secretaries or public relations people may be delegated to read to the press the message of their superior. Furthermore, in the case of an oral reading of a poetic or prose selection, the purpose frequently is to evoke a feeling rather than to relay information or to persuade. These kinds of situations have so dominated the definition of presenting material from a manuscript that very few people (including textbook writers) are careful to differentiate between that and *speaking* from manuscript.

Actually, speaking from manuscript *should* involve some deviation and interpolation. For instance, one may want to refer to someone in the audience. One may want to inject a recent experience or refer to a relevant article in the morning paper. An appropriate bit of humor may suddenly come to mind. Speaking from manuscript, then, is a speech using a prepared manuscript but with appropriate impromptu modifications, if desired, as the speech progresses.

Utilization   Speaking from manuscript is becoming increasingly employed, for better or ill. The strict time limits imposed by, and the large heterogeneous audiences of, radio and television make a manuscript mandatory. At conventions the numerous speeches have to be carefully timed, and hence a manuscript is expected. Complaints are made increasingly that parliamentary and congressional debates are becoming too much a series of unrelated set speeches from manuscript instead of the cut and thrust of more extemporaneous or impromptu debating. Community leaders as well as political figures are becoming more dependent on a script. With the increasing availability of secretarial assistance in preparing manuscripts, the practice is likely to increase.

Advantages   A number of significant advantages could result from speaking from manuscript. The likelihood is increased, but not guaranteed, that one will say what one wants to say in the manner in which one wishes to say it. Greater clarity of thought and organization, greater soundness of logic, and better supporting materials often will result. Irrelevant excursions, needless repetition, and wordiness can be carefully controlled. The speech can be precisely timed. Vagueness and ambiguity can be reduced, and the desired mood can be created. One is more likely to employ a broader and richer vocabulary, to utilize figurative language more effectively, to construct transitional bridges with greater care. One is likely to achieve greater variety of sentence constructions, to vary the declarative with occasional interrogative and imperative expressions. One may wisely rely more heavily on the active voice, but also use the passive where appropriate. One is more likely to vary the length of the sentences in a manner that is both arresting and meaningful. Proper emphasis is more likely to be achieved. That is, the coordinate elements are seen as equals, and the subordinate are clearly placed in a lesser role. More effective utilization of appropriate alliteration, balanced phraseology, repetition, and rhythm is possible. Variations in pause, stress, pitch, rate, and volume can be more carefully practiced and executed. Proper pronunciations are more likley to be checked out ahead of time. Inaccurate, incomplete, careless, and tactless remarks can be sharply reduced if not totally eliminated. By eliminating the fear of forgetting, a manuscript permits one to approach the rostrum with considerable confidence. Finally, it provides a good, permanent product to file for future reference.

Disadvantages   A number of disadvantages are likely to be present if the speaker is ineffective. Many people, perhaps most, simply do not read well. This is understandable, for most people are accustomed to silently skimming the newspaper. Little or no time is given anymore to reading aloud for family recreation as earlier generations did. Students have to engage in swift and silent reading.

Ineffective manuscript speakers lose the sense of spontaneity, directness, animation, and involvement that are so necessary to good communication. Stumbling along in a stiff and mechanical manner, they do not extract the proper meaning and mood from the written material. The language may be in the style of an essay rather than in an oral style. A monotone may develop, the rate of speaking frequently becomes too rapid and constant, and projection of the voice is lessened because the head is down. Adaptation to the listeners is often at a minimum, and they become bored and inattentive. The manuscript, through excessive handling, may serve as a distraction. Usually gestures and body movements are held to a monotonous minimum. A major problem is that speakers adopt a false goal. That is, they assume their task is to repeat the words that are written rather than to communicate the meaning the words are intended to convey.

Furthermore, since a manuscript obviously can be, and frequently is, written by someone other than the speaker, the audience may lose respect for the communicator. The audience may interpret a poor presentation as an example of a ghostwritten speech inadequately practiced or comprehended by the speaker. This decline in the speaker's ethos will seriously detract from what may be excellent substance.

Suggestions for improvement   A number of specific suggestions may be of help as one endeavors to speak better from a manuscript. One will find it helpful, especially during rehearsal, to mark one's manuscript in some meaningful, uncluttered manner. Underscoring, typing in capital letters, or printing those words and phrases intended to be stressed may be useful. One may also want to insert marks at places where pauses are to be employed and to use other marks to indicate an increase or decrease in rate and volume. One may write brief notes or ciphers in the margins. Some speakers use such a marked copy for rehearsal only, but others use notations in their speech script as well. The manuscript from which one speaks should be easily readable. It should be clearly typewritten, approximately triple-spaced, and, of course, typed on only one side of the paper.

Clergy and other experienced public speakers find it helpful to make use of the vertical (top to bottom) as well as the usual horizontal (left to right) dimension in their script, especially at key places and when utilizing words or phrases in a series. For example, the following illustrates the use of the vertical dimension in order to see more clearly the relationship of ideas to the balance and rhythm of expression:

We must build a more
    just and
    humane society.
We must work
    to secure our freedoms,
    to extend equality in
        housing,
        employment, and
        education, and
    to build respect for democratic processes.
The task
    will not be easy,
    nor will it be glamorous, but
the rewards will be
    many and
    satisfying.

The audience will not easily forgive mispronunciations in speaking from manuscript, so one should consult the dictionary for any doubtful terms. If words or combinations of sounds prove to be stumbling blocks, search for appropriate synonyms or other expressions. Avoid too many lengthy, complex sentence constructions. Write for the ear, not for the eye. Many inexperienced speakers make the mistake of trying to read too much in a single period of exhalation and create irregular and uncontrolled breathing patterns. If they paused more frequently, they would be amazed at their increased effectiveness and reduced tension.

One should try to extend the eye-voice span, that is, the distance between where one's voice is and where the eye has advanced to. A good oral reader has an eye-voice span of about seven or eight words. Furthermore, one ought to be able to look at one's audience at least half of the time.

The rate of delivery should be slower than in extemporaneous speaking in order to achieve clear articulation and appropriate variety in pitch, stress, and volume. Many inexperienced speakers simply race through the words in front of them. The tendency is to assume that all printed words are created equal, and to utter them with no sense of relative importance.

One should concentrate throughout the speech on meaning and ideas. One should create a sense of communication with one's audience, and should feel free to insert, delete, or alter content as the circumstances seem to suggest. One should not consider oneself a slave to what has been written on the paper. The speaker is still the master.

Speaking from memory

Definition and utilization   In addition to impromptu comments, extemporaneous speaking, or speaking from a manuscript, one may utilize in some situations a fourth mode—one may deliver one's speech from memory. Without manuscript or notes of any kind to aid one in expressing one's carefully prepared statements, one relies totally on memory.

Ancient storytellers relied on memory to pass on to following generations the heritage of their culture.[5] In this oral tradition Greek and Roman orators held forth in great grandeur. The great first century Roman teacher of rhetoric, Quintilian, provided the most complete discussion of the role of memory in speech-making to that time. The discussion of memory by teachers of rhetoric gradually declined and virtually disappeared in the eighteenth and nineteenth centuries. But twentieth century American speech textbooks are beginning to include again some discussion of the role of memory in oral communication. It is still valuable in some formalized speaking situations, such as a sermon, or a memorial address.

5. Many readers may be unfamiliar with these traditions in the Arab world. A brief insight can be secured from H. Samuel Hamod, "Arab and Moslem Rhetorical Theory and Practice," *Central States Speech Journal*, 14 (1963): 97–102.

Advantages   To have gone through the laborious and meticulous procedures needed to commit a speech to memory usually leaves one with an assurance that is difficult to match. One may well feel a great command over ideas and wording. Unimpeded by manuscript or notes, one is totally free to interact with the audience. Gestures and body movements frequently come much more easily. Experienced speakers feel no sense of slavery to repeating words exactly as they were rehearsed, and phrasing and vocabulary will be altered during the presentation, as seems appropriate. Finally, the timing of the speech is usually carefully worked out.

Disadvantages   There are some disadvantages to speaking from memory. It requires what most people would consider an unreasonable amount of time and effort. Few speakers want to invest so heavy a commitment for what they feel would be rather limited returns. If not handled well, a memorized speech can be inflexible in phraseology and wooden in delivery, in other words, it sounds "memorized" or "canned." That is, the sense of audience contact is missing, and speakers seem to be talking *at* their listeners, rather than communicating *with* them. The speaker may put a disproportionate amount of attention on delivery and not enough on the message. Finally, the danger of forgetting is fearsome and creates an unnecessary obstacle. There are enough things for speakers to worry about without adding the burden of recalling from memory the language they have prepared.

Suggestions for improvement   When delivering a memorized speech, one should follow most of the guidelines already discussed in connection with extemporaneous and manuscript speaking. The object is to be as conversational as when speaking extemporaneously. Work for spontaneous and natural gesturing. Be sure to avoid uttering all the words at the same speed and with the same emphasis. Work for rate and stress variety, and utilize pauses effectively.

Interrelationships

It is a mistake to think of these four modes of delivery as distinct, mutually exclusive methods. They often are combined in some way, as has already been emphasized throughout this chapter. The impromptu remark is highly welcome in the extemporaneous and manuscript speech. The memorized item is an appropriate insert into any of the other methods. An appropriate number of written quotations or statistical data are effectively employed in an extemporaneous speech.

Before leaving the discussion of the different modes of delivery, it ought to be made clear that no one method is superior and another inferior. Many textbooks unfortunately assert or imply that the extemporaneous mode is the best. But each method has its advantages and disadvantages, as we have noted. Thus, it is not the mode that determines effectiveness but, instead, the ability of the speaker to use the chosen method. Therefore, one should choose the mode in which one is the most proficient. On the other hand, since the occasion often dictates which mode ought to be employed (a script is needed for a radio address, for example), one needs to arm oneself by becoming trained and experienced in all modes. This demands, among other things, a full understanding of the role of systematic and careful rehearsing.

REHEARSING

Importance and rewards

Rehearsing for any public speech is an extremely significant phase. It must be done thoroughly and well if the speech is to realize its maximum success. After the basic steps of research and composition have been completed, the task of rehearsing is a vital link to the moment in which one will deliver the speech before the designated audience. After spending several hours preparing the speech it is incredibly unwise not to devote enough time to molding and polishing the delivery of the material. A speech is not the composition, but rather composition plus delivery. Intelligent rehearsal will embed the material more firmly in one's mind, will improve the organization and transitions, and will greatly increase one's confidence and will help get rid of aimless worrying about the speech. Appropriate rehearsal will very often be the determining factor whether or not the speaker (and the audience) will have an enjoyable and profitable experience. It must be admitted that careful rehearsal will not guarantee a successful speech, for too many things may go wrong at the last minute. But conscientious rehearsal is one of the soundest investments of time that can be made. With it, the odds of future success go up considerably. One ought not to be discouraged if in a few instances exhaustive rehearsal does not seem to bring proportionate immediate rewards. The long-run rewards are almost sure to come.

When to rehearse

One should begin one's rehearsal as early as possible. Finish composing the speech a few days prior to its due date. Allow at least a two- or three-day buffer zone (of course, major addresses should be completed much earlier). This is extremely important, for one's rehearsal may reveal weak spots that can be bolstered with more information, thought, and polish.

Letting a completed speech lie untouched for a day or so enables one to back away from it and to see it afresh. Generally avoid making major changes immediately prior to presentation; frequently these alterations do not improve the speech as much as we think they do. Instead they usually increase our tension and confusion. Of course, *some* last-minute changes may be valuable, and the desire to improve one's presentation to the very end is commendable.

One should practice whenever one has free minutes. Many students do not rehearse because they think they do not have the block of time necessary for it. While a block of time is important, especially in the final stages of rehearsal, short moments of free time can also be well used. It may be possible to review the material while working at such jobs as washing dishes in some restaurant, attending to a parking lot, or baby-sitting. Riding on the bus, standing in line at the cafeteria, and a host of other everyday situations may also offer valuable moments.

Where to rehearse

The place of rehearsal can be virtually anywhere, at least in preliminary stages. Do not wait for ideal surroundings before beginning. When one is ready to rehearse the whole completed speech, then seek a location that would approximate as closely as possible the room in which the speech will be given. It would be ideal to use the very same room when it is empty, such as might often be the case on many campuses in the late afternoon or evening. Seeing the room from the front can be quite different from seeing it from one's normal location in the audience. If the room is not available, then some other classroom of similar size would be helpful. Otherwise, use the largest room available wherever one is living. One should use the same kind of notes that one will have in the speech, and should employ a rostrum, or a makeshift one, similar to what one will be using in the classroom. One might even find it helpful to go through the motion of rising from a chair and walking to the front of the room. In other words, duplicate the actual setting as closely as possible.

How to rehearse

It is mandatory that one devotes much rehearsal time to audible practice. One needs to become psychologically accustomed to hearing one's voice break the silence. Frequently during a speech the one thing that unnerves inexperienced speakers is to realize suddenly that the only thing breaking the silence of the classroom is their voice. Since they are not accustomed to this, they fall apart. Rehearsing aloud also helps one to time the speech more accurately and to know better what to exclude or alter. It helps one to test how the material sounds and to polish the transitional and other phraseology. Clarity in articulation and variety in pitch, stress, and rate cannot be practiced well unless one rehearses audibly.

There also is a place for spot practice as well as for going through the whole speech. Most textbooks appropriately emphasize the importance of continuing on through the whole speech without stopping. But too little emphasis is placed on the helpfulness of spot practice, that is, practicing only a troublesome segment of the speech. A piano student, for instance, when beginning a new composition, practices only the two or three measures that are difficult rather than going over the entire piece. Some speakers waste time going over the whole speech just because certain segments give difficulty. But in late stages of rehearsal one needs to go through the whole speech many times without interruption and without repeating.

It is also extremely important in the rehearsal phase to get as much response as possible. One might listen to oneself on a tape recorder. If one does not possess one, most colleges and universities now have tape recorders available for student rehearsals, or perhaps a friend has one. Recording permits one to improve the vocal aspects, to polish the phraseology, and to eliminate needless details and wordiness. It permits one to hear the need to define and clarify terms and ideas, and to clearly identify those people one has mentioned in the speech.

The old standby—a full-length mirror—can also help. This frequently reveals that with a fuller movement of the jaw and with more energetic and precise movement of lips and tongue one's articulation could be improved. It may show an expressionless face, immobility of body, a rigid or slouchy posture, inadequate gesturing, or distracting mannerisms. On the other hand the mirror may reflect some excellent habits, and thus give a person considerable confidence. It can help one to look up from one's manuscript at appropriate intervals.

It is also helpful to secure a response from a second person—a friend, or member of the family—whose opinion of one's strengths and weaknesses one would respect. Other people often can hear and see things that the individual involved would miss. But one should not let the critics mislead one by their excessive complaints or praise.

In closing, we should remind ourselves that the development of our oral skills depends in large part on our willingness and effort to take part in all the various forms of oral communication which may be available to us in our college and university classes. One should not think that giving set formal speeches in speech class is the only way in which to improve as an oral arguer. We are greatly aided by taking advantage of all opportunities to speak up, such as in informal class discussion, panels, symposiums, individual oral reports, question and answer periods, brainstorming sessions, and classroom debates.[6]

SUMMARY

The importance of fluent delivery has to be understood and appreciated by all who wish to be effective oral communicators. If one wishes to speak well, one will endeavor to improve one's command over articulation, pronunciation, pitch, volume, rate, and stress. Seeking to improve one's command over gestures, facial expressions, and movements of the body, one will want them to be purposeful, fully executed, spontaneous, varied, economically used, coordinated, and appropriate.

One will want to understand the nature, advantages, and disadvantages of each of the four general modes of delivery: impromptu speaking, extemporaneous speaking, speaking from manuscript, and speaking from memory. One will want to study and put into practice specific suggestions for improving one's use of each mode.

Careful and conscientious rehearsal is mandatory if one is to grow and fulfill one's potential as a speaker. A number of specific suggestions as to when, where, and how to engage in meaningful rehearsal should open up a number of possibilities for improvement.

The perceptive reader will have noted that some basic qualities of effective delivery are habitually alluded to throughout this chapter. That is, it is urged that one should present one's material with clarity, vitality,

6. See J. Vernon Jensen, "Oral Skills Enhance Learning," *Improving College and University Teaching*, 28 (1980): 78–80.

directness, appropriateness, sincerity, and confidence. One's command over voice and gesture should contribute to the clarity of one's message. A sense of vitality, of liveliness, of appropriate enthusiasm, of animation should pervade. One should talk *with* the members of the audience, not *at* them; a sense of conversational directness should be maintained. The use of voice and gesture should be appropriate to the subject matter, the audience, the occasion, and oneself as speaker. This means that one should be natural, not mechanical, in one's delivery. One should be oneself, but oneself at one's best.

EXERCISES

1. Keep a log of the activities you go through in preparing for and delivering a speech in class. Begin with how you went about choosing the topic, researching the subject, writing and rehearsing the speech, and reactions to how you felt during and immediately after the speech. Include a summary of any oral and written responses from the audience and instructor. Conclude with a concise, one-page answer to the question: "How can I improve my speech preparation, rehearsal, and delivery habits?"

2. Present a five-minute extemporaneous speech on any subject about which you feel strongly. Any topic dealing with religious beliefs, social attitudes, political views, or educational philosophy would serve as meaningful subjects. But something less formidable would also be appropriate. Make every effort to put into practice many of the suggestions discussed in this chapter. Give the instructor a list of five specific things you consciously did in an effort to improve your oral presentation.

3. Listen to a tape recording of a speech which your department, college or university library possesses, or which you might secure from some other source. You may want to listen to the tape at least twice if possible. Carefully analyze all aspects of the vocal dimension: articulation, pronunciation, pitch, volume, rate, and stress. Summarize your observations in a concise 300-word essay.

4. Observe and record the gestures used by people in a variety of natural settings, such as:
   a. A salesperson trying to sell something to a customer
   b. Excited children talking with each other

    c. Some lecturer, panelist, or announcer on television (turn down the volume)

    d. A person talking on the telephone

Summarize your material in a 500-word essay.

5. For a few days observe and record all of the characteristics of voice and gesture of one of your professors, or someone else to whom you listen frequently (a television personality, an employer, or a member of your family). Which characteristics are assets and which are liabilities? Which characteristics do you think would be appropriate for you to use or avoid in the future? Summarize in a 500-word essay.

Suggested Readings

ANDERSEN, KENNETH E. *Persuasion: Theory and Practice*, 2nd ed.; Boston: Allyn and Bacon, 1978.

Introductory textbook in persuasion which includes an interesting chapter on totalitarian persuasion. Helpful discussion questions and projects at end of chapters. Mary Andersen coauthored chapter on ethics.

ANDERSON, JERRY M.; and Dovre, Paul J. (eds.). *Readings in Argumentation*. Boston: Allyn and Bacon, 1968.

Handy collection of thirty-three articles on most of the fundamental aspects of argumentation, written by various contemporary scholars, but also including Baker, Whately, Cicero, and Aristotle.

ARNOLD, CARROLL. "What's Reasonable?" *Today's Speech*, 19 (1971): 19–23.

A leading scholar emphasizes that speech communication teachers need to honor sound reasoning but at the same time need to realize that it is different from the inherent worth of the claims being made. Students need to see reason not as some irrelevant pietism but as a realistic tool which admittedly possesses some limitations in certain situations.

BEARDSLEY, MONROE C. *Writing With Reason: Logic for Composition*. Englewood Cliffs, N.J.: Prentice-Hall, 1976.

Brief survey of basic principles of logical thought aimed at improving writing skills. Good practical exercises throughout. Informality of style increases the appeal of this famous logician.

BEARDSLEY, MONROE C. *Thinking Straight: Principles of Reasoning for Readers and Writers*, 4th Ed.,; Englewood Cliffs, N.J.: Prentice-Hall, 1975.

Updated version of a highly successful practical logic textbook; analyzes deduction and induction, and explores such language factors as ambiguity, equivocation, vagueness, metaphors, emotive language, slanting, and controlling of definitions. New examples and exercises in this edition.

BERNINGHAUSEN, DAVID K. *The Flight from Reason.* Chicago: American Library Assoc., 1975.

Vigorous essays reaffirming faith in reason, dialogue and objectivity, and denouncing efforts from extreme Right and Left to infringe on intellectual freedom in academia, libraries, and the press.

BETTINGHAUS, ERWIN P. *The Nature of Proof*, 2nd ed.; Indianapolis: Bobbs-Merrill, 1972.

A brief volume which discusses the nature of proof, belief, and motivation in the communication context; surveys substantive proof (evidence) modes of proof (inference), and rhetorical strategies and tactics.

BETTINGHAUS, ERWIN P. *Persuasive Communication*, 3rd ed.; New York: Holt, Rinehart and Winston, 1980.

Recent revision of a good textbook in persuasion which includes a discussion of persuasion in mass media, small groups, formal organizations, and various social action contexts. Extensive footnoting and lengthy bibliography.

BREMBECK, WINSTON L.; and Howell, William S. *Persuasion: A Means of Social Influence*, 2nd ed.; Englewood Cliffs, N.J.: Prentice-Hall, 1976.

Updated version of a highly successful pioneering textbook in persuasion, which explores the role of drives, emotions, attitudes, critical thinking, social pressures, cultural values, ethics, ethos, attention, perception, and nonverbal cues. This edition analyzes persuasion in campaign contexts.

CHURCH, RUSSELL T. "A Bibliography of Argumentation and Debate for 1975–76," *Journal of the American Forensic Association*, 15(1979): 228–43.

An example of an important on-going bibliographical aid available to the student of argumentation and debate. Organized by history and practice of argumentation, theory of argumentation, scholastic forensics, experimental studies, interpersonal conflicts, and political campaign communication.

CLEVENGER, THEODORE, JR. *Audience Analysis.* Indianapolis: Bobbs-Merrill, 1966.

Part of a series of paperbacks on speech communication, this small volume explores the audience dimension much more fully than most general textbooks do. Helpful for teaching a speaker to adapt appropriately to the audience.

CORBETT, EDWARD P.J. "The Rhetoric of the Open Hand and the Rhetoric of the Closed Fist," *College Composition and Communication*, 20 (1969): 288–96.

The author characterizes the contemporary rhetoric of the closed fist as mainly nonverbal, group oriented, coercive, and nonconciliatory, whereas the rhetoric of the open hand is persuasive, conciliatory, and reasoned. He calls for renewed faith in the latter, but acknowledges that the closed fist may have a role to play in certain situations.

CRABLE, RICHARD E. *Argumentation as Communication: Reasoning with Receivers.* Columbus, Ohio: Charles E. Merrill, 1976.

This receiver-oriented text deals with argumentation as a complex communicative process. Heavily indebted to Toulmin, the author emphasizes function of argument rather than its form, and focuses on the informal unstructured argumentaion of everyday situations. Practical guidelines grow out of a descriptive rather than prescriptive approach. Includes analyses of case studies.

CROSSLEY, DAVID J.; and Wilson, Peter A. *How to Argue: An Introduction to Logical Thinking.* New York: Random House, 1979.

These Canadian authors present a cursory traditional treatment of argumentation with a heavy focus on deduction. Helpful exercises and case studies.

DICK, ROBERT C. *Argumentation and Rational Debating*. Dubuque, Iowa: William C. Brown, 1972.

This paperback serves as a brief handbook of specific practical guidance for debaters. Includes a National Debate Tournament final debate in the appendix.

EHNINGER, DOUGLAS. *Influence, Belief, and Argument: An Introduction to Responsible Persuasion*. Glenview, Ill.: Scott, Foresman, 1974.

A brief sound survey of a few of the components of argumentation by a leading scholar, recently deceased. An unusually large number of interesting exercises. Appendix includes newspaper and magazine articles and case studies for analysis.

EHNINGER, DOUGLAS; and Brockriede, Wayne. *Decision by Debate*, 2nd ed.; New York: Harper & Row, 1978.

Omitting some material from the first landmark edition, this shortened, updated version sharpens the focus on "argument as a person-centered method in the process of debate." Thoughtful and sound, this edition again relies on the Toulmin model of analysis. Three chapters are contributed by additional authors.

EISENBERG, ABNE M.; and Ilardo, Joseph A. *Argument: A Guide to Formal and Informal Debate*, 2nd ed.; Englewood Cliffs, N.J.: Prentice-Hall, 1979.

Adding material on formal contest debating, this second edition now balances the original emphasis on improving students' command of argument in informal dyadic or small group situations in everyday life. Analyzes opponent and audience as well as evidence, reasoning, and common fallacies. Quite a few practical illustrations and examples.

FEARNSIDE, W. WARD. *About Thinking*. Englewood Cliffs, N.J.: Prentice-Hall, 1980.

Beginning with three chapters on fallacies, this volume is reminiscent of an earlier one by Fearnside and W. B. Holther, *Fallacy, The Counterfeit of Argument* (1959). Traditional treatment of deduction and most subjects, and dependent on older materials and examples. Covers a large number of subjects but in a cursory manner. Helpful aids such as exercises and quizzes.

FISHER, WALTER R. "Toward a Logic of Good Reasons," *Quarterly Journal of Speech,* 64 (1978): 376–84.

He feels we "need to reaffirm the place of value as a component of knowledge." Thoughtful and carefully reasoned, this article seeks to clarify what logic in this context means, and proceeds to "restructure the concept of 'good reasons,' propose a design for a 'logic of "good reasons",' and recommend ways to implement it."

FOGELIN, ROBERT J. *Understanding Arguments: An Introduction to Informal Logic.* New York: Harcourt Brace Jovanovich, 1978.

The first part of this introductory logic textbook is an analysis of argument, a combination of theoretical substance which discusses fundamentals of logic. Part two provides specimens of argument for analytical practice and for illustrating the distinctive features of argumentation in fields of law, science, religion, morality, and philosophy.

FREELEY, AUSTIN J. *Argumentation and Debate: Rational Decision Making,* 4th ed.; Belmont, Calif.: Wadsworth, 1976.

An argumentation textbook directed mainly at the specific needs and interests of the intercollegiate debater. Includes sample debates in the appendix.

GEACH, P.T. *Reason and Argument.* Berkeley: University of California Press, 1976.

Aimed at an introductory philosophy course, this brief paperback by a British logician surveys a number of fundamental factors in argumentation in an attempt to apply logic to everyday situations.

GOODWIN, PAUL D.; and Wenzel, Joseph W. "Proverbs and Practical Reasoning: A Study in Socio-Logic," *Quarterly Journal of Speech,* 65 (1979): 289–302.

A provocative and interesting article which demonstrates how proverbs illustrate "a significant number of logical principles," and thus serve a sort of "common folk's equivalent of a logic textbook," warning people against faulty reasoning from sign, cause-and-effect, generalization, analogy, and other modes.

HAIMAN, FRANKLYN S. "The Rhetoric of 1968: A Farewell to Rational Discourse," in Johannesen, Richard L. *Ethics in Human Communication*. Wayne, N.J.: Avery Publishing Group, 1978, pp. 108–121.

A lively presentation in which Haiman describes and evaluates what he perceived at that time to be the trend away from rational discourse, characterized by emotionalization of verbal discourse, body rhetoric, and civil disobedience.

HAMPLE, DALE. "The Toulmin Model and the Syllogism," *Journal of the American Forensic Association*, 24 (1977): 1–9.

To balance the heavy swing toward Toulmin analysis of argument, the author thoughtfully calls for a return to the syllogism, emphasizing that each approach has much to offer the student of argumentation.

HOLTZMAN, PAUL D. *The Psychology of Speakers' Audiences*. Glenview, Ill.: Scott, Foresman, 1970.

A brief paperback which explores the types of listening, audience influence, general factors in listening, audience analysis, and audience adaptation more fully than general textbooks can do.

HUNSAKER, DAVID M. "Freedom and Responsibility in First Amendment Theory: Defamation Law and Media Credibility," *Quarterly Journal of Speech*, 65 (1979): 25–35.

A recent updating on the delicate balance between freedom and responsibility of the press, between vigorous journalism and the rights of the public to redress grievance through defamation complaints in the courts, in order to maintain public trust in the media, which in turn is necessary to the successful functioning of a democratic self-governing society.

JOHANNESEN, RICHARD L. "Richard M. Weaver on Standards for Ethical Rhetoric," *Central States Speech Journal*, 29 (1978): 127–37.

Concise summary of one aspect of Weaver's philosophy of rhetoric. Surveys Weaver's hierarchy of message-centered standards for an ethical rhetorician: argument from genus at the top, followed by argument from similitude, cause and effect, and circumstance. Emphasizes that language is sermonic, thus pseudo neutrality is ethically suspect.

JOHANNESEN, RICHARD L. *Ethics in Human Communication*. Wayne, N.J.: Avery Publishing Group, 1978.

A leading scholar in ethics in communication discusses religious, utilitarian, legal, political, ontological, dialogical, and situational perspectives on ethics, and then analyzes some basic issues. Includes four case studies in the appendix, and includes an extensive bibliography.

JOHNSON, RALPH H.; and Blair, J. Anthony. *Logical Self Defense*. Toronto: McGraw-Hill Ryerson, 1977.

In the tradition of the Kahane textbook, these Canadian authors focus on informal fallacies in order to help readers become more intelligent consumers of everyday persuasion encountered in the mass media and elsewhere. Contains many examples from Canadian newspapers, magazines and books, thus it is a broadening experience for students in the United States.

KAHANE, HOWARD. *Logic and Contemporary Rhetoric: The Use of Reason in Everyday Life*. 2nd ed., Belmont, Calif.: Wadsworth, 1976.

Exposing fallicies, emphasizing what to avoid, forms the framework of this induction-oriented textbook designed to help readers better defend themselves against, and improve the level of reasoning in political and other everyday persuasion. Examples drawn from contemporary newspapers, magazines, speeches, television, and public school textbooks. Helpful exercises.

KELLERMANN, KATHY. "The Concept of Evidence: A Critical Review," *Journal of the American Forensic Association*, 16 (1980): 159–72.

She claims that past research on the role of evidence in argumentation is not very helpful as it has not accounted for variables carefully enough; the nature and effect of evidence have not been clearly handled, thus there is need for methodological improvements in this area.

KLOPF, DONALD; and McCroskey, James. "Ethical Practices in Debate," *Journal of the American Forensic Association*, 1 (1964): 14–16.

A questionnaire was answered by 244 debate instructors some years ago in an endeavor to ascertain practices that could be labeled unethical. It was concluded that variables of intent, degree, and circumstances of each situation were too powerful to isolate inherent ethical quality of any particular practice, but thirty-one practices were identified by a significant number as having at least some questionable ethics.

KRUGER, ARTHUR N. *Modern Debate: Its Logic and Strategy*. New York: McGraw-Hill, 1960.

An older practical textbook focusing mainly on training college and university debaters and orators. It includes an analysis of a sample debate, chapters on speaking contests, various kinds of debate formats, judging debate, and directing a forensic program.

LAMBERT, KAREL; and Ulrich, William. *The Nature of Argument*. New York: Macmillan, 1980.

A new textbook for an introductory philosophy course, but also applicable to speech communication. Aims at identifying arguments in everyday discourse, clarifying them in more formal phrasing, and evaluating them more effectively.

LARSON, CHARLES U. *Persuasion: Reception and Responsibility*, 2nd ed.; Belmont, Calif.: Wadsworth, 1979.

Retains the receiver-centered approach of the first edition, updates the discussion of persuasive campaigns and movements, and adds chapters on the mass media and on becoming a persuader. Richard Johannesen again supplies the chapter on ethics.

McBATH, JAMES H. (ED.). *Argumentation and Debate: Principles and Practices*, rev. ed.; New York: Holt, Rinehart and Winston, 1963.

Essays contributed by twenty authorities in the field, surveying historical roots, research processes, proving one's case, oral presentation, and educational debate activities. A sample debate in the appendix.

McBATH, JAMES H.; and Cripe, Nicholas M. "Delivery: Rhetoric's Rusty Canon," *Journal of the American Forensic Association*, 2 (1965): 1–6.

The authors stress the importance of delivery in debate, and lament that many debaters, teachers, and critics overlook it. Survey empirical studies which confirm the importance of delivery.

McBurney, James H.; and Mills, Glen E. *Argumentation and Debate: Techniques of a Free Society*. New York: Macmillan, 1964.

An older widely used textbook, geared for college and university debaters. Traditional treatment of deduction. Appendix includes sample debates and a brief.

McCroskey, James C. *An Introduction to Rhetorical Communications*, 3rd ed.; Englewood Cliffs, N.J.: Prentice-Hall, 1978.

A thorough well documented survey of the fundamentals of communication with much attention given to factors central to argumentation. Ten speeches in the appendix for analysis.

McDonald, Daniel. *The Language of Argument*, 3rd ed.; New York: Harper & Row, 1980.

Aimed at an English composition course but is easily applicable to speech communication. Cursory discussion of substance but contains numerous short essays which are helpful aids for analysis and illustration and for generating subjects for student argumentative presentations.

McGuire, Michael. "The Ethics of Rhetoric: "The Morality of Knowledge," *Southern Speech Communication Journal*, 45 (1980): 133–48.

Drawing mainly on the writings of Friedrich Nietzsche and contemporary rhetorical scholars who advocate that knowledge is created, not merely transmitted, by rhetorical activity, the author arrives at the assertion that "As a guiding ethic for rhetoric, the will to power judges knowledge to be moral to the extent that it enhances life's value to the individual."

McQuade, Donald; and Atwan, Robert. *Thinking in Writing: Structures for Composition*. New York: Alfred A. Knopf, 1980.

Aimed at improving thinking and writing, this introductory composition textbook has a section on argument which includes contemporary argumentative articles, essays, and book excerpts for analysis.

MILLER, GERALD R.; and Nilsen, Thomas R. (eds.). *Perspectives on Argumentation*. Chicago: Scott, Foresman, 1966.

For the advanced student, these essays are written by various experts in argumentation. Nature and functions of argument, and the roles of evidence, reasoning, motivation, structure, language, and ethics are treated in depth.

MILLS, GLEN E. *Reason in Controversy: An Introduction to General Argumentation*. Boston: Allyn and Bacon, 1964.

An early textbook to aim argumentation not at the limited audience of debaters but at the general student seeking a liberal education and seeking improvement in everyday reasoning. Lengthy appendix includes materials for illustration and analysis.

NEWMAN, ROBERT P.; and Newman, Dale R. *Evidence*. Boston: Houghton Mifflin, 1969.

This volume probes the uses, credibility, and sources of evidence in greater depth than most general textbooks can do. Relies heavily on political issues of the 1960s for examples and analysis. Helpful bibliographical material.

NILSEN, THOMAS R. *Ethics of Speech Communication*, 2nd ed.; Indianapolis: Bobbs-Merrill, 1974.

A leading scholar thoughtfully discusses ethical concerns involving truth telling, persuasive tactics, achieving a meaningful free choice, and approximating the "optimific" act.

PERELMAN, CHAIM; and Olbrechts-Tyteca, L. *The New Rhetoric: A Treatise on Argumentation*. Trans. by John Wilkinson and Purcell Weaver. Notre Dame, Indiana: University of Notre Dame Press, 1969.

A speculative yet practical volume which roams over an incredibly broad landscape, probing a host of factors relevant to theory and technique in argumentation.

RAY, JOHN W. "Perelman's Universal Audience," *Quarterly Journal of Speech*, 64 (1978): 361–75.

Perelman's concept of the universal audience, a basic element in his theory of rhetoric, is clarified as an ideal model audience of competent and reasonable human beings which exists only in the mind of the speaker. Ray reveals Perelman's close affinity to Rousseau, Diderot, and Kant.

RIEKE, RICHARD D.; and Sillars, Malcolm O. *Argumentation and the Decision Making Process.* New York: John Wiley & Sons, 1975.

Influenced by Perelman and Toulmin, this audience-centered textbook is an eclectic presentation of varied concepts about argumentation. Though not prescriptive, it seeks to improve general argumentation in everyday situations, and seeks to increase understanding of the role of argumentation in such specialized areas as law, scholarship, and educational debate.

RUGGIERO, VINCENT RYAN. *Beyond Feelings: A guide to Critical Thinking.* Port Washington, N.Y.: Alfred Publishing Co., 1975.

An example of the trend back to reasoning from the emotionalism of the 1960s in order to better appreciate the complementary roles of both. Cursory sketch of practical psychological and logical considerations.

SCHUETZ, JAN. "Argumentative Competence and the Negotiation of Henry Kissinger," *Journal of the American Forensic Association,* 15 (1978): 1–16.

An interesting analysis of a secretary of state's shuttle diplomacy to negotiate peace between Israel and the Arab world in 1973. Despite some shortcomings, he did succeed in generating their trust and generating communication between the disputants.

SCRIVEN, MICHAEL. *Reasoning.* New York: McGraw-Hill, 1976.

An innovative and provocative logic textbook designed to be practical in improving one's skill in analyzing, evaluating, and presenting arguments in everyday discourse, and in strengthening the attitude of reasonableness. Extensive helpful quizzes and answers at the end of each chapter.

SEMLAK, WILLIAM D.; and Shields, Donald C. "The Effect of Debate Training on Students Participating in the Bicentennial Youth Debates," *Journal of the American Forensic Association,* 13 (1977): 192–96.

This study supports the contention that skills learned in participation in competitive educatonal debate, particularly in delivery, organization, and analysis, do transfer to other considerably different speaking activities.

SHURTER, ROBERT L.; and Pierce, John R. *Critical Thinking: Its Expression in Argument*. New York: McGraw-Hill, 1966.

A brief survey of basic substantive material aimed at improving thinking and writing. Most of the book is devoted to a large number of exercises, essays on contemporary subjects for analysis, and case studies.

SIMONS, HERBERT W. *Persuasion: Understanding, Practice, and Analysis*. Reading, Mass.: Addison-Wesley, 1976.

As the title indicates, this textbook seeks to strengthen the students' understanding of persuasion, their ability to practice it, and their ability to analyze it when it is used by others. Good list of references at the end.

SMITH, CRAIG R.; and Hunsaker, David M. *The Bases of Argument: Ideas in Conflict*.

Part of a paperback series in speech communication, this text gives impetus to the move toward studying argumentation as it applies not to a few debaters but to all students, meeting their needs in everyday life and in the public arena.

SPROULE, J. MICHAEL. *Argument: Language and Its Influence*. New York: McGraw-Hill, 1980.

Heavily documented, this recent textbook is aimed at advanced students of argumentation. Both theoretical and practical, it is unusually comprehensive, touching on a large number of factors. Contains numerous exercises.

THOMPSON, WAYNE N. *Modern Argumentation and Debate: Principles and Practices*. New York: Harper & Row, 1971.

Draws on time-tested theories and modern experimental findings to create a theoretical and practical textbook aimed primarily at debaters. Traditional but solid discussion of deduction and induction. Includes chapters on debate judging and on participation in debate. At the end of each chapter are useful exercises and references.

TOULMIN, STEPHEN; Rieke, Richard; and Janik, Allan. *An Introduction to Reasoning*. New York: Macmillan, 1979.

A thorough discussion of the Toulmin pattern of analysis, followed by practical applications in the criticism of arguments. A final section treats reasoning as it relates to law, science, the arts, management, and ethics.

VASILIUS, JANET M.; and DeStephen, Dan. "An Investigation of the Relationship Between Debate Tournament Success and Rate, Evidence, and Jargon," *Journal of the American Forensic Association*, 15 (1979): 197–204.

Focusing only on the quantitative dimension, this study concludes that while large quantities of words, evidence, and jargon may seem to accompany success, they can not be attributed as causes for it.

WALTER, OTIS M. *Speaking Intelligently: Communication for Problem Solving*. New York: Macmillan, 1976.

A pioneering textbook in speech communication, focusing solely on problem solving, which he feels needs more attention in the field than it is getting. Appendix contains sample speech assignments.

WEDDLE, PERRY. *Argument: A Guide to Critical Thinking*. New York: McGraw-Hill, 1978.

A cursory, traditional discussion of deduction, comparison, causation, and fallacies, this brief textbook is aimed at a broad range of communication students, to enable them to better handle everyday argumentation in interpersonal, commercial, and political settings. Helpful exercises.

WENZEL, JOSEPH W. "Jürgen Habermas and the Dialectical Perspective on Argumentation," *Journal of the American Forensic Association*, 16 (1979): 83–94.

One of six articles in a recent issue of the *Journal of the American Forensic Association*, which is totally devoted to an analysis of the implications for argumentation of the work of the influential German philosopher.

WINDES, RUSSEL R.; and Hastings, Arthur. *Argumentation and Advocacy.* New York: Random House, 1965.

An introduction to the principles of argumentation as applied to decision-making in all areas of public life. An example of the move to expand argumentation books away from the narrow debate focus to a broader perspective.

ZIEGELMUELLER, GEORGE W.; and Dause, Charles A. *Argumentation: Inquiry and Advocacy.* Englewood Cliffs, N.J.: Prentice-Hall, 1975.

Inquiry and advocacy provide the structure of this practical textbook geared mainly to the interests and needs of the college and university debater. Includes sample debates in the appendix.

Name Index

Andersen, Kenneth E., 200, 214, 223, 240–242, 299
Andersen, Martin P., 194
Anderson, Chester G., 8
Anderson, Raymond E., 32
Aristotle, 2, 67, 194, 200
Auden, W. H., 28

Baird, A. Craig, 4
Barton, H. Arnold, 206
Barzun, Jacques, 114, 196
Beardsley, Monroe C., 141
Bentham, Jeremy, 34
Bethge, Eberhard, 28
Bettinghaus, Erwin P., 306
Bitzer, Lloyd, 170
Blair, J. Anthony, 175
Blankenship, Jane, 255
Bohman, George V., 4
Bonhoeffer, Dietrich, 28
Bormann, Ernest G., 239
Bosmajian, Haig A., 2
Braden, Waldo W., 107
Brembeck, Winston L., 33–34, 178, 205, 207, 214, 217
Brock, Bernard L., 236
Brockriede, Wayne, 10, 14, 236

Chesebro, James W., 236
Churchill, Sir Winston, 2
Clevenger, Theodore, Jr., 194, 197, 214
Congalton, David, 4
Cowperthwaite, L. Leroy, 4
Crable, Richard, 3, 57, 194–195

Cragan, John, 236
Cronen, Vernon E., 255

Dause, Charles A., 4, 139, 246, 259
Day, Dennis, 38
Dick, Robert C., 237
Diggs, B. J., 37–39

Ehninger, Douglas, 10–11, 14, 123, 236
Engel, S. Morris, 175
Lord Erskine, 2

Freeley, Austin, J., 12, 236, 240, 246

Goodwin, Paul D., 157
Graff, Henry F., 114, 196
Greeves, Arthur, 9

Hagood, Annabel D., 4
Haiman, Franklyn S., 296
Hammarskjold, Dag, 28
Hamod, H. Samuel, 318
Hample, Dale, 162
Hitler, 24, 188
Holtzman, Paul D., 194
Hooper, Walter, 9
Howell, William S., 33–34, 178, 205, 207, 214, 217

Janik, Allan, 43, 156
Jensen, J. Vernon, 2, 64, 291–292, 323
Johannesen, Richard L., 20, 296
Johnson, Arlee, 230
Johnson, Ralph H., 175

Subject Index